THE LIVING AND THE DEAD

SUNY series in Hindu Studies
Wendy Doniger, Editor

The Living and the Dead

Social Dimensions of Death in South Asian Religions

EDITED BY

Liz Wilson

State University of New York Press

Published by
State University of New York Press, Albany

Printed in the United States of America

Cover photo courtesy of the author; the Hindu Destroyer God Shiva and an undead sidekick.

For information, address State University of New York Press,
90 State Street, Suite 700, Albany, N.Y., 12207

Production by Diane Ganeles
Marketing by Anne M. Valentine

Library of Congress Cataloging-in-Publication Data

The living and the dead : social dimensions of death in South Asian religions / Liz Wilson, editor.
p. cm. — (Suny series in Hindu studies)
Includes bibliographical references and index.
ISBN 0-7914-5677-3 (alk. paper) —ISBN 0-7914-5678-1 (pbk. : alk. paper)
1. Death—Religious aspects 2. Funeral rites and ceremonies—South Asia. 3. South Asia—Religious life and customs. I. Wilson, Liz. II. Series.

BL504 .L58 2003
291.2'3—dc21

2002067042

10 9 8 7 6 5 4 3 2 1

Contents

Illustrations

Acknowledgments

The editor would like to thank Mary Denney and Ryan Siney for their help in preparing the manuscript for this volume. The Miami University Office of Research and Scholarship provided funding needed for the preparation of this volume.

Note on Transliteration and Transcription

We have retained the various types of transliteration and transcription used by the contributors to this volume. Where diacritical marks have been used, the standard academic conventions have been followed.

Introduction: Passing On: The Social Life of Death in South Asian Religions

Liz Wilson

In his classic study of the collective representation of death, Robert Hertz suggested that death is best understood as a rite of passage in which the deceased makes a transition from the visible "here and now" to an invisible hereafter.[1] Death is thus the ultimate experience of passage; it is a threshold through which one passes beyond the house of life to some unknown place. As the termination of life, death is both a terminus ad quem and a terminus a quo, both an "end to which," or conclusion, and an "end from which," or commencement. In many South Asian religious traditions, death constitutes a particularly important moment of passage since it offers the deceased the opportunity to pass beyond the dissatisfactory and often painful cycle of repeated birth and death *(saṃsāra)* and to experience liberation (*mokṣa* or *nirvāṇa*). It is through the terminal of death that those who are ready for it pass into the deathless interminability of the unconditioned.

For those who are not yet ready for this ultimate passage out of the realm of conditioned existence, death entails a transition to another life. As this transition is represented in many South Asian traditions, the assistance of the living is vital. To ensure safe passage of the deceased to his or her postmortem destination, a great deal of sustained ritual activity is required. Without the ritual intervention of the living—the provision of sustenance and the ritual manipulation of various surrogates for the dead, for example—the deceased may fail to achieve a satisfactory postmortem condition and end up instead suspended in limbo between life and death. Hindus perform ancestral rites *(śrāddha)* in order to provide sustenance for the deceased on the year-long journey to the abode of the ancestors (*pitṛ-loka*). Tibetan Buddhist mourners sponsor recitations of texts such as the *Bar do thos grol* (known in the West as the *Bardo Thödol* or Tibetan Book of the Dead) in the presence of the dying/dead person to provide guidance on what to expect at each stage of the postmortem journey. It behooves the living to provide such care for the dead, since those who lose their way along their postmortem journeys are often said to return to the realm of the living in unwelcome forms. The disgruntled dead whose exit from human life is untimely or inadequately effected through ritual means may pose a considerable threat to the ongoing vitality of the living.

The chapters in this volume describe various forms of passage associated with death and dying as well as the handling of, provision for, and disposal of the dead in South Asian religious practice. Exploring traditions followed by Hindus, Buddhists, Muslims, and tribal groups of South Asia, the contributors examine beliefs and practices associated with the moment of death itself, mortuary rituals by which the deceased are ushered into a new postmortem status, rites of mourning by which the survivors reconstitute and reconfigure their social ties to the deceased, and healing rituals in which the living are restored to health through ritual mimicry of death as well as through the intervention of the dead. In the passages from life to death and from death to postmortem states that contributors analyze here, a wide variety of surrogates serve as stand-ins for the dying and the dead. Effigies, monuments, plants, animals, and living persons provide temporary bodies for the disembodied dead. Human surrogates give voice to the concerns of the dead. The provision of food and the manipulation of ritually effective substitutes ensure that the dead can successfully navigate the uncertainties of the postmortem journey. In some cases, these ritual operations follow protocols laid down in canonical texts; in other cases, the rituals have little or no textual precedent.

Interpretations of the social history of death in South Asia as advanced by pioneers in the field tend to rely on texts composed by elites, such as literate brahmins.[2] We have had until very recently little idea of the considerable differences between social groups in the 'management' of death and the customs and rituals that attend to it. Recent ethnographic work by scholars such as David G. Mandelbaum and Jonathan Parry have to a certain extent remedied this situation.[3] Such ethnographic investigations have expanded our knowledge of the relationship between textual ideals and actual practice and have supplemented the testimony of elite informants with ethnographic data representing more restricted social categories. The chapters in this volume carry forward this important project. Drawing on the oral testimony of illiterate people as well as tribal groups just beginning to be drawn into the dominant South Asian cultural ethos, many of the chapters presented here shed light on the practices of those in marginalized social categories.

Death by Design: Voluntary Death as a Means and Mark of Transcendence

Symbolic enactments of death are common in the history of religions. In the physical ordeals often associated with rites of passage in societies throughout the world, ritual enactments of death "kill" the initiand and herald the birth of a new social being. It is only by a ritually enacted death in which one dies to the social world, obliterating one's social identity, that one can return to that world as a new being with a new station in life. Arnold Van Gennep—the trailblazing student of the anthropology of rites of passage—observed that funerary symbolism often plays a role in passage rituals, especially in the initial rites of separation and in the intermediary rites of transition that lead to the final rites of incorporation.[4]

Dying in a ritually controlled manner while yet alive is also an important feature of specialized rites of passage associated with the vocation of the religious virtuoso. The visionary journeys to heaven and hell that play such a central role in shamanic initiations are often preceded by the visionary death of the candidate.[5] Neophytes commonly lose consciousness for prolonged periods of time, during which time their bodies are subject to dismemberment and renewal. In some instances, the candidate is symbolically killed and revived by the initiation master. Without such ritually controlled enactments of death, the shaman would be ill-equipped to communicate with ancestors, deities, demons, and other supernatural beings and hence less able to perform healing work on behalf of others.

South Asian religious texts and funerary performances place a high premium on the ritually controlled release of life, as S. Settar, Parry, Christopher Justice, and others have demonstrated in ethnographic and textual explorations of Hindu deathways.[6] Although the voluntary termination of life is sometimes regarded as a superordinate pious practice undertaken only by a few saintly members of the Jain community (a minority community in Hindu-majority India), it is far from an isolated phenomenon. Settar demonstrates that the idea of death by design has great appeal to a variety of religious communities in South Asia. Elisabeth Schömbucher and Claus Peter Zoller indicate that the voluntary termination of life stands out as a central theme in a variety of South Asian religious traditions. In their introduction to *Ways of Dying* (as well as in the chapters in this collection), the editors demonstrate that many mainstream South Asian religious actors aspire to die by their own hands, as it were, through a voluntary relinquishing of the life force.[7]

David Gordon White examines ritual enactments of death and cremation performed by *yogin*s of the Śaiva sect known as the Nāth Siddhas or "Perfect Masters" in "Ashes to Nectar." Death is the royal road to the state of liberation that Nāth Siddhas, following medieval traditions, seek to attain. Eschewing disembodied liberation, their goal is bodily immortality or liberation while still alive *(jīvanmukti)*. White's study of the alchemical and yogic practices of Nāth Siddhas suggests that the attainment *(siddhi)* of bodily immortality is only available to those who are willing to die for it. Without "killing off" the gross body, there is no chance of bodily immortality. The *yogin* who is willing to die lives forever by committing yogic or alchemical suicide—from yogic breath-control practices by which one suspends the body's vital functions and thus "swoons" in mimicry of death to alchemical lab-work in which one cooks oneself in a vat of "swooned" mercury and boiling oil.

The alchemical and yogic forms of ritual suicide that such *yogin*s perform are modeled on the death and regeneration of the cosmos. They reenact on a microcosmic level the macrocosmic *pralāya* or "cosmic dissolution" by which the world itself is incinerated and re-created at the end of each cycle of existence. Thus the *yogin* who seeks immortality in this very body wears ashes specially prepared to represent the dissolution of the cosmos. In addition to the outer chemical process of incineration that produces the holy ash, internally the *yogin* burns with ascetic heat. Unleashing inner and outer forms of radiant energy, *yogin*s who desire liberation in the body transform the gross material elements of the body into their subtle correlates. This is done by incinerating the gross body through yogic breathing practices that generate ascetic heat or by alchemical practices that "cook" and thus transform the gross body. "Dying is sweet" either way, whether yogic or alchemical, for the conflagration that consumes the *yogin* also burns up the fire of aging and death *(kālāgni)* and thus deprives death of its dominion.

Liz Wilson also takes up the themes of voluntary death and fire as an agent of transformation in her chapter, "Human Torches of Enlightenment." South Asian Buddhist hagiographies often attribute masterful powers over the circumstances of death to Buddhas and to Buddhist saints. It is customary for Buddhas, scriptural reports suggest, to die by choice, voluntarily giving up a portion of their allotted span of life. Likewise, many saints are said to determine the precise moment of their deaths well in advance. Rather than being taken by death unaware, Buddhas and Buddhist saints relinquish life voluntarily, declaring that they have achieved what they set out to achieve in life and that there is no point in remaining any longer. Rather than being a feared event, death becomes a ceremonial occasion and a teaching opportunity by which central points of Buddhist doctrine are wordlessly conveyed in the manner in which a Buddha or saint passes away.

Hagiographic accounts describe a variety of spectacular means by which Buddhas and Buddhist saints pass out of conditioned existence, but burning oneself in the flames of one's own inner radiance appears most frequently in hagiographies relating the deaths of saints. Saints who die by self-incineration thereby demonstrate meditative mastery over the elements that comprise the physical body, making manifest the radiance that always exists within, but is not normally visible to the untrained eye. In this fiery manner of departing from the world of conditioned existence, Buddhas and Buddhist saints follow ancient Indian precedents. The cultivation of radiant energy as a means of transformation plays a central role in Vedic descriptions of the ritual work of sacrifice. Buddhist texts describe the disciplined life as an internalized kindling of the Vedic fire sacrifice; the practice of self-immolation may be seen as the culmination of a life of sacrificially conceived self-discipline. Contextualizing self-immolation and other acts of self-ignition (e.g., the spontaneous combustion of the funeral pyres of the awakened ones) by reference to Vedic-Hindu sacrificial practices, Wilson explores themes that cut across the boundaries of South Asian religious communities while highlighting a practice that has been developed to a unique extent by Buddhist practioners not only in South Asia but also in Southeast and East Asia.

Labor Pains: The Ritual Work of Death and Rebirth

In his influential study of collective representations of death, Robert Hertz demonstrated the extent to which the boundaries between life and death vary from culture to culture. Arguing that death is a social fact rather than simply a biological occurrence, Hertz demonstrated his thesis by reference to a variety of cultures in which death is not seen as an instantaneous event but rather as a gradual process that takes months or even years. Many cultures, for example, enact a second burial long after the initial disposal of the corpse. Intended to ensure that the deceased has successfully completed the postmortem journey, this secondary disposal of the corpse operates on the premise that the dead are not truly gone until the bones of the deceased have become dry and free of decaying flesh. It is often only at this second funeral that ties between the deceased and the survivors (e.g., the marriage bond) are broken.

David Knipe's "When a Wife Dies First" explores postcremation rituals that ensure the controlled passage of the deceased from an earthly locale to an ultimate destination. Knipe observed a dramatic ritual of transformation performed for deceased Hindu women in Andhra Pradesh. When a woman predeceases her husband, she is ritually transformed ten or eleven days after her cremation into the goddess Gaurī, who was once herself transfomed by the creator-god Brahmā. Formerly the dark goddess (Kālī), Gaurī received her golden *(gaurī)*, luminous form in recognition of her unwavering devotion to her husband Śiva. To die before one's husband marks a woman as an exemplar of wifely devotion—the antithesis of the wife whose husband dies before her, ostensibly because of her failure to carry out the vows that devoted wives are said to perform to ensure the longevity of their husbands. Just as Gaurī was rewarded for her wifely devotion, so too the wife who dies before her husband is rewarded with a divine status.

As Knipe demonstrates, however, there is much ambiguity in her transformation into Gaurī. The ritual both deifies and dismisses the deceased wife. It ensures her transformation into a goddess, but it also signals that her husband is free to marry again and has no more ritual obligations toward his dead wife. Marital symbolism is used in the ritual functions so as to turn back the clock, as it were, presenting an already married woman as a maiden on the eve of her wedding, still identified with her family of birth and not yet connected by affinal ties to her bridegroom's family. Marital imagery thus serves to uncouple the couple, disjoining the wife from her husband.

In "Return to Tears, " Richard K. Wolf draws attention to the significance of music in mourning observances, and its mutability as a sign of affect. Wolf examines the narrowing of the spectrum of emotional display seen over the past century in the funeral practices of a tribal group living in the Nilgiri hills as well as in urban Indian and Pakistani Shī'ah observances of Muḥarram, a festival commemorating slain Muslim martyrs. The Kotas, who are classified by the government of India as a tribal people, practice secondary funeral rituals that traditionally included rites that might be described as life-affirming ritual markers of the termination of mourning. Many Kota communities follow the immediate postmortem cremation of the dead (known as the green funeral) with a collective annual ceremony (the dry funeral). Bones remaining from the first cremation are carried on decorated biers to be recremated at a special "dry" cremation ground; the soul of the deceased is thereby sent off to the "mother land" or land of the ancestors. In contrast to the green funeral with its emphasis on loss and grieving, the dry funeral is not a somber affair but a celebration of the ongoing life of the community. The more celebratory aspects of the dry funeral have been attenuated in some villages, while the ceremony itself has been completely abandoned in one. As Wolf indicates, there are conflicting views on the status of certain practices, competitive displays involving buffalo sacrifice, dancing, and drinking, as regards the proper affective comportment toward the dead. These areas of ambivalence have been particularly vulnerable to change in a changing social and political climate.

Wolf sees a similar narrowing of the spectrum of permissible emotions in the musical and dramatic performances accompanying Muḥarram observances in twentieth-century urban centers in North India and Pakistan. He links this narrowing of the permitted range of emotions to colonial encounters with more austere ritual performance moods and iconoclastic discourse about ritual, as well as to Islamist reform rhetoric that degrades Shī'ī ritual "excess" and "superstition" as signs of Hindu influence on Muslim life in India. Disagreements about the appropriate manner of memorializing dead leaders during Muḥarram has polarized urban South Asian Shī'ī and Sunni communities of the twentieth century.

Wolf documents the violence that has erupted in urban centers (e.g., riots in Lucknow in the early decades of the twentieth century) over the manner in which to remember long-dead Muslim leaders. Wolf's emphasis on memorialization as a site of communal tension (between Sunnis and Shī'as and by extension between Muslims and Hindus) underscores a theme that is often overlooked in the treakly, self-congratulatory trend in contemporary popular writing on death and dying epitomized by Mitch Albom's best seller *Tuesdays with Morrie:* caring for the dying, and remembering/memorializing the dead do not always inspire noble sentiments.[9]

Remembering and Demembering the Dead: The Social Lives (and Deaths) of the Dead

As Knipe's chapter suggests, funerary rituals can be read as codes that determine how the dead remain socially significant in the world of the living, encoding such features of identity as the kinship ties that will henceforth connect the deceased to the living community. In "Deanimating and Reanimating the Dead in Rural Sri Lanka," Jonathan S. Walters explores various ways in which Sri Lankan mortuary rituals enact continued relationships with the dead. Walters separates out the different strands of tradition that have contributed to contemporary mortuary practices in Sri Lanka, noting the divergent conceptions of death that these strands entail. Theravāda Buddhist rituals stress the inescapable reality of death and are orchestrated by monks whose social status as renouncers mirrors the condition of the dead. Like the deceased, monks are no longer members of the world of production and reproduction. In their professed and constantly reaffirmed renunciation of familial ties and hence separation from loved ones in this life, Buddhist monks and nuns take great solace in the idea that such a social separation in this life can serve as an antidote to the painful emotional separation that takes place at the death of a loved one. By going forth while still young and while one's loved ones still thrive, one anticipates and "works through" the pain of saying goodbye to those loved ones that death inevitably snatches from the clinging arms of the living. Thus for Sri Lankan Buddhists, a visit to the village cemetery or cremation-ground is an educational experience; the cemetery is a locus of insight where the implacable reality of death is made evident in the piling up of bones in grave upon grave and by the convention of providing no grave-marker for the deceased. Unmarked graves underscore the essential Buddhist teachings of impermanence and lack of abiding essence or selfhood. The discourse of monks during mortuary rites drives home the lesson that the dead are truly gone, never having existed in any abiding sense in the first place.

But if the Sri Lankan village cemetery is place where the dead are socially deanimated, where their continued presence among the living is shown to be nil, it is also the locus of ritual reanimations where the dead return to the world of the living in response to necromantic spells. Sri Lankan cemeteries are also said to be visited by sorcerers who, in contrast to the monks whose liturgical function in the cemetery is to stress the fact that the dead are truly gone, are hired by clients to reanimate the dead for various necromantic purposes. These sorcerers rely on the help of a divine pantheon imported from Hindu South India that since the eighteenth century has been well-known and often resorted to by Sri Lankan Buddhists (although Buddhists relegate these Hindu gods to an inferior cosmological level below that of the Buddhas). *Sohon deviyo,* the "god of graves," is said to cause the dead to rise again as zombies when called to action by powerful mantras that combine incantatory syllables from the Tamil and Pāli languages.

Walters thus sets up a contrast between those who deanimate or ritually enact the social death of the deceased and those who reanimate the dead for necromantic purposes. In the cemetery, forces of deanimation work at cross-purposes with forces of reanimation. But, as Walters goes on to suggest, the distinction is by no means absolute. Sometimes in order to protect a client, sorcerers also deanimate or terminate the renewed existence of a deceased being whom some other sorcerer had animated for nefarious purposes. These necromantic killings or deanimations are not all that different in practice from the liturgical chanting of unintelligible Pāli verses; as mantra-driven rites of separation, Buddhist and theistic deanimations share the same basic liturgical forms.

Gregory Schopen's "Suppression of Nuns and the Ritual Murder of Their Special Dead in Two Buddhist Monastic Texts" shows that Buddhist monks and nuns were well aware of the necromantic possibilites afforded by the ongoing presence of the special dead. Housed in their funerary monuments *(stūpa*s*)*—monuments that are the primary focus of Buddhist devotional activity throughout the Buddhist world—the special dead are very much alive. In his groundbreaking analysis of Buddhist mortuary deposits, Schopen provided archaeological and epigraphic evidence to support the idea (suggested but inconclusively proved by more textually oriented scholars) that *stūpa*s are imbued with the living presence of the Buddhas and saints whose relics are there enshrined.[8] If a *stūpa* can live, Schopen argues, then "it also—by necessity—should be able to die or even, indeed, be murdered." To destroy a *stūpa* is clearly an act of ritual murder and is condemned as such by Buddhist authorities. But Schopen's reading of monastic codes redacted at different times in different parts of the South Asian Buddhist world shows the act going uncensured when it takes the form of a political assassination of another group's very special dead. When these ritual murders are directed against "heretical" groups on the margins of the Buddhist fold or against the order of Buddhist nuns, standing (by virtue of its administrative subordination to the order of Buddhist monks) on the margins of the Buddhist monastic community, then these killings evidently went uncensured.

In her chapter on Tamil countersorcery rites, Isabelle Nabokov also examines ritual processes of killing those who are in some sense already dead. This vivid first-person account entitled "A Funeral to Part With the Living" deals with Tamil healing rituals that bring those "killed" by sorcery (i.e., understood by the community to be socially dead) back from the state of death to the state of life. These countersorcery rituals operate under the premise that further destruction is necessary for healing to occur. In order to neutralize the social annihilation effected by the sorcerer, it is necessary for the victim to terminate his or her relationship with the sorcerer's client (the individual whom the victim believes to have paid the sorcerer to annihilate the victim) by a rite that is in some ways the ritual equivalent of a murder-suicide. The ritual of healing involves two phases: first, the creation and animation of an effigy that represents both the suffering victim and the sorcerer's client; second, the destruction of the effigy, at the conclusion of which the sorcerer's spell is presumed to have been neutralized and the victim is declared to have returned to life as a newly born self. With one effigy representing both parties, the victim "killed" by sorcery and the presumed culprit are both symbolically terminated with the termination of the "life" of the effigy. The ritual enactment is thus a homicidal act but not necessarily a malevolent one because in the "killing" of the effigy, it is essentially the relationship between victim and tormentor that is killed. With this relationship terminated, the victim is able to return to life as a new social being with new possiblities. Nabokov suggests that in their regenerative capacity, the countersorcery rites she observed in Tamil Nadu are comparable to the initiatory rites that render a Hindu man "twice-born" and enable him to engage in a career of regenerative ritual acts. But unlike the initiatory and sacrificial rites for which only certain Hindu men are eligible, these Tamil counter-sorcery rites can be performed on behalf of anyone, regardless of their gender or caste identity. If death is, as many Indologists have suggested, the ultimate *saṁskāra* or "ritual of perfection/transformation," then rituals that allow the individual to enact his or her death can lead the individual to new and better ontological states.

Where the chapters by Walters, Schopen, and Nabokov reveal an unexpected level of factionalism, rivalry, and intrigue with regard to the treatment of the dead and of the living in the name of the dead, Peter Gottschalk's chapter, "Dead Healers and Living Identities," suggests a surprising level of communal harmony where one might not expect it—in relationships between Hindus and Muslims who rely for healing on the powers of the dead in a North Indian village. In the village of Arampur, those who seek relief from various physical ailments, psychological afflictions, and possessing spirits can resort to the healing powers of two men who died in the fifteenth century: a Muslim saint known as Makhūm Ṣāhib and a Hindu royal minister known as Harsū Brahm. Muslim and Hindu residents of Arampur proudly claim both men as key figures in the history of their village. And narratives about the two figures connect them both to the fifteenth-century ruler Rājā Vicitra, who through his civic-building projects shaped Arampur more than any other ruler. Gottschalk found that local narratives about Makhūm Ṣāhib and Harsū Brahm are divided along communal lines in some ways but not in others. When the narrator attempts to demonstrate the figure's authority as an agent of healing, the narration will tend to stress Makhūm Ṣāhib's Muslim identity and Harsū Brahm's Hindu identity. But in describing the efficacy of Makhūm Ṣāhib and Harsū Brahm as healers, residents of Arampur produce narratives that elide the religious identity of these figures in interesting ways. Thus in Arampur, civic pride and common reverence for the dead unites the living through intercommunal narratives and activities that go beyond the confines of communal boundaries.

Passing On: Transitions and Transformations

In this brief synopsis of some of the customs and rituals that accompany death and dying in South Asian religious traditions, various levels of transformation can be seen involving both the individual who confronts death and the community that lives on after the death of one of its members. The deceased, in transit between this life and the beyond, undergoes a transformation commensurate with the postmortem status to be achieved. For some women who die before their husbands, this transformation is an apotheosization: the deceased becomes a goddess. In the case of ritual enactments of death performed by the living, radical transformations are possible. Victims of sorcery emerge as new social beings and *yogin*s as living immortals. But death not only transforms the deceased; it also shapes the surviving community. In mortuary rituals in which the living help transfer the dead to their proper levels in the world beyond, social ties are reconfigured and new social orders are established. These ritual activities not only patch up holes in the social fabric rended by death but creatively reconstruct kinship bonds and other social ties in such a way as to produce new relationships. Exercising transformative power from beyond the grave, the dead never sleep. The social consequences of the dead may continue to be felt long after the death of an individual and those consequences may change, as Wolf's chapter shows, to a considerable degree over the years. Having passed beyond life, the dead are often thought to be able to mediate between domains normally considered incommensurate. Due to their powers of mediation and their role as icons and touchstones for the living, the dead can thus sustain and heal the living as well as generate conflict and legitimate violence.

That the dead are standard-bearers for the living who aid in the process of communal identity formation and expression is not exactly late-breaking news in anthropological or religious studies circles. But this volume explores some of the less-explored tributaries of the stream of theory on how attitudes toward the dead shape living communities. We demonstrate how riots in early twentieth-century India have erupted out of communal conflict over proper decorum in remembering the deaths of Muslim leaders who died centuries ago in other lands. We show how conflict between Buddhists and outsiders and also between Buddhist nuns and monks in competition for lay support was expressed as a ritual homicide that took the form of destroying rival monuments as well as ritual cannibalism, or the eating of food in a ritually provocative way that expressed homicidal or communicidal intent. Those who wish to see more comfort with ambivalence in scholarly and popular discourse on death and dying will appreciate the importance given to anger, hatred, and communal conflict in this volume's explorations of how memorializing the dead can engender certain unpleasant moods and motivations among the living.

While significant work has been done on protocols surrounding death and the handling of the dead within specific religious traditions in South Asia, there is much comparative work to be done on patterns and themes that cut across the boundaries of religious communities. This is especially the case now that scholars are moving outside the narrow confines of what can be learned from texts and from the practices of cultural elites. We hope that the chapters in this volume contribute not only to the growing conversation on death and dying among students of the history of religions but also to the emerging interest in ethnographic methods that shed light on the social life of death in underrepresented groups.

Notes

1. Robert Hertz, "A Contribution to the Study of the Collective Representation of Death," in *Death and the Right Hand,* trans. R. C. Needham (London: Cohen and West, 1960).

2. See, for example, A. Hillebrandt, "Death and the Disposal of the Dead (Hindu)," in *Encyclopaedia of Religion and Ethics*, ed. James Hastings (Edinburgh, Scotland: T. & T. Clark; New York: C. Scribner's Sons, 1908–26), pp. 475–79.

3. See Jonathan Parry, *Death in Banaras* (New York: Cambridge University Press, 1994). See also the editorial comments of Elisabeth Schömbucher and Claus Peter Zoller, eds., *Ways of Dying: Death and Its Meanings in South Asia* (New Delhi: Manohar, 1999) (South Asia Institute, Heidelberg University South Asian Studies Series, no. 33).

4. Arnold Van Gennep, *The Rites of Passage,* trans. M. B. Visedom and G. L. Caffee (Chicago: University of Chicago Press, 1960), pp. 81–115.

5. See Mircea Eliade, *Shamanism: Archaic Techniques of Ecstasy,* trans. Willard R. Trask (Princeton, N.J.: Princeton University Press, 1964), pp. 53–66.

6. See S. Settar, *Inviting Death: Indian Attitude Towards the Ritual Death* (Leiden, Netherlands: E. J. Brill, 1989); Parry, *Death in Banaras*; Christopher Justice, *Dying*

the Good Death: The Pilgrimage to Die in India's Holy City (Albany: State University of New York Press, 1997).

7. Schömbucher and Zoller, Ways of Dying, pp. 20–24.

8. "Burial 'Ad Sanctos' and the Physical Presence of the Buddha in Early Indian Buddhism," *Religion* 17 (1987): 193–225.

9. Mitch Albom, *Tuesdays with Morrie: An Old Man, A Young Man, and Life's Greatest Lesson* (New York: Doubleday, 1997).

1

Ashes to Nectar: Death and Regeneration among the *Rasa Siddhas* and *Nāth Siddhas**

David Gordon White

What does it mean to be born again? Across a wide array of world religions and several millennia, people have devised a number of strategies for denying the finality of death; indeed, the problem of death may be said to lie at the heart if not at the origin of religious thought and practice.[1] Two strategies have dominated: the one posits an afterlife to which the lifebody goes following the transitional event of death; the other goes yet a step further and denies the importance, if not the reality, of death itself. It is a specific Indian application of this latter strategy that we will address here.

How may one deny death its sting? By dying before death, by orchestrating the dissolution of one's self before someone or something else (Time) does, one may live eternally in an immortal, invulnerable body. Different traditions have conceived this project in different ways, ranging from the quite literal experience of bodily dismemberment and rememberment (with metallic prostheses) of shamans, to the gnoseological death experience of the philosopher praised by Socrates in the *Phaedo* (64a): "The sole occupation of the philosopher is to die before he is dead."

What all of these approaches seem to have in common is the notion that one ought not to be dragged helplessly into death like some brute animal, but should rather anticipate it through a meditative self-dissolution, in such a way that death becomes rendered inoffensive and incapable of inspiring fear. The practical concomitant to this notion is a body of exercises, often initiatory in nature, which permit one to advance as far as possible in life along the path of a

* Portions of this chapter are reprinted from *The Alchemical Body: Siddha Traditions in Medieval India* published by The University of Chicago Press.

death of one's own making. Such exercises, both physical and psychological, are aimed at triggering the "limit situation" of one's own death, such that one becomes totally open to what is to follow. According to the logic of such practices, he who is able to look unflinchingly into the face of death will see that it is *impossible*, and that it can never really take place for anyone.[2]

We are all familiar with the classical Hindu strategy for denying the reality of death. This is the practice of the renouncer who self-consciously dies by performing his own funeral rites and laying together *(sannyāsa)* and internalizing his sacrificial fires as a means to burning away his socially constructed self. The fires that have been so gathered up serve both as a cremation pyre—by which the now obsolete mundane, social body is shown to have truly died to the world—and, in the postcrematory existence of the renouncer, as the seat of his internalized sacrifice,[3] the fire of his austerities. Already in the *Śvetāśvatara Upaniṣad* (2.12), this inner fire is termed *yogāgni,* the "fire of yoga" which, this source states, generates a new body unaffected by disease, old age, or death.[4]

As we know, the end product of combustion, of calcination by fire, is ashes; and ashes—the residue of the combustion process have, since at least the time of the *Mahābhārata,* played an initiatory role in Hindu throught. This is the case in the epic myth of Kāvya Uśanas and his disciple Kaca, in which the latter is initiated into the secret of immortality only after he has been reduced to ashes and swallowed by the former in his evening cordial.[5] In a parallel myth, Kāvya Uśanas himself enters into the body of Śiva, exiting in the form of Śukra (semen) as the result of that god's prodigious yogic powers of digestion.[6]

The connection between ashes and semen is made most explicitly in Śaiva metaphysics for which the sole essence in the universe is Śiva's seed, which is identified with ashes, whence the cyclic necessity for that phallic god to reduce the universe—all the "accidental" forms that have proliferated and degenerated over a cosmic aeon—to ashes. It is in the same Śaiva context that we encounter the sacramental use of ashes in religious practice: since at least the time of the Pāśupatas, ashes have been integral to Śaiva initiation and worship. Two terms predominate in Śaiva parlance. The first of these is *bhasma,* a participial form of the verbal root *bhas,* which literally means "consuming," but also "shining"; the second is *vibhūti,* which literally means "all-pervasive, omnipresent," but that is also used as a synonym for *siddhi,* "supernatural power," or for the eight *siddhi*s taken as an aggregate, *siddhi*s that are the prerogative of *sādhu*s, Śaiva sectarians, or Siddhas, the "Perfected Ones," to whom we will return shortly. Initiation involves bathing in ashes *(bhasma-snāna),* while the worship of Bhairava, a terrible, tantric form of Śiva, entails smearing cowdung ash on the forehead—in place of the normal bloodred *sindura*—as well as consuming a pinch of said ash.[7]

The Śaiva symbolism of ashes is explicable through the role played by the great god in the universal dissolution. It is Śiva who incinerates the universe, reduces it to ashes, in order that a new universe might be regenerated from the ashen remains (Śeṣa) of the former. Universes may rise and fall, but ashes are forever. More than this, ashes are creative, even procreative, in the generation of new universes. Therefore, the ashes with which Śiva besmears himself are, like the garland of skulls he wears around his neck, emblems of his eternity. Śiva is like ash, in that he outlives the universe and all the gods. In the words of the twelfth-century Vīraśaiva founder and poet Basavaṇṇa,[9] "When the ghosts read the writing on the skulls Śiva wears around his neck, they know, 'This one is Brahmā, this one is Viṣṇu, this one is Indra, this is Death,' and as they play happily with them, Śiva smiles, he laughs, our god." The Śaiva identification, between regenerative ash and generative seed, *rasa*, is explained, in what may be termed a "theology of ashes" at the conclusion of a Pāśupata inspired variant on the myth of Śiva in the Pine Forest. Here, after the phallic god has brought a group of uncomprehending Vedic sages to heel and before he initiates them after the Pāśupata fashion with an "ashen bath," a *bhasma-snāna*, he explains to them the importance of ashes.

> "I am Agni joined with Soma. . . . The supreme purification of the universe is to be accomplished by ashes; I place my seed in ashes and sprinkle creatures with it. . . . Ashes are known as my seed, and I bear my own seed upon my body. . . . Let a man smear his body until it is pale with ashes: . . . then he . . . grasps the supreme ambrosia."[9]

Now, the *bhasma* with which Śaiva *sādhus* besmear their bodies is not just any ash; it is ash that has been treated, and the way in which it has been treated tells us two things about Śiva's sectarian followers. First, the ashes they view and wear as symbols of transformation are ashes that have themselves been transformed, refined, or perfected *(saṃskṛta)*; second, this transformation is one that they themselves effect: every ash-smeared *sādhu* one sees in India is a Śaiva possessed of a practical knowledge of chemistry that has been handed down for centuries if not millennia. The preparation of *bhasma* is of a piece with the science of alchemy that has been a Śaiva specialty since its inception in India.

Here then is an account of the preparation of this ash of immortality:

> "*Bhasma* is made from the dung dropped in forests by grazing cows, which the *[sādhu]* collects when it has dried. It is then burnt. The ash is mixed in water and filtered with a piece of cloth. The ash suspended in water is allowed to settle for a night. While the water is decanted, the ash is shaped into small wicks, which are burnt once more in a pit well by dry dungcakes. The ash from the second burning becomes the white, sacred *bhasma*."[10]

In this "boilerplate" piece of Śaiva renunciant practice then, we find ourselves in the presence of a number of operations that closely resemble alchemical operations, and that concretely reproduce the Śaiva symbolism of ashes inasmuch as *bhasma* is itself—like the universe—subjected to a sequence of purificatory processes that involve burning, flooding, and burning again.

In Śaiva alchemy, the primary object of the *samskāras,* the ordered series of chemical operations that ultimately issue in the generation of a perfected, immortal, unaging and invulnerable body, is precisely the preparation of calcinated mineral oxides or ashes *(bhasma).* When they are consumed by the alchemist, these ashes, and most particularly the calcinated preparation called killed mercury (*mṛtasūtaka* or *mṛtabhasma*), will transform him—if it does not kill him—into a perfected immortal, a Siddha. Indeed, it is only when it has been killed, reduced to ashes, that mercury, the alchemical equivalent of Śiva's seed, is capable of resurrecting (and thereby fundamentally transmuting, transforming) other bodies, both metallic and human.[11] It is no coincidence that in the alchemical tradition, the most common term for mercury is *rasa;* the same term as is used for Śiva's seed as well as for any vital fluid, divine, human, animal, or vegetable; and so it was that India's medieval alchemists, who regenerated and perfected their bodies through the consumption of *rasa,* called themselves the "Rasa Siddhas."

My first taste of ashes was at the Benares temple of Kāla Bhairava or Bhaironāth, of which the important medieval Śaiva sect known as the Nāth Siddhas, the "Perfect Masters," were custodians until recent date. While this sect, which traces its origins back to the tenth century C.E. figure of Matsyendranātha, is best known today for its major innovations in the practice of *haṭha yoga*—innovations made by its late twelfth- to early thirteenth-century C.E. founder Gorakhnāth—it is also that sect that was most responsible for integrating the already existing discipline of Hindu alchemy into its broader practice. (Here, by the way, I take issue with present-day scholarly consensus, which maintains that the Kaula *paścimāmnāya* or "Western Transmission," whose core text is the *Kubjikāmata,* innovated Hindu *haṭha yoga.* On the basis of a close study of Matsyendranātha's *Kaulajñānanirṇaya*[12] and the *Kubjikāmata,*[13] I would maintain that the former is the original work on the subject; it is not, however, until the later works of Gorakhnāth himself that one can truly speak of a hathayogic system.)

What the Nāth Siddhas in fact did was to carry out to its logical conclusions the project of the Hindu alchemists, the Rasa Siddhas, whose core textual tradition predates Gorakhnāth's hathayogic synthesis by about two centuries. It is quite correct, I believe, to see in the *haṭha yoga* of the Nāth Siddhas the culmination of the mercury-based alchemy of the earlier Rasa Siddhas inasmuch as *haṭha yoga* is, to a great extent, an internalization, onto the grid of the subtle body, of external alchemy. In order to provide some context for this assertion, I cite here passages from the introduction and conclusion of the eleventh-century C.E. *Rasārṇava* (RA), the "Flood of Mercury," the classic text of the North Indian Rasa Siddhas. What these passages indicate, more than anything else, is the altogether *concrete* (as opposed to symbolic or gnoseological) nature of alchemical transformation.

> Eternal youth, bodily immortality, and the attainment of an identity of nature with Śiva—that is, liberation in the body *(jīvanmukti)*—is difficult even for the gods to attain. The liberation which occurs when one drops dead, that liberation is worthless. For in that case, a donkey would also be liberated when it dropped dead. If liberation is to be identified with the excitation of the female genitilia, would not even donkeys be liberated? Indeed, why are rams and bulls not liberated? Therefore, one should safeguard one's body with mercury and mercurial elixirs. . . . Liberation is indeed viewed in the six schools as occuring when one drops dead, but that kind of liberation is not directly perceivable, in the manner of a myrobolan fruit in the hand *(karāmalakavat)*.[14]

Tropical fruits are good to think with. For the Hindu alchemists, bodily immortality was something to be grasped, like a fruit, not in some nonverifiable future existence following the death of the gross body, but in the here and now. The final fifteen verses of the *Rasārṇava* (18.213–227) tell us how:

> Let the alchemist place thirty-six pellets of "diamond-bound" mercury [that has proven its efficacity by restoring cripples, freaks, and mutants to wholeness and by transmuting ten million times its mass of base metals into gold] in a copper cauldron of oil and clarified butter that is of the same measure as himself in height and half his measure in diameter. Let him place a four-sided wooden frame around the mouth of this cauldron. Then, let him worship the cauldron, the regents of the four quarters, and a virgin. . . . When he sees that the oil has stopped smoking, he should then bow to his *guru,* the sun, moon, planets, and stars, and then leap into the cauldron.

At this point, the text (*Rasārṇava* 18.217) explains the principle behind this operation: the five gross elements—"*earth, water, fire, air, and ether*"—of his material body will be serially transformed into their subtle correlates (*tanmātras*), beginnining with that of earth, and ending with that of ether. And, as the alchemist boils down, the RA continues with instructions for his faithful laboratory assistant, noting what he is to add as the body in the cauldron disintegrates (and here I abridge the description):

When he has been [reduced to] a ball of flesh *(maṁsapiṇḍa)*, [the assistant] should add the [chemical equivalent of] the element air. When the mix has taken on a beautiful appearance, he should place mica [*kha,* the alchemical equivalent of the fifth element, ether] in the skull. Then, pumping the bellows [until the mix has] the look of molten gold, [the assistant] should add an alkaline substance *(kṣāra)*. No sooner has this been done than [the Alchemical Man] rises up with a mighty roar: "Hum!". His flesh entirely restored, his body is massive, and shines with a divine brilliance, like the sun. Possessed of great strength, he has the power of divine sight. . . . He mounts into an aerial car made of divine gold . . . and a divine maiden . . . comes to him, and takes that consummate practitioner [with her] to dwell in the world of the Siddhas.

As this classic description of alchemical apotheosis makes clear, the Rasa Siddha must, in order to be reborn, first die in a cauldron of burning oil. But clearly, it is in his own body, now entirely transformed, that he is reborn, and that he mounts to the atmospheric realms of the Siddhas, the "self-made gods"[15] of this medieval tradition, to enjoy an existence of eternal felicity.

The link between the theory and practice of the Rasa Siddhas and the later Nāth Siddhas is already intimated in the *Rasārṇava* (1.18–19) itself, which indicates the complementarity of outer alchemy and inner yogic practice in its introductory verses: "The preservation of the body is realized through the Work *(karmayoga)*. Mercury and breath [control]: these are known as the Work in two parts. When swooned, mercury, like the breath, carries off disease; when killed, it reanimates itself; when bound, it affords the power of flight."

This statement is echoed in Gorakhnāth's *Amaraughaprabodha* (v. 5), which describes the twofold *rājayoga* as botanical and spiritual, and the twofold *haṭha yoga* as the "practice of breath and seed."[16] Still more striking is a passage from the fifteenth-century *Haṭhayogapradīpikā* of Svātmarāman, an author who acknowledges Gorakhnāth as his prinicipal source, and whose work is, for the most part, a systematic recapitulation of the principles set forth in the *Gorakṣa Śataka,* in the *Yogamārtaṇḍa,* and in other hathayogic works of Gorakhnāth. What is remarkable about this passage (*Haṭhayogapradīpikā* 4.27) is that it is identical to the *Rasārṇava* (1.19) passage I quoted a moment ago (as well as to analogous passages in nearly every other major Hindu alchemical work). In other words, Svātmarāma is self-consciously employing "alchemical" terminology to make a yogic point. That is, the same verse may be read on two different registers, the one alchemical and the other yogic. Once again, the verse in question reads as follows: "When swooned, *rasa,* like the breath, drives away diseases; when killed, it reanimates itself; and when bound, it affords the power of flight."[17] In the alchemical *Rasārṇava,* the term *rasa* refers to swooned, bound, and killed mercury, the ingestion of which, in tandem with the practice of breath control, renders the practitioner healthy, immortal, and possessed of the power of flight. The hathayogic *Haṭhayogapradīpikā* promises the same results, but takes *rasa* to mean "semen," the immobilization and retention of which are paramount to the hathayogic discipline, as witnessed in a poem attributed to the Nāth Siddha Gopīcand:

> Steady goes the breath, and the mind is steadied, steady goes the mind, the semen;
> Steady goes the semen, and the body is steadied, that's what Gopīcand is sayin'.[18]

What I wish to indicate here is not only that the alchemical synthesis of the Rasa Siddhas anticipated the hathayogic synthesis of the Nāth Siddhas by a number of centuries, but also that for Gorakhnāth—both the great systematizer of *haṭha yoga* and a highly reputed alchemist[19] in his day—the chemical reactions he observed in his laboratory provided food for thought regarding the internal processes of yogic transformation. I would go so far as to say that it was by observing the behavior of metals and minerals undergoing the alchemical processes of steaming, rubbing, roasting, trituration, calcination, and so on that Gorakhnāth reached a number of his original insights concerning the practice and effects of *haṭha yoga*.

In a unified universe in which transformations in the macrocosm and its human replica, the microcosm, were effected through the dynamic interaction of the same three elements—fire, wind, and fluid—deductive changes of register, from the metallic to the corporeal would have been self-evident.[20] Among these would have been the basic notion that such poisons as mercury, when reduced to ashes, were not only detoxified but also transformed into ambrosial elixirs of eternal life. This is in fact what the alchemist did in his laboratory and, as the *Rasārṇava* makes clear, it was only possible for him to absorb the potions he produced by combining his alchemical practice with hathayogic breath control: this was the Work in two parts.

In addition to his Sanskrit works on the technical theory and practice of *haṭha yoga,* Gorakhnāth was also the author of a body of mystic poetry on the concrete *experience* of the practitioner. Among his most powerful verses on these matters is the following, which underscores the continuity of Rasa Siddha and Nāth Siddha concepts concerning death and regeneration: "Die yogi die, dying is sweet [when you] die that death by which Gorakh, in dying, gained his vision [of the absolute, immortality]."[21]

An alchemical echo is provided in Muhammad Jayasi's sixteenth-century *Padmāvat,* a romance in which the hero is a prince-turned-Nāth Siddha: "The Siddha's immortal body is like mercury. You can break it down, you can kill it, but you can't make it die."[22]

What is it, then, that dies? It is the gross, biologically given body, a husk that is to be cast off like the slough of a snake. How is this body made to die, in order that the golden, adamantine, or *siddha* body may emerge? In *haṭha yoga,* it is breath control that plays a central role in this transformation. So too, however, does the generation of yogic heat, of the fire of yoga *(yogāgni)* that burns up the fire of time or death *(kālāgni)*. Here, the focus of breath control is on the three central channels (*nāḍī*s) of the subtle body. In order to reverse the normal downward, death-laden flow of existence, the practitioner first must concentrate all of his vital breaths and energy into the *iḍā* and *piṅgalā* channels, which are peripheral to the central *suṣumṇā*. Then through a "pumping technique," the yogin first inflates and then empties these two peripheral *nāḍī*s of breath. This emptying is likened to a death that generates new life, in this case through the resulting opening and inflation of the upward-tending medial *suṣumṇā*. In its description of the yogic seal called the *mahāvedha* (the great penetration), the *Amaraughaprabodha* states that "the breath, overflowing the two vessels [the *iḍā* and *piṅgalā* channels] . . . suddenly bursts [into the medial channel]. The union of moon, sun, and fire which then occurs surely results in immortality. When the condition of death *(mṛtāvasthā)* occurs, how can there be fear of death?"[23] Passing through a state of death to bodily immortality is also effected, in hathayogic practice, through the mediation of fire, since it is a fiery breath, called the *brahmāgni,* which rises through the medial channel, rendering it a microcosmic cremation ground *(śmaśāna)*,[24] at the upper end of which gross semen *(rasa)* is transformed into vivifying rejuvenating nectar *(amṛta)*. To this corresponds the macrocosmic cremation ground, which is nothing other than the entire universe, that Śiva "saves" by reducing it to ashes, at the end of an aeon. On the mesocosmic level, the cremation ground is also the site of the final sacrificial offering *(antyeṣṭi)*, the last of a long series of life cycle rites (*samskāra*s), many of which are portrayed, symbolically, as so many sacrifices. Of course, sacrifice is, in its original Vedic context, the transformation of a fluid offering *(rasa)*, through cooking in fire *(agni)*, into an ambrosial offering fit for the gods.[25] In this perspective, all of the transformations we have been discussing, are so many variations on this fundamental Vedic dynamic of cooking, with two important changes. One of these is the intensity of the cooking process. If Vedic sacrifice was "cooking to a turn,"[26] Tantric calcination is "cooking the hell out of": indeed, the object of these Tantric transformations is Time or Death (Kāla) itself, "which cooks all beings."[27] In order to cook Time itself, one needs to turn up the heat a number of extra notches: this is precisely what the yogin does when he cooks the fire of time *(kālāgni)* in the fires of yoga *(yogāgni)*. The mythological correlate to this practice are the many legends in which Nāth Siddhas skew time (*kāla-vañcana*) or trick Death,[28] thrashing Yama, the god of the dead when he attempts to carry off one of their number.

The second shift, from Vedic to Tantic or Siddha practice, involves the locus of transformation; for whereas in the Vedic sacrifice or in the ultimate sacrifice that is cremation the cooked or ashen residue that remained in this world was an indication that the nectar of the sacrifice was being enjoyed by the gods or by the transformed person in that other world, in the transformations we have been discussing, both the ashen residue and the alchemically- or yogically-produced nectar are enjoyed in this world, by the practitioner himself. The alchemical synthesis takes things one step further: ashes *are* the nectar that the practitioner enjoys in this world; his body is immortal because it has been calcinated.

Mercury and its compounds in flux are never anthropomorphized in the Indian alchemical texts as they are in Western alchemical traditions (in which the *corpus alchymicum* of the "Ethiopian" or "Son of God" is dismembered, crushed, cooked, etc. to be resuscitated in a new divine form). It is rather in the legends of the Nāth Siddhas that such allegorical dismemberments and tortures occur; and while the origins of these accounts may be as old as religion itself, the "gloss" they receive in Nāth Siddha legend appears to be both alchemical and yogic. Nowhere are these themes as evident as in the best-known and perhaps the oldest of such accounts, the legend of Caurangī (Four-Limbs) or Pūraṇ Bhagat.[29]

While Pūraṇ Bhagat is generally held to be the son of King Śālivāhana (Sāl Vāhan, Salwān, Sulivān, and Sulwahan in vernacular transcriptions), the principal Punjabi recension of his legend first calls this figure King Śaṅkh. One source maintains that Pūraṇ Bhagat was born of Śiva's seed.[30] Pūraṇ Bhagat is the son of Śaṅkh/Salwān's first queen Acchrān, and it is not until the age of twelve that has his first audience with the junior queen, Lūṇā (or Lūṇān/Nūṇān/Noṇān). This queen, who is in reality a terrible witch,[31] falls in love with her adolescent stepson, and attempts to seduce him. When he refuses her advances, she denounces him to the king, claiming that he had seduced her.[32]

At her urging, the king orders that Pūraṇ Bhagat be bound *(bandhke)* hand and foot, and that his head be cut off and kebab'ed.[33] When the boy is brought before the king, he takes a vow of truth: let the king plunge him into a cauldron of boiling oil; his innocence will be proven if no part of his body, not even one of his fingers, be burned. Lūṇā lights the fire and puts on the cauldron, and Pūraṇ Bhagat is plunged into the boiling oil for four hours, from which he emerges unscathed.[34] Lūṇā nevertheless has her way, and an outcaste is ordered to cut off Pūraṇ Bhagat's hands, gouge out his eyes, and throw him down a well.[35] The outcaste, pitying the young prince, spares him, and instead slays a fawn and brings its eyes and blood to Lūṇā; she, however, tests this blood by plunging a pearl into it, and sees that it is not that of her stepson.[36] The outcaste, fearing for his own life, goes to the forest where Pūraṇ Bhagat has hidden. In order to spare him, Pūraṇ Bhagat has him do Lūṇā's bidding. His arms and legs are cut off, his eyes gouged out, and his body thrown down a dry, broken-down well *(jīrṇāndhakūpa)*. Also at Pūraṇ Bhagat's request, he returns to the city to tell Acchrān that her son will return after twelve years.[37]

Acchrān, turned out of the city by the king, comes to the well into which Pūraṇ Bhagat has been thrown. He cries up to her, "Set my elephant free, mother, to go to the Kajali Forest. . . ."[38] Twelve years pass, until one day Gorakhnāth and his retinue of yogins come to Pūraṇ Bhagat's well on their way from their monastery at Ṭilla to Sialkot. There they find the young man, and draw him out with a single thread of spun cotton. Gorakhnāth then restores his eyes, and, sprinkling nectar *(amṛta)* over him, restores his limbs.[39] Twenty-four years later, Gorakhnāth again returns to the well, and finds that Pūraṇ Bhagat has remained inside, in the practice of asceticism. When Pūraṇ Bhagat asks Gorakh to initiate him into the Nāth order, he and his disciple Kānīpā (Kanha-pā) initiate him with ashes and earrings.[40]

Now a full-fledged yogin, Pūraṇ Bhagat returns to Sialkot, his childhood home, where his mere presence causes his garden to burst into bloom. He restores his mother Acchrān's sight, and forgives Salwān and Lūṇā. To the latter he gives grains of *dhāk* and rice from his yogin's wallet, promising that by swallowing them whole, she will conceive and bear a son, Rasālū.[41]

It is possible to view the legend of Pūraṇ Bhagat as a medieval Indian alchemical allegory. Like mercury, its hero is born of Śiva's seed; his human father, Śaṅkh (*saṅ-khad,* "chew up," "consume") and stepmother Lūṇā (*lavaṇa,* corrosive "salt")[42] cause him to be bound *(baddha)*, boiled in oil *(sāraṇa)*, and dismembered *(mardana, māraṇa)*. All of these are alchemical operations, by means of which mercury is reduced to a "dead ash," at which point it "reanimates itself" and is rendered capable of transmuting base metals into gold.[43] The well he is thrown into is *jīrṇāndha,* which evokes the closed *(andha)* crucible in which mercury is calcinated (*jīrṇa,* the past passive participial form of the same root *jṛ* that generates *jāraṇa,* "calcinate," the alchemical operation in which mercury is "killed"). This well is moreover identified with Kajalī Van, the "forest of black mercuric sulphide" (*kajjalī*, one of the most common forms of processed mercury). After twelve years, he is drawn out of his well and restored through the magical techniques of Gorakhnāth, who restores him to wholeness with *amṛta*. The legend ends with Pūraṇ Bhagat offering Lūṇā seeds to eat, by which she conceives Rasālu, the mercurial one *(rasa)*.[44] Is Pūraṇ Bhagat then the Hindu "Alchemical Man" whose death and resurrection out of a crucible renders him capable of creating life? Perhaps.

Less alchemical in their allegorical content but more to the point of the life-giving properties of ash are two other legends of the Nāth Siddhas. These are the legends of the birth of Gorakhnāth, and of the initiation of Gopīcand. In the first of these, a solitary Brahman woman who desires a son is given a pinch of ash (i.e., *rasa,* "vital seed") by Matsyendra, who instructs her to consume it, together with milk, following her purificatory bath after her next menses. Instead of eating the ash, she throws it onto a heap of cowdung behind her house. Twelve years later, Matsyendra returns and asks for news of his son. When the woman avows that she had discarded the ash, Matsyendra scoops away twelve years of accumulated cowdung to reveal a perfectly formed twelve-year-old child yogin—for the boy has been practicing his *sādhana*s there since birth—whom he names Gorakh (*go-rākh:* "cow [dung]-ash) and makes his disciple.[45]

Ashes are also brought to the fore in a version of the classic legend of Gopīcand, whom his guru Jālandharanāth rescues from death by making him a yogin; that is, by initiating him through a process that is described by the young Gopīcand in the following terms: "I used to be an unfired pot, thrown whichever way [the wheel] turned. When I was made a *jogī* my *guru* did the firing."[46] Here, it is useful to recall that when earthen pots are fired, they are placed in the midst of a wood and dung fire inside an oven; at the end of the firing process, they are pulled out of the piled-up ash of the burnt combustibles. Like Gorakhnāth, the initiated Gopīcand is born out of the ashes.

Gorakhnāth's ashen dungheap and Gopīcand's dung-en ash-heap, both wombs (like the wells in which such Nāth Siddhas as Pūraṇ Bhagat are wont to meditate for twelve years) and tumuli (like the *samādhi*s under which Nāth Siddhas are buried), have their most significant structural parallel in what is perhaps the order's most important external attribute. This is the *dhūni,* a conical pile of wood- and cowdung-ash that the wandering yogin heaps up wherever he alights. Its fire warms him, its coals serve to light his chillum-pipe, and its ash is both the present or grace *(prasāda)* he bestows upon all who come to visit him, and the substance with which he smears his own body in imitation of Śiva. More than a movable hearth, the *dhūni* is, quite literally, a double of the yogin's subtle body, a body that has already been cooked and transformed through his yogic austerities. The ashes of the *dhūni* represent the continuity of his unending *sādhana*s and thereby of his immortal subtle body. Long after a yogin has quit his mundane body, his *dhūni* (maintained and kept burning, in some cases, for centuries), like his *samādhi,* remains as a memorial and testimony to his continuing presence in the world. India is a country dotted with the *samādhi*s and *dhūni*s of its great yogins, whose undying nature is epitomized through ashes. Like his Rasa Siddha forebears, the Nāth Siddha, by virtue of having calcinated and reduced his yogic body to ashes, himself becomes uncalcinable and all-calcinating, an ashen, ash-smeared, ash-producing, alchemical touchstone.

Notes

1. Edmund Leach, "Genesis as Myth," in *Genesis as Myth* (London: Grossman, 1969), pp. 8–11.

2. This discussion draws on Michel Hulin, *La face cachée du temps* (Paris: Fayard, 1985), pp. 35–36, 44.

3. On dying to the world and performing one's cremations rites, see P. V. Kane, *History of Dharamaśāstra,* 5 vols. 2d ed. (Poona: Bhandarkar Oriental Research Institute, 1968–75), vol. 2, part 2, pp. 954–55, 985. On the *prāṇāgnihotra,* see *Vaikhānasa Smārta Sūtra* 2.18. This tradition goes back to the *Taittirīya Āraṇyaka*: Madeleine Biardeau and Charles Malamoud, *Le sacrifice dans l'Inde Ancienne* (Paris: Presses Universitaires de France, 1976), pp. 67–68. A *Prāṇāgnihotra Upaniṣad,* a compilation of earlier Upanishadic descriptions of this practice, is found in Paul Deussen, *Sixty Upanisads,* 2 vols. (Delhi: Motilal Banarsidass, 1975), 2: pp. 645–51. Because the renouncer has performed his own cremation rites upon taking up *sannyās*, his body is not burned, but rather inhumed or set adrift, upon its apparent "death." On this see *Paiṅgala Upaniṣad* 4.5–8, cited in Lakshmi Kapani, *La notion du saṁskāra,* 2 vols. Publications de l'Institut de Civilisation Indienne, no. 59 (Paris: De Boccard, 1991, 1993), 1: 153.

4. *na tasya rogo na jarā na mṛtyuḥ prāptasya yogāgnimayaṃ śarīram/.*

5. The myth is found in *Mahābhārata* 1.71.2–1.72.25.

6. Georges Dumézil, *Mythe et épopée*, 3 vols. 2. *Types épiques Indo-Européens: un héros, un sorcier, un roi,* 4th ed. (Paris: Gallimard, 1986) 2: 200–204.

7. On the Pāśupatas, see David Lorenzen, "Śaivism: Pāśupatas," in *Encyclopedia of Religion,* ed. by Mircea Eliade (New York: Macmillan, 1986), 13: 18. On *vibhūti,* Sir Monier Monier-Williams, *A Sanskrit-English Dictionary* (London: Oxford University Press, 1899; reprint Delhi: Motilal Banarsidass, 1984), s.v. "vibhūti. On the consumption of ashes as a component of *dīkṣā,* see *Manu Smṛti* 6.25, 38 (*Manu Smṛti,* with the commentary of Kullūka Bhaṭṭa, ed. Pandit Gopala Sastri Nene, Kashi Sanskrit Series, no. 114 (Benares: Chowkhamba Sanskrit Series Office, 1970).

8. Basavaṇṇa 537, trans. A. K. Ramanujan, "The Myths of Bhakti: Images of Śiva in Śaiva Poetry," in *Discourses on Śiva: Proceedings of a Symposium on the Nature of Religious Imagery,* ed. Michael Meister (Philadelphia: University of Pennsylvania Press, 1984), p. 213.

9. *Brahmāṇḍa Purāṇa* 1.2.27.91b–123, trans. in Wendy Doniger O'Flaherty, *Hindu Myths* (Harmondsworth: Penguin, 1980), pp. 147–48.

10. Rajesh Bedi and Ramesh Bedi, *Sadhus, The Holy Men of India* (New Delhi: Brijbasi Printers Private, 1991), pp. 78–79. Cf. Raya Bahadur Munshi Haradayal Singh, *Riporṭ Mardumaśumārī Rāja Mārvāḍ Bābat san[vat] 1891 Īsvī, Tīsarāhissā,* 2 vols. (Jodhpur: Vidyasal, 1895), 2: 244.

11. *Rasārṇava* 7.142, 12.79 (*Rasārṇavam nama Rasatantram,* ed. with Hindi trans. by Indradeo Tripathi and notes by Taradatta Panta, Haridas Sanskrit Series, no. 88 (Banares: Chowkhamba, 1978); *Rasaratnasamucchaya* 11.75–76 (*Śrīvāgbhaṭācāryaviracitaḥ Rasaratnasamucchaya,* ed. with a Hindi commentary by Dharmananda Sharma (Benares: Motilal Banarsidass, 1962).

12. *Kaulajñānanirṇaya and Some Minor Texts of the School of Matysyendranātha,* ed. Prabodh Chandra Bagchi, Calcutta Sanskrit Series, no. 3 (Calcutta: Metropolitan, 1934). A mention of the Siddha[-amṛta] Kaula in the *Kaulajñānanirṇaya* (16.47a, 48c;

21.4–7), is significant inasmuch as Śiva-Bhairava is praised as the leader of the Siddha Kaulas in an opening verse of the *Rasārṇava* (1.4b); the same alchemical work (18.228a) closes with—and perhaps takes its title from—a verse it appears to borrow from the *Kaulajñānanirṇaya* (17.7a).

13. *Kubjikāmata Tantra, Kulālikāmnāya Version*, eds. Teun Goudriaan and Jan A. Schoterman, Orientalia Rheno-Traiectina, no. 30 (Leiden, Netherlands: Brill, 1988). For a more detailed discussion of the issue, see White, *Alchemical Body,* chapter 5, part 2.

14. *Rasārṇava* 1.8–13.

15. I own this felicitous appellation to Charlotte Vaudeville, *Kabīr,* vol. 1 (Oxford: Clarendon Press, 1974), p. 96.

16. *auṣadhyo'dhyātmakaśceti rājayogo dvidhā kvacit / haṭho 'pi dvividhaḥ kvāpi vāyubindunisevanāt //* (*Amaraughaprabodha* of Gorakhnāth, in Kalyani Mallik, *Siddha Siddhānta Paddhati and Other Works of the Natha Yogis* (Poona: Oriental Book House, 1954). Cf. *Rasārṇava* 4.23, which calls for the conjoined use of botanicals and *mantras*.

17. *Haṭhayogapradīpikā of Svātmarāman,* with the commentary of Brahmānanda, ed. and trans. Srinivasa Iyengar (Madras: Adyar, 1972). Verse 4.27 reads: *mūrchito harate vyādhīn mṛto jīvayati svayam / baddhaḥ khecaratāṃdhatte raso vāyuśca [parvati] //*. Cf. *Rasārṇava* 1.19: *mūrchito harate vyādhiṃ mṛto jīvayati svayam / baddhaḥ khecaratāṃ kuryyāt raso vāyuśca [bhairavi]//.*

18. *Rājā rāṇī sambād*, v. 18 in Hazariprasad Dvivedi, ed., *Nāth siddoṃ kī bāniyāṃ,* 2d ed. (Benares: Kasi Nagarapracarini Sabha, 1980), p. 9. Statements of this kind are legion in the hathyogic sources. Cf. *Haṭhayogapradīpikā* 2.2 and 4.26, 28 for more sober formulations.

19. In addition to being the purported author of the thirteenth-century alchemical *Bhūtiprakaraṇa* (published under the title *Gorakṣa Saṁhitā* (part 2), ed. Janardana Pandeya, Sarasvatibhavana-Granthamala, vol. 110 (Benares: Sampurnananda Sanskrit Visvavidyalaya, 1979); Gorakhnāth figures in a number of Rasa Siddha lists, and in a number of alchemical legends. On these, see White, *Alchemical Body*, chapter 4.

20. Such is also anticipated in the *Rasārṇava* 17.165: "As in metal, so in the body."

21. *Gorakh Bānī* Sabadi 26: *marau be jogī marau, maraṇ hai mīṭhā/ tis maranīṃ marau jis maranīṃ Goraṣ mari dīṭhā //* (Pitambaradatta Barthwal, *Gorakh Bānī* [Allahabad: Hindi Sahitya Sammelan, 1955]). Cf. Kabir, *Sākhī* 19.13 (= *Doha* 41.8), in Vaudeville, *Kabīr*, p. 260.

22. *Padmāvat* 24.2, in *The Padumawāti of Malik Muhammad Jaisī,* ed. with a [Hindi] commentary, translation, and critical notes by George Grierson and Sudhakara Dvivedi, Bibliotheca Indica, n.s. 877 (Calcutta: Baptist Mission Press, 1896), p. 530.

23. *Amaraughaprabodha* 40b–41, which is nearly identical to *Haṭhayogapradīpikā* 3.27b–28. I have translated the problematic *jānīyāt* in this passage as a gerundive. The fourth state of consciousness is called either *mūrcchā* or *turīya* ("trance"). A fifth may be

added. This is *maraṇa*, "death": commentary to the English translation of *Haṭhayogapradīpikā* 4.107 (p. 107).

24. *Haṭhayogapradīpikā* 3.4.

25. For a discussion of this symbolism in the context of the Hindu practice of *satī*, see the masterful synthesis of Catherine Weinberger-Thomas, *Ashes of Immortality: Widow-Burning in India,* trans. Jeffrey Mehlman and David Gordon White (Chicago: University of Chicago Press, 1999).

26. Charles Malamoud, "Village et forêt dans l'idéologie de l'Inde brahmanique," in *Cuire le monde* (Paris: Editions de la Découverte, 1989), p. 102; Kapani, *Notion du saṁskāra,* vol. 1, p. 60, note 34, citing *Śatapatha Brāhmaṇa* 6.2.2.6; 6.3.1.1.; and 6.5.3.1.

27. *Maitrī Upaniṣad* 6.15.

28. *Haṭhayogapradīpikā* 3.3; *Kaulajñānanirṇaya* 17.17.

29. The principal recensions of the Pūraṇ Bhagat/Caurаṅgīnāth legend are those found in Richard Carnac Temple, *The Legends of the Panjāb,* 3 vols. (London: Turner and Company, 1884–86; reprint Patiala: Department of Languages, Punjab, 1963), 2: 375–455, no. 34; Charles Swynnerton, *Romantic Tales from the Panjāb* (Westminster, England: Archibald Constable, 1903), pp. 411–41, both of which are Punjabi; and the twenty opening verses of the fourteenth-fifteenth-century. *Prāṇ Sāṅkalī* of Caurаṅgīnāth (in Dvivedi, *Nāth Siddhoṃ*, pp. 19–20), written in a medieval eastern Rajasthani dialect (ibid., p. 16 of the preface). It is also recounted in the *Yogīsampradāyāviṣkṛti*, a work of Nāth Siddha hagiography attributed to the late thirteenth-century Marathi saint Jñāneśvara (p. 372, cited in Hazariprasad Dvivedi, *Nāth Sampradāy*, 3d ed. [Allahabad: Lokabharati Prakashan, 1981], p. 177); and in Camanlal Gautama, *Śrī Gorakhnāth Caritr* (Bareilly: Samskrti Samsthan, 1981), pp. 81–89.

30. *Prāṇ Sāṅkalī,* in Dvivedi, ed. *Nāth Siddhoṃ*, p. 19 [= v. 206]. On the Śaṅkh/Salwān alternation, see Temple, *Legends*, 2:376, 378 [legend 34, vv. 5, 28], who says in a note that Śaṅkh is Salwān's father. Gautama (*Srī Gorakhnāth Caritra,* p. 82) maintains that Caurаṅgīnāth was born from Śiva's seed, and that King "Śaśāṅga" was Caurаṅgī's surrogate father. The Punjabi legend recounted in Temple states that Pūraṇ Bhagat was conceived by Acchrān "as soon as the Sun saw her" (*Legends,* 2: 384 [v. 93]).

31. Lūṇā, who is said in Temple's Punjabi recension of this legend (*Legends,* 2: 392 [v. 187]) to be of the Chamāri (currier) subcaste, is widely known as Loṇā (or Noṇā) Chamāri, the most terrible sorceress of North India. She is said to have gained her powers by eating the corpse of Dhanvantari, the divine founder of Āyurveda, who had died of snakebite at the fangs of the great *nāga* Takṣaka: William Crooke, *The Popular Religion and Folklore of Northern India,* 2d ed. (London: Constable, 1896: reprint Delhi: Munshiram Manoharlal, 1968), p. 437. Veiled references are given in Temple, *Legends,* 2: 386 and 413 (vv. 118–19, 441). Curiously, Sālwan is himself said to be the son of another great *nāga*, Vasuki (Bāsak) in another version of this legend: Briggs, *Gorakhnāth,* p. 184.

32. Temple, *Legends*, 2: 408 (vv. 383–86).

33. Ibid., 2: 411 (vv. 418–19).

34. Ibid., 2: 414–15 (vv. 457–468).

35. Ibid., 2: 417 (vv. 498–502).

36. Ibid., 2: 419–20 (vv. 517–33).

37. Ibid., p. 422–23 (vv. 555–67). The well is described as such in the *Śrīnātha-kathāsāra* of Dwarkanāth (ed. Narharinath [Benares: n.p., 1951], p. 18).

38. Ibid., 2: 426 (v. 604). Cf. Kabir, *Sākhī* 29.2 (in Vaudeville, *Kabīr,* p. 290): "This body is a *kajarī bana* and the mind is an elephant gone mad, the jewel of wisdom is the goad but few are the Saints who can apply it!"

39. Temple, *Legends*, 2: 428–34 (vv. 630–701).

40. Ibid., 2: 440–46 (vv. 774–846).

41. Ibid., 2: 448–55 (vv. 875–968).

42. Both *śaṅkha* and *(birwā) loṇa* are also herbs used in alchemical operations: *Kākacaṇḍeśvarīmata* (Kathmandu, Nepal National Archives mss. no. 5–3969) fol. 12a.9; and *Padmāvat* 310 [=27.3].

43. For a detailed description of these alchemical operations, see White, *Alchemical Body*, chapter 9, especially parts 2 and 4.

44. This would parallel such Hindi constructions as *dayālū*, from *dayā*, "kindness": thus "kind"; or *kṛpālū,* from *kṛpa,* "mercy": thus "merciful."

45. Sylvain Lévi, *Le Népal,* 3 vols. (Paris: Ernest Leroux, 1905; reprint Paris: Toit du Monde & Errance, 1985), 1: 351, 372 citing the *Buddha Purāṇa*; and Dvivedi, *Nāth Sampradāy,* p. 47, citing the *Yogīsampradāyāviṣkṛti* (see note 29). This latter account, which includes the detail concerning milk and menses, is adapted into Hindi in Gautama, *Śrī Gorakhnāth Caritr*, p. 6. A Punjabi variant is briefly recounted in H. A. Rose, *A Glossary of the Tribes and Castes of the Punjab and Northwest Frontier Province*, 3 vols. (Lahore: Superintendant, Government Printing, Punjab, 1911–19; reprint Delhi: Asian Educational Services, 1990), 2: 393. Another version of the same account, from the *Tahqiqat-i-Chishti*, is cited in George Weston Briggs, *Gorakhnāth and the Kānphaṭa Yogis* (Calcutta: YMCA Press, 1938; reprint New Delhi: Motilal Banarsidass, 1982), pp. 182–83.

46. Gopīcand's statement (in Temple, *Legends,* 2: 48 [legend no. 18, vv. 499–500]) reads *kachā bartan hove jidhar phere phir jāe / ham to jogī hūe gurū ne dīe pakāe//.* Cf. Gorakhnāth's *Yogabīja* 34–35, 51, which distinguishes between a body that is cooked or fired *(pakvā)* by yoga and one that is not *(apakva)*; and evokes a "seven-*dhātu* body fired in the fire of yoga"; and the Vedic invocation to Agni and the gods, "May we be well cooked!" (*Ṛg Veda* 9.83.1).

2

Human Torches of Enlightenment: Autocremation and Spontaneous Combustion as Marks of Sanctity in South Asian Buddhism

Liz Wilson

Flames! Blazing flames rushing up the Lotus Throne!
From eight points, the flesh-bodies and worldly dust-hearts
Into poetry they all melt. . . .
The Great Monk emerges from night's darkness and earth's thickness,
He advances, sits in meditation, his face to the West turning,
Evoking the flames to enter his flesh and skin defenseless.
Hieratic, he prays, his arms hold the ritual position. . . .
A sharp breath, He expires, and stops the Great Wheel's roll.

The poet Vũ-Hoáng-Chu'o'ng describes in these lines the death of the Vietnamese monk Thich Quang-Duc, who resolved in May of 1963 to end his life through self-immolation in response to the persecution of Buddhists by the Diem regime.[1] Seating himself in the lotus position at the busy intersection of Le Van Duying in Saigon, Quang-Duc lit a match and calmly ignited his gasoline-soaked robes while chanting Buddhist scripture. In sharp contrast to the keen emotion of the wailing crowds who watched his death, the monk's outward composure was one of complete self-control; observers noted that Quang-Duc never deviated from his steady chanting as the flames consumed his body. Thich Quang-Duc's decision to go out in a blaze of fire was not an isolated event. His self-immolation followed the pattern of medieval Chinese rituals of self-destruction involving fire—from the burning of isolated body parts to complete autocremation—and was in turn followed by the self-immolations of other Vietnamese monks and nuns.[2]

Although the question of to what extent such actions are sanctioned by Buddhist monastic rules is certainly an interesting one, it is not my concern here.[3] This chapter also brackets the question of how political events in medieval China and twentieth-century Vietnam may have fanned the flames of religious fervor, if you will, to the point where autocremation and the ritualized burning of body parts came to be a standard practice for those Buddhists willing to sacrifice themselves to shed light on a benighted world. My concern here is with the idiom of self-combustion that pervades these various acts of fiery self-destruction. I will explore Indian Buddhist texts that praise autocremation and other igneous displays at death. The death they describe is a sacrificial one: it is the natural (albeit spectacular) terminus of a disciplined life that is envisioned as a kind of slow-burning holocaust, an offering of oneself to the inner flames of austerity. The incandescent lifestyle praised in these texts eventuates in a fiery termination or burning out that is both hot and cool, conceived as both a conflagration and a complete extinguishing of a fire (*parinirvāṇa,* literally, "the complete blowing out" of a flame).[4] By burning oneself, then, one eventually burns out; this self-consuming conflagration is envisaged as a passing on to an unconditioned state. Although it is fruitless to inquire about the condition of the person who has passed through what Walter Kaelber in his study of Vedic heat imagery has called the "heated passage" of incandescent asceticism (since Buddhist doctrine holds that the person in question never existed in the first place), it is nevertheless fruitful to regard this final passing as a passage to an unconditioned state.[5] Contextualizing self-immolation and other acts of self-ignition (e.g., the spontaneous combustion of the funeral pyres of the awakened ones) by reference to Vedic-Hindu sacrificial practices and to Buddhist notions of mastery achieved through insight, I argue that this dramatic form of self-destruction may be understood as both a sacrificial act in which one willingly offers oneself to the flames and as a form of teaching in which one proclaims one's lack of essential nature in a wordless display of evanescence.

Self-immolation may appear to be an act of self-destruction toute courte. But as a sacrificial act in which one makes oneself a holocaust willingly offered to, and consumed by, the transformative element of fire, self-immolation can never be a wholly destructive act. As a sacrificium, something holy or sacred is produced (literally, "shaped or molded") at the moment of committing oneself to the flames. Such a destruction must also be a construction, a productive act. Not only is self-immolation a potentially creative act, it is also an act of communication. Something is transmitted to the eyes when a person goes up in flames; it is literally a phenomenal thing, a shining forth in which something appears. What appears in the flames of an auto-immolation is, of course, no longer the person who lit the match (or otherwise ignited the fire). What appears is a negative, if you will, of the flesh and blood person, an outline of what is absent or rapidly absenting itself. Thus auto-immolation is an act of communication in which the onlookers see something with which they cannot communicate. What the onlooker sees is a noumenon rather than a phenomenon; it is a sensory apprehension of some object that is itself inaccessible to sense experience (or rapidly becoming so, depending on the speed of the combustive process).

The Decision to Pass Away

Controlling the circumstances of one's death deprives death of its sting, and thus many South Asian religious traditions attempt to limit the contingency of death by offering ritualized means of achieving mastery over the end of life. For example, the ideal death that many contemporary Hindus strive for is one in which the dying person gives up the life force willingly and passes away surrounded by family members, in full command of his or her faculties, having previously predicted the time of his or her death.[6] Less accomplished people are caught unaware by death and their passing from this world is anything but a ritual act. They die with their pants down, as it were, in the midst of doing something else. Such persons, Hindus believe, inevitably cling to life in ways that endanger the well-being of the living; their dissatisfaction at being forced to relinquish their lives prematurely translates into malevolence as they continue to seek gratification in the world of the living from which they have been so unceremoniously wrenched. By contrast with the "bad" or unanticipated death of such persons, the "good" death that Hindus aspire to is a controlled, highly ritualized release of life. The more spiritually accomplished the dying person, the more control he or she has over the circumstances of death. Jonathan Parry describes the case of one exemplary man who performed intense austerities for nine months prior to his death, predicted the moment of his death, and died sitting upright while listening to a recitation of Hindu scripture.[7] As this pious man's body was being cremated, it successively manifested itself in the forms of several deities and famous religious teachers.[8]

Buddhist literature also places a high premium on taking control of the circumstances of one's passing from this world. Not only is the decision to terminate life at a moment of one's choosing an act commonly attributed to Buddhas and Buddhist saints, but Buddhist texts even go so far as to suggest that every Buddha voluntarily relinquishes the remainder of his allotted life span. The *Mahāparinibbāna Sutta,* for example, suggests that the letting go of one's vital forces is an act that every Tathāgata performs. When thunder and earthquake follow the Buddha's decision to let go of his life force, Ānanda asks about the cause of these celestial events and is told that just as the cosmos rises up in acknowledgment whenever someone destined to become a Buddha achieves awakening as a Tathāgata, so too there are bursts of thunder and a hair-raising earthquake when the Tathāgatas deliberately dismiss their allotted sum of life.[9]

Typical of Indian Buddhist accounts is the judgment that the Buddhist saint in question—be it a Buddha or awakened one, a *pratyekabuddha* or "solitary

Buddha," or an *arhat* or "worthy one"—has done what is needed to be done in order to alleviate suffering. Having accomplished what they set out to accomplish and transcended the forces of rebirth, Buddhas and Buddhist saints make the decision to enter *parinirvāṇa,* the "state of passing away completely." At the Cāpāla cairn in the city of Vaiśalī, for example, the Buddha Shākyamuni decided that he had accomplished his aims in life. The *Mahāparinibbāna Sutta* reports that the Buddha voluntarily relinquished at Vaiśalī the concomitant forces that would have allowed him to go on living, declaring that in three months time he would surely pass away:

> "The passing away of the Tathāgata will occur before long. At the end of three months, the Tathāgata will pass away." Thus the Blessed One while at the Cāpāla cairn consciously and deliberately let go of *(ossaji)* his vital force (*āyusaṅkhāraṁ,* literally, "life-construction"), and when he let go of his vital force there was an awful, hair-raising earthquake and there were bursts of thunder.[10]

The Buddha's decision to relinquish his vital force is a perfectly sensible act, given the view that death is the culmination of a life well lived, a life in which one has achieved all of one's aims. At Vaiśalī the Buddha of this epoch knew that he had accomplished what he took birth as a human to achieve. There was much to be gained by a decision that would circumvent death's unpredictability and show the Buddha's control over the forces of life and death.[11] Hence even though the Buddha reportedly chose to relinquish his remaining life span in response to an entreaty by Māra, the god of death and enemy of the Buddhas, this agreement to die should not be understood as a capitulation to the Deadly One.[12] Taking control of the circumstances of one's death is the ultimate act of mastery. By such means, Death is deprived of his dominion.

It is not only Buddhas who conquer death by seeming to fall into Māra's clutches. A number of Buddhist schools held that *arhats* also have the power to prolong or cut short life. There was considerable controversy over whether the power to alter one's life span is a power that abrogates or works within the laws of karma, with some schools (e.g., the Mahāsanghikas) maintaining that the laws of karma do not apply to awakened ones and others (e.g., the Sthaviravādins) maintaining that the power to alter one's life span does not abrogate the laws of karma.[13] Although the great Sthaviravādin commentator Buddhaghosa is critical of those who assert that the Buddha could have extended his life for billions of years in flagrant violation of the laws of karma, in his *Visuddhimagga* Buddhaghosa declares that anyone who has become an *arhat* through the practice of mindfulness with regard to breathing *(ānāpāṇasati)* can limit his life span and take control of the circumstances of his death: "Knowing that 'for this long and no longer my vital forces *(āyusaṅkhārā)* will continue,' he does what is proper with regard to himself—tending to his body, covering it with clothing, doing everything that is required—and shuts his eyes like Tissa the Elder of Koṭapabbata monastery, etc."[14] Buddhaghosa then lists a number of monks who were thus able to relinquish their vital forces and to orchestrate their own passages from terrestrial life. One monk mentioned by Buddhaghosa drew a line on the ground in his walking path and, predicting that when he walked across the line, he would expire, passed away just as his foot touched the line.[15]

Buddhas and Buddhist saints use the mastery over matter they attain through their meditative practices not only to control the moment of death but also to orchestrate magisterial displays at the time of death. Numerous Buddhist saints are said to have passed from this world by rising up in the air and entering into *parinirvāṇa* by resolving their bodies into one of the four material elements that constitute the body, namely, earth/solidity, water/fluidity, fire/heat, and air/movement. Some rise up into the air and draw the water-element out from their bodies; others enter into *parinirvāṇa* by resolving their bodies into the air-element.[16] Some emit both fire and water. But the method of passing away that is most commonly attributed to Buddhas and Buddhist saints is autocremation. Entering into meditative absorption (Pāli, *jhāna*; Sanskrit, *dhyāna*) by way of the fire-element *(tejo-dhātum)*, it is possible for the accomplished meditator to make the body burst into flames, going out in a fiery conflagration.[17] But before we can fully appreciate the significance of such acts of self-immolation at the moment of passing out of the cycle of birth and death, it is necessary to understand the importance of fire as a symbol of transcendence in the Indian cultural milieu in which Buddhism arose.

Burning Out

If Mircea Eliade is correct in his assertion that fire holds a unique place in the history of religions as the symbol of trancendence par excellence, then it should come as no surprise that for so many Buddhist saints the moment of passage from the cycle of birth and death should take the form of a conflagration in which matter is resolved into heat and light.[18] Having perfectly understood the cycle of cause and effect that leads to further birth and death in this world of dissatisfying addictions, and having achieved what they set out to achieve, Buddhas and Buddhist saints are said to pass out of existence like a flame that is extinguished for lack of fuel. But as images produced by Buddhist artists throughout Asia testify, that snuffing out of the fires of ignorance, passion, and hatred that lead to further existence is itself often envisioned as a fiery state. The fiery luminosity of the awakened ones is suggested by the halos of flame that surround Buddha images from India to Japan and by the flame finials that surmount the heads of Southeast Asian Buddha images.[19] The luminous power of the awakened ones also manifests itself as a pillar of fire in Buddhist iconography—a motif that draws on Vedic images of Agni, the god of fire, as a flaming pillar extending between heaven and earth.[20]

As Eliade and others have shown, the generation of radiant energy *(tapas)* through self-discipline is a practice that has ancient roots in India.[21] Vedic cosmological myths identify *tapas* as the force behind creation; various cosmogonic agents mentioned in the *Rig Veda* are said to create the world out of radiant energy.[22] The cultivation of radiant energy as a means of transformation and regeneration plays such a central role in Vedic descriptions of the ritual work of sacrifice that *tapas* has been called "the essence of the sacrifice."[23] Not only was the generation of *tapas* through self-imposed austerities such as fasting, seclusion, and chastity central to the rituals of consecration that qualified the Vedic sacrificer to enter the sacred space of the sacrificial arena, but homologies between the sacrificer and Agni, the igneous principle of transformation that glows within the sacrificial fire, suggest that ritual labor and its afterlife consequences were understood as a regenerative self-immolation. The sacrificer offered himself up to the womb-like fire (through the medium of an animal intermediary) in order to be reborn as a divine self in a divine abode.[24]

In the Upanishadic age the cultivation of radiant energy continued to play a key role in religious practice as Vedic sacrificial rituals were transposed into inner forms of sacrifice achieved through knowledge and asceticism.[25] The Buddha of the *Saṃyutta Nikāya* presents his celibate path, for example, as an internalized kindling of the Vedic fire sacrifice: "I ignite an inward fire . . . the heart is the altar, self-discipline the flame."[26] With its capacity for effecting purification and refinement, fire is commonly used in Buddhist discourse to symbolize the purity and power acquired through self-discipline.[27] The *Milindapañha* describes the wisdom, zeal, and other virtues that monks ought to cultivate as fires that burn away all impurities.[28] In the *Dhammapada,* the Buddha is depicted as burning with radiance *(tapati tejasā)* day and night, outshining the sun and moon that only glow by day or by night.[29] Various Buddhist saints are said to shine like fireballs or masses of fire *(aggikkhanda)*.[30] According to the *Dīpavaṃsa*, for example, it was the radiant appearance of the monk Nigrodha who blazed light like a fireball *(aggikkhandaṃ va tejitaṃ)* that attracted the attention of King Aśoka and led to the conversion of this key figure in the history of Indian Buddhism.[31] Fire imagery also holds a prominent place in descriptions of Buddhist *samādhi*s or "states of meditative absorption" and the realms to which such meditations give access, suggesting that higher levels of contemplative practice lead to the attainment of radiant states of being.[32]

The image of the saint who, having burned away inner impurities, blazes with light is apt on a number of levels. The defilements that are eliminated through Buddhist practice are often represented as liquid in nature. Since eliminating those "wet" emotional and cognitive states (known in Pāli as *āsava* and in Sanskrit as *āśrava*) that are usually rendered in English as "outflows" or "cankers" is the essence of liberation, the liberated saint may be said to have burned away the dross of desire and ignorance in the fire of self-discipline.

Mastery over the Elements: Taking Matter Into One's Own Hands

Those who blaze like fire can do so because they are said to have attained a special mastery over the element of fire as one of the physical elements that can be correctly apprehended and manipulated through meditation. Abhidharmic discussions of the four physical elements suggest that they exist in equal quantity in every material form, even though they may not be visible as such.[33] Because heat and fluidity are properties of everything, the "spontaneous" combustion or "spontaneous" liquification of any phenomenon is only a matter of making manifest what is not normally visible to the untrained eye. Buddhaghosa's discussion of the benefits of meditating on *kasina*s suggests that a wide array of abilities to influence material conditions can be achieved through meditative practice.[34] Using *kasina*-devices such as disks made of earth, bowls of water, lamps, and other embodiments of the four elements (as well as colored disks that embody qualities of the four elements), the accomplished meditator can perform various feats of mastery involving the four elements and their qualities.[35] Concentrating on water, for example, enables one to produce rain, create rivers, and dive headlong into the earth. Those who focus on earth can walk on land created in space or on water as well as reduplicate themselves so to appear in two different places at once. By using fire-devices such as lamps, one can produce smoke and various forms of fire and burn whatever one wishes, including one's own body at the time of death.

As signals of meditative prowess, fiery displays that underscore the mutability of matter are common in South Asian Buddhist hagiographic literature. Pāli sources attribute some spectacular examples of mastery over the element of fire, for example, to the *arhat* Dabba. Dabba's mastery over fire began early in life. Dhammapāla's commentary to the *Theragāthā* reports that he was born in the midst of flames, emerging miraculously from his mother's womb as his mother's body was being cremated. His grandmother found him laying on one of the posts of the pyre *(ekasmin dabbatthambhe)* and so gave him the name Dabba, "Post."[36] He was ordained at the age of seven and became an *arhat* while his head was being shaved during the ordination ceremony. Assigned the job of overseeing the assignment of lodgings to members of the monastic order, Dabba had a special method for dealing with monks who arrived at the monastery late at night seeking lodging: entering into the element of fire *(tejodhātuṃ samāpajjitvā)*, Dabba's fingers would begin to glow, the Pāli *Vinaya* indicates, and he would light the way holding his hand in the air.[37] Monks began to arrive late at night just to see the marvel of his supernormal powers *(iddhipāṭihāriyaṃ).* Requesting that Dabba convey them to distant lodgings on cliffs and mountaintops, they came up with various far-flung destinations just for the opportunity of observing how well Dabba's digital torch illuminated the surrounding landscape.[38] The account of Dabba's final *nirvāṇa* in the *Udāna* suggests that Dabba passed away in the same igneous manner in which he was born. Dabba attained the Buddha's permission to pass away, then rose up into the air in the lotus position, and, entering into the element of fire *(tejodhātuṃ samāpajjitvā),* was completely consumed, leaving not a speck of ash or soot behind, much less tissue or organ.[39]

Clearly, one who has developed mastery over the physical elements that comprise the body can perform amazing deeds. And yet such fiery displays are not really all that extraordinary when one considers the fact that the four elements of fire, water, air, and earth that comprise one's body are the same four great elements found outside the body. The element of fire/heat in one's belly responsible for the digesting of food is no different from the fire that consumes corpses on the cremation pyre. The fire within and the fire without are not two different things, but two forms of the same radiant energy that exists in all physical things. As the Buddha explains in the *Aṅguttara Nikāya,* one should see the fire within the body *(yā ajjhattikā tejodhātu)* as it really is, from the perspective of perfect wisdom *(evam etaṃ yathābhūtaṁ sammappaññāya daṭṭhabbaṃ)* and recognize that I am not this *(n' eso 'ham asmi)*; this [radiant energy] is not mine *(taṃ n' etaṃ mama).*[40] Just as the solid tissues in the body are simply forms of the earth element that are "on loan" to a person, having constituted in the past the solid tissues of billions of animals, vegetables, and other beings, so too the body's heat is not one's own but a particularized form of fire. Entering into the element of fire, one beholds no self there that is to be burned. Thus one passes away without leaving a terrestrial trace, as Dabba did and as so many other Buddhist saints are also reported to have done.

Autocremation as a Sacrificial Rite

Like the Hindu paragons of virtue that Jonathan Parry describes in his monograph *Death in Banaras,* the Buddhas do not die but rather give up their bodies willingly and pass away in ritually controlled circumstances.[41] Surrounded by their disciples (just as aged Hindu patriarchs are surrounded by their sons at death), in full command of their faculties, having previously predicted the time of their going, the Buddhas pass away with the decorum befitting a master of ceremonies. In that they describe a controlled and highly ceremonialized release of life, descriptions of the death of the Buddhas may be compared to accounts of Vedic-Hindu mortuary practices, in which the termination of life is understood as the ultimate act of sacrifice that culminates a career of sacrificial offerings.[42] To be acceptable as an offering, the life of the deceased must be freely given, for the essence of Vedic sacrifice and its Hindu counterparts is the sacrificer's willing renunciation or abandonment *(tyāga)* of self.[43] Cremation in the Vedic-Hindu tradition is thus the final sacrifice *(antyeṣṭi)*, the offering up of the body to the sacrificial fire as a voluntary sacrificial offering. If the Buddhist practitioner who has internalized the sacrificial fire, whose heart is the altar and whose self-disipline is the flame of an ongoing fire-sacrifice, wishes to culminate his or her career as one who burns away the dross of egoism in the inner flames of asceticism, what could be a more fit ending than the destruction of one's body in the flames of one's own inner heat? Exploding the illusion that there is an enduring essence within the composite of material and psychic elements that constitute the person, it is fitting that one who has achieved insight should simply burn out like the *arhat* Dabba is reported to have done.

Although the Buddha's passing from this world did not take the form of an autocremation like Dabba's in which the body went up in flames by virtue of its own inner heat at the moment of death, it is possible to construe the cremation of the Buddha's body as an autocremation, a voluntary self-incineration. The event was certainly not a typical cremation, for the pyre beneath the Buddha's body reportedly ignited of its own accord. Attempting to cremate the body of the Buddha, the Malla chieftains found that they could not light the pyre. It was only with the arrival of Mahākāśyapa (Pāli, Mahākassapa) along with a company of five hundred monks that the funeral pyre began to burn. The majority of the extant accounts of the Buddha's last days attribute the pyre's spontaneous combustion to the will of the deities, but one Chinese text attributes it to the will of the Tathāgata: "It is by the occult action of the Tathāgata himself."[44] Although as J. Przyluski has suggested, this attribution of agency to the deceased Buddha would seem to be a contradiction of the very meaning of *parinirvāṇa* as a complete passing away, Gregory Schopen's analysis of archaeological and epigraphic evidence for the ongoing presence of the deceased Buddhas in *stūpa*s (Buddhist funerary monuments) would suggest that Buddhas who have passed on are still capable of exercising considerable agency in this world.[45] Even though nothing remains of them but relics interred in a reliquary monument, deceased Buddhas nevertheless exercise certain of the legal rights of living persons, as evidenced, for example, by their right to own property.

If we view the events surrounding the death of the Buddha through the lenses provided by Vedic-Hindu mortuary rites, there is an additional reason to regard the cremation of the Buddha as an autocremation. The pyre of the Buddha only ignited after the arrival of Mahākāśyapa, the respected elder who is widely (although not universally) regarded in a variety of Indian Buddhist texts as the Buddha's legitimate successor.[46] Once Mahākāśyapa and the five hundred monks in his company had shown reverence to the body of their departed master, the pyre spontaneously combusted, catching fire of its own accord.[47] It is fitting that Mahākāśyapa should play the role of the catalyst whose presence ignites the pyre of the Buddha. As the Buddha's putative successor, he is equivalent to the eldest son who as chief mourner in Vedic-Hindu cremation ceremonies is responsible for lighting the pyre and releasing the life force of his father. Identified in Vedic literature as the father's double on earth, the son acts in accordance with the father's wishes in releasing his father's vital force by crushing the skull as it lays burning on the pyre. Indeed, their identification is so complete that one can say that it is the father who terminates his own existence on the cremation pyre.[48] Given that realized disciples of the Buddha are identified in Buddhist literature as heirs not only of his Dharma but of his *Dharmakaya,* his eternal teaching body, one can say that even while passing out of conditioned existence through the destruction of his physical body, the Buddha lives on in his teaching body incarnate in the form of his "son" Mahākāśyapa, who in the *Mahāvastu* identifies himself as "a true son of the Blessed One, born of the Dharma, created by the Dharma, an heir to the Dharma."[49] And because his son Mahākāśyapa acts in accordance with the Buddha's wishes as the heir not only to his teachings but to his person, the cremation of the Buddha is tantamount to autocremation.[50]

We might also compare the fiery termination of the Buddhas to the ceremonial deaths enacted by *satī*s, or virtuous Hindu widows who cremate themselves on their husbands' funeral pyres. Not only is the death of the *satī* described as a self-willed act, but the pyres of truly virtuous widows are often said to spontaneously ignite.[51] Since the *sat* or "goodness" of a devoted wife manifests itself in a fiery form akin to the *tapas* or "radiant energy" generated by asceticism, the spontaneous ignition of the *satī*'s pyre is explained as an effect of the radiance of the *satī*'s virtue.[52] That the pyre of the *satī* is said to spontaneously combust is not surprising, for it reinforces the idea that the death of the *satī* is a self-willed termination of life, thus absolving the relatives of any complicity in the "crime" of a widow's immolation.[53] Thus accounts of the passing away of *satī*s often underscore the voluntary nature of the widow's death by suggesting that—as Roop Kanwar's relatives asserted in 1987—no one lit the pyre of the widow in question.[54]

Autocremation as a Response to the Buddha's Passing On

Judging from scriptural accounts of the Buddha's death, it seems that reactions to the passing away of the Buddha varied considerably, from the abject weeping of Ānanda to the rejoicing of one monk—variously named—who gleefully anticipates a relaxation of monastic rules.[55] One theme, however, that is consistently stressed in the accounts is the desire of many members of the monastic order *(sangha)* to join the Blessed One in passing out of conditioned existence.

Thousands of *arhats* are reported to have entered into complete *nirvāṇa* upon hearing of the death of the Buddha. The Tibetan *Vinaya,* for example, reports that eighteen thousand *arhats* passed away on that day.[56] Typical of those saints who herald the passing away of the Buddha with their own final passing is the *arhat* Gavāṃpati.[57] Gavāṃpati not only went out in a shower of flames but also orchestrated an elaborate display at the moment of his passage.[58] Declaring that there was no point in his remaining any longer since no abiding essence ever remains, Gavāṃpati emitted both fire and water from his body, thus imitating the miracle of gleaming with burning flames and showers that the Buddha performed when manifesting the twin miracle (Pāli, *yamaka-pāṭihāriya;* Sanskrit, *yamaka-prātihārya*) at Shrāvastī.[59]

An equally stupendous exit is attributed to Gotamī Mahāprajāpatī, the Buddha's foster-mother and founder of the order of nuns *(bhikṣunī-sangha).* Unlike Gavāṃpati, however, Gotamī did not enter into final *nirvāṇa* as a response to the *parinirvāṇa* of the Buddha. She chose rather to predecease her stepson because she did not want to live to see the passing away of the Buddha and his chief disciples.[60] As reported in the *Sūtrālaṃkāra,* Gotamī and her five hundred companions put on an extraordinary show as they passed away. They touched the sun and moon with their hands, plunged into the earth as if it were a body of water, walked on water as if it were earth, and then performed the miracle of gleaming with burning flames and showers as they entered into final *nirvāṇa.* [61]

The aged monk Subhadra (Pāli, Subhadda) reportedly terminated his existence for the same reason as Gotamī and her five hundred companions: he did not wish to live to see the Buddha pass away. Subhadra learned of the immanent death of the Buddha in a dream and went to the dying master to ask about the path. Achieving *arhatship* upon hearing the Buddha's answers to his questions, Subhadra thought to himself, "I should not enter *parinirvāṇa* after the Buddha."[62] He then seated himself in the lotus position before the Buddha and incinerated his body completely, passing into final *nirvāṇa* as the Buddha lay dying.

With so many members of the sangha choosing to predecease the Buddha or passing out of existence after learning that Shākyamuni had passed away, it is no wonder that there were concerns about the decimation of the *sangha* and the consequent demise of the Buddha's teachings. Such concerns informed Mahākāśyapa's decision to convene the First Buddhist Council so that the teachings of the Buddha could be collected and preserved. To ensure that the teachings lodged in the collective memory of the *sangha* would be fully recollected and remembered (constituting a complete corpus or teaching body of the Buddha), Mahākāśyapa prohibited anyone from entering into final *nirvāṇa* until the canon had been compiled in its totality. Charged with preserving the teaching, *arhats* were to defer their own passing away. Many *arhats*, most notably Mahākāśyapa himself, are said to have used powers of longevity achieved through meditation to defer their deaths for many millennia; they have not yet passed on but reportedly live on to this day in a state of suspended animation. John Strong reads Mahākāśyapa's proclamation and his own postponing of *nirvāṇa* as an indication that even within "Hīnayāna" traditions proclaiming the ideal of the *arhat*, there is an emphasis on delaying out of compassion an enlightenment that is already within the arhat's power to realize.[63] In this suggestion "that the attainment of final *nirvāṇa* should somehow be postponed," Strong asserts, "We have a sentiment that could be seen to be the root of the [classical Mahāyāna] bodhisattva ideal."[64]

As Paul Griffiths has pointed out, however, the good of all sentient beings is not always well served by postponing the attainment of final *nirvāṇa*. Separation surely does make the heart grow fond, and therefore to have constant access to Buddhas and Buddhas-in-the-making is not always desirable. Griffiths notes that Buddhist scholastic theorists were very concerned about the dangers of overexposure to the presence of Buddhas, suggesting that zeal for the practice of the path would diminish if the physical presence of the awakened ones was not limited to reasonable life spans.[65] The self-immolations of the Buddhas who deliberately pass on—and of their disciples who follow—suggest that a good preacher is one who knows when to stop. If their words are to be heard and ring true in the minds of their audiences, the best preachers know, sometimes it is best to simply stop speaking.

Seeing Is Believing

A stanza in the *Theragāthā* compares Buddhas to fires that burn in the night, their wisdom giving light and the power of sight to dispel doubt of all who come to them.[66] The radiance of Buddhist saints at the moment of entry into *parinirvāṇa* can, like the radiance of the Buddhas, serve as a source of illumination for others. Thus pyrotechnic displays at death may be understood not only as epiphenomena of the process of entry into *parinirvāṇa* but also as forms of teaching. Harnessing the radiance of fire for the purpose of illustrating the abstract truths of the Dharma for those who need to see the Dharma in order to believe, Buddhas and Buddhist saints perform a pedagogical service through their displays of incandescence. Such nonverbal displays are frequently attributed to the solitary or self-awakened Buddhas (Pāli, *paccekabuddha*s; Sanskrit, *pratyekabuddha*s) who play such an important role as exemplars of the Dharma at times when no Buddha is present in the world.[67] These Buddhas are often described as having taken vows of silence; hence one of the primary means by which they propagate the Dharma is through providing opportunities for *darśana*, or "participatory seeing," as Reginald Ray puts it.[68] Since *pratyekabuddha*s generally transmit their teachings visually rather than aurally, textual descriptions emphasize the wondrous appearance of the solitary Buddhas, especially their radiance (Sanskrit, *śobhā*). In the Pāli *Jātakas*, they are described as suns *(suriyā)*; they are said to resemble deities because of their flame-like forms.[69] In the *Mahāvastu,* the solitary Buddhas are described as having the radiance of silence (*tūṣṇīkaśobhana*) about them: they shine out rather than speak out.[70] Objects that *pratyekabuddhas* come into contact with partake of the glow that surrounds these radiant saints. The *Mahāvastu,* for example, tells of a lotus once held in the hand of a *pratyekabuddha* that shone with brilliance; likewise a garland of flowers placed on the *stūpa* of a *pratyekabuddha* emitted brilliant light.[71]

At the time of their passing away, the luminosity of *pratyekabuddhas* finds full expression in the pyrotechnic displays that so often accompany the solitary Buddhas' achievement of *parinirvāṇa*. When Shākyamuni took the form of a white elephant in order to enter his mother's body, the *Mahāvastu* reports, five hundred *pratyekabuddhas* assembled at Deer Park (the site where Shākyamuni would later teach the Dharma) and passed out of existence in a phenomenal manner. They immolated themselves by rising up in the air to a height of seven palm trees and bursting into flames.[72] The appearance of the Buddha of this epoch rendering their continued existence in this world superfluous, these solitary Buddhas committed their bodies to the flames in what may be seen through the lenses of Vedic-Hindu mortuary rites as a sacrificial act of passing the torch to their successor. And in so doing, these shining ones in effect taught a sermon with their bodies at the moment of their passing away. Teaching by example being the only kind of teaching that *pratyekabuddhas* typically engage in, the autocremation of these solitary Buddhas constitutes an iconic foreshadowing of Shākyamuni's first teaching at Deer Park.

Like the fire Blaise Pascal spoke of in "The Memorial," the fire of self-combustion is a numinous fire. The incandescent preaching of the Buddhas and Buddhist saints points to an alternative reality of which apprehension is impossible. But unlike the fire of Pascal's ecstasy, which was "not of the philosophers," the fiery passing of the awakened ones and their disciples is also a communication of wisdom.[73] Passing the torch of enlightenment while themselves passing on, those who pass out of this world in incandescence demonstrate to others the fruits of their perfection of wisdom, a wisdom that is often and aptly described as "gone beyond."

Notes

1. Cited in Thich Thien-An, *Buddhism and Zen in Vietnam in Relation to the Development of Buddhism in Asia* (Tokyo: Charles E. Tuttle Company, 1975), p. 175.

2. Six other Vietnamese Buddhists, female as well as male, immolated themselves between May and October of 1963. The practice of self-immolation as an act of protest

continues to play a role among dissident Buddhist groups in Vietnam today. In May of 1993 in the city of Hue, a monk's death by self-immolation at a pagoda with a history of antigovernment activities led to the arrest of the abbot, Tri Tuu, and of two other monks on charges of breaching public security. Abbot Tri Tuu warned, in a letter released in Paris by a Vietnamese dissident group, that unless the government relents in its persecution of Buddhists, he too would self-immolate: "I will make my body a torch to light the truth." See the *New York Times,* International Edition, October 20, 1993, p. A4. On self-immolations by medieval Chinese Buddhists, see Jacques Gernet, "Les suicides par le feu chez les Bouddhistes Chinois du V́ an X siécle," *Mélanges Publiés par l'Institute des Hautes Études Chinoises* 2 (1960): 527-58; Jan Yün-hua, "Buddhist Self-Immolation in Medieval China," *History of Religions* 4 (1964): 243–68.

3. On the question of whether these self-immolations should be seen as a deviation from the precept against taking life, see Étienne Lamotte, "Le suicide religieux dans le Bouddhisme," *Bulletin de las Classe des Lettres et des Sciences de l'Académie Royale Belgique* 51 (1965): 156–68; Jean Filliozat, "Le mort voluntaire par le feu et la tradition Bouddhique Indienne," *Journal Asiatique* 251 (1963): 21–51; Charles D. Orzeck, "Provoked Suicide and the Victim's Behavior," in *Curing Violence*, eds. Mark I. Wallace and Theophus H. Smith (Sonoma, CA: Polebridge Press, 1994), pp. 141–60; Damien Keown, "Buddhism and Suicide: The Case of Channa," *Journal of Buddhist Ethics* 3 (1996). Jaina texts commend the voluntary termination of life through fasting while condemning those who commit suicide, which is classified as an act involving passion *(rāga)* and violence *(himsā)*. See Shadashari Settar, *Inviting Death: Indian Attitudes towards the Ritual Death* (Leiden, Netherlands: E. J. Brill, 1989).

4. Many of the terms used in this work exist in both Pāli and Sanskrit forms. Some of these terms—such as *parinirvāṇa*—are best left untranslated because there is no satisfactory English equivalent. For the sake of stylistic consistency, I have given preference to the Sanskritic forms of such terms (even though this work deals extensively with Pāli texts) since many of the most untranslatable Buddhist terms have become well-known to English speakers in their Sanskrit forms (e.g., *nirvana*).

5. Walter Kaelber, *Tapta Marga: Asceticism and Initation in Vedic India* (Albany: State University of New York Press, 1989).

6. See Jonathan Parry, *Death in Banaras* (New York: Cambridge University Press, 1994).

7. See ibid., p. 161.

8. Ibid.

9. Thunder and earthquake also herald the moment when those who are destined to become Buddhas are born as well as the moment in which they achieve *parinibbāna*. See *Dīgha Nikāya,* eds. T. W. Rhys Davids and J. Estlin Carpenter, 3 vols. (London: Pali Text Society, 1947), 2: 108.

10. *Mahāparinibbāna Sutta* 3.9–10. *Dīgha Nikāya,* 2: 106. All translations from the Pāli or Sanskrit in this paper are my own unless otherwise specified.

11. In "The Buddha's Prolongation of Life," *Bulletin of the School of Oriental and African Studies* 21 (1958): 546–52, Padmanabh S. Jaini discusses the role that mastery over the forces of life and death plays in the Buddha's decision; see esp. 547.

12. *Mahāparinibbāna Sutta* 3.7–9; *Dīgha Nikāya,* (cited above), 2: 104–6.

13. On the various interpretations of the Buddha's claim in the *Mahāparinibbāna Sutta* that whoever has developed the four bases of *ṛddhi* or "supernormal power" can remain alive for a *kappa,* see Jaini, "Buddha's Prolongation of Life," 546–52. At *Abhidharmakośa* 2.10, Vasubandhu summarizes a range of views on the means by which one can alter one's life span. Vasubandhu begins by surveying Vaibhāṣika attempts to produce an account of how *arhat*s can prolong or cut short life within the laws of karma. According to one view, there are two kinds of karma and the *arhat* is able to transform the one into the other. One is the karma that at the moment of conception determines one's life span *(āyur-vipāka-karma)* and the other *(bhoga-vipāka-karma)* is the sum total of all past karmas; it continuously yields fruit during one's life but does not directly effect one's life span. An *arhat* who is absolutely liberated *(asamayavimukta)* can relinquish life by entering into the fourth *dhyana* (Pāli, *jhāna*) and transforming the *āyur-vipāka-karma* into *bhoga-vipāka-karma.* By the same method of transferring between karmic accounts, an *arhat* who wishes to prolong life has only to transform *bhoga-vipāka-karma* into *āyur-vipāka-karma.* After giving these views, Vasubandhu concludes with his own view that one can put aside the life span determined at birth by one's past actions through the power of meditation. See Louis de la Vallée Poussin, *Abhidharmakośabhāṣyam,* trans. Leo Pruden (Berkeley: Asian Humanities Press, 1988), pp. 165–67.

14. *Visuddhimagga* 2.8.9; C. A. F. Rhys Davids, ed., *The Visuddhimagga of Buddhaghosa* (London: Pali Text Society, 1920–21; reprint London: Routledge & Kegan Paul, 1975), p. 292. *The Path of Purity,* trans. Pe Maung Tin (London: Pali Text Society, 1975), p. 336. On mindful breathing in the Theravāda tradition, see Paravahera Vajirañāṇa Mahāthera, *Buddhist Meditation in Theory and Practice: A General Exposition according to the Pāli Canon of the Theravāda School* (Colombo: MD Gunasena and Co., 1962), pp. 227–58.

15. *Visuddhimagga* 2.8.9; Rhys Davids, ed., *Visuddhimagga of Buddhaghosa,* p. 292.

16. See Isshi Yamada, *Karuṇāpuṇḍarīka* (London: School of Oriental and African Studies, 1968), pp. 241ff. on the various methods of entering into *parinirvāṇa* associated with the cult of Akṣobhya in India, Nepal, and Tibet.

17. Accomplished meditators who focus on the element of fire can, as Buddhaghosa explains in the *Visuddhimagga*, produce fire, smoke, and showers of embers, burn whatever they wish, and cremate their own bodies at will. See Rhys Davids, ed., *Visuddhimagga of Buddhaghosa,* p. 177.

18. On fire as a symbol of transcendence, see Mircea Eliade, *The Two and the One,* trans. J. Cohen (London: Harvill Press, 1965), pp. 19-77; on Indo-European terms for the divine that are derived from roots that connote radiance, see Carl Darling Buck's *Dictionary of Selected Synonymns in the Principle on Indo-European Languages* (Chicago: University of Chicago Press, 1949), p. 1455.

19. On flame finials in Buddhist iconography, see Hiram Woodward, "The Buddha's Radiance," *Journal of the Siam Society* 61 (1973): 187-91; see also Woodward, "Some Buddhist Symbols and Their Ancestry," in *Kalādarśana: American Studies in the Art of India,* ed. Joanna G. Williams (Leiden, Netherlands: E. J. Brill, 1981): 165–73. Benjamin Rowland discusses the Gandhāran convention of representing Buddhas and *arhat*s with flames issuing from the shoulders in "The Iconography of the Flame Halo," *Bulletin of the Fogg Museum of Art* 11 (1962): 10–16. His discussion of iconographic elements associated with Persian and Greek fire-deities on Kushan coins is particularly noteworthy (pp. 11–13), as is his summary of A. Grünwedel's analysis of Central Asian wall-paintings in which flames of various forms and colors are used to designate different levels of attainment, with *arhat*s burning with flames of flat gold and Buddhas giving off multicolored flame aureoles (p. 10).

20. On reliefs from Amarāvatī representing the Buddha as a pillar of fire, see Ānanda K. Coomaraswamy, *Elements of Buddhist Iconography* (Cambridge: Harvard University Press, 1935), p. 10 and figs. 4–10. The Hindu god Shiva is also represented in the form of a fiery *liṇgam* which, like the pillar of fire in which Agni is represented, serves as an *axis mundi* linking this world and the beyond.

21. On the cultivation of radiant energy in South Asian traditions, see Eliade, *Yoga, Immortality, and Freedom,* trans. Willard Trask (Princeton, N.J.: Princeton University Press, 1958), pp. 106–8, 330–34; see also David Knipe, *In the Image of Fire: The Vedic Experience of Heat* (Delhi: Motilal Banarsidass, 1975); Uma Marina Vesci, *Heat and Sacrifice in the Vedas* (Delhi: Motilal Banarsidass, 1985); Kaelber, *Tapta Marga.*

22. On the cosmogonic role of *tapas* in Vedic literature, see Knipe, *In the Image of Fire,* pp. 107–21.

23. Vesci, *Heat and Sacrifice in the Vedas,* p. 60.

24. On the generation of *tapas* in the rite of *Dīkṣā* or consecration, see Kaelber, *Tapta Marga,* pp. 34–36. In Southeast Asian Buddhist cremation rites, the ascension imagery of Vedic rites is well preserved in the shape and symbolism of the pyre. As Charles F. Keyes suggests in his "Tug of War for Merit: Cremation of a Senior Monk," *Journal of Siam Society* 63 (1975): 44–62, the cremation pyre of constructed for monks and high-ranking laypeople in northwestern Thailand "is recognized by local people as a model of the cosmos. The tiered rooves represent the levels of existence or heavens located on Mount Meru. Through the fire of cremation, the deceased monk's earthly heaven becomes transformed into an actual heaven, that is the abode for the soul of this virtuous man" (p. 52).

25. This transposition was already prefigured in the *Veda Samhitā*s, as Ā. K. Coomaraswami notes in his discussion of the inner *agnihotra* in "Ātmayajña: Self-Sacrifice," *Harvard Journal of Asiatic Studies* 6 (1941): 358–98.

26. *Saṃutta Nikāya,* ed. L. Feer, 5 vols. (London: Pali Text Society, 1884–98), 1: 169.

27. Textual descriptions of the radiant powers of Buddhas and Buddhist saints often underscore the link between ascetic exertion and radiant heat *(tapas).* Sri Lankan

accounts of how the Buddha vanquished the bloodthirsty *yakkhas* (Sanskrit, *yakṣas*) and *pisācas* (Sanskrit, *piśācas*) who once inhabited Sri Lanka describe the Buddha causing the hide on which he sat meditating to rise up in the air and radiate heat like the doomsday fire. Since animal hides of various kinds have long served in South Asia as symbols of asceticism, this is a clear indication that the source of the Buddha's radiant energy is his contemplative self-discipline. "I have power over fire," he announced as he turned the seat of his asceticism into a blazing fire hotter than four suns put together, thus driving the ogres and ghouls off the island. See Herman Oldenberg, ed., The *Dīpavaṃsa* (New Delhi: Asian Educational Services, 1982), pp. 17–18; see also *Thūpavaṃsa,* ed. N. A. Jayawickrama (London: Pali Text Society, 1971), pp. 209–10.

28. V. Trenckner, ed. *Milindapañha* (London: Pali Text Society, 1880; reprint London: Luzac and Co., 1962), pp. 384–85.

29. *Dhammapada* 387: *Divā tapati ādicco rattiṃ ābhāti candimā / sannaddho khattiyo tapati jhāyī tapati brāhmaṇo / atha sabbam ahorattiṃ buddho tapati tejasā*. See John Ross Carter and Mahinda Palihawadane, trans. and ed., The *Dhammapada* (New York: Oxford University Press, 1987), pp. 394–95.

30. Mahādhammarakkhita is so described in the commentary to the Pāli Vinaya. See *Samantāpaśādikā,* eds. J. Takakusa and M. Nagai, 7 vols. (London: Pali Text Society, 1924–47), 1: 67. See also the description of the saints of the second council, ibid., p. 69.

31. *Dīpavaṃsa* 6.38; Oldenberg, *Dīpavaṃsa,* p. 44. In addition to the *Dīpavaṃsa*'s account of the conversion of King Aśoka, see also the *Mahāvaṃsa;* Wilhelm Geiger, trans., *The Mahāvaṃsa or the Great Chronicle of Ceylon* (London: Pali Text Society, 1908; reprint Luzac and Co., 1958), pp. 28–32.

32. In his analysis of lists of *samādhi*-names found in Buddhist literature, Lewis Lancaster found that light imagery pervades many of these lists. Of the 156 *samādhis* listed in the *Shatasāhasrikāprajñāpāramitā,* for example, 28 names refer to radiant objects of various forms such as flaming mountains, and lightning bolts. See Lancaster, "Samādhi Names in Buddhist Texts," in *Malalasekera Commemoration Volume,* ed. O. H. de A. Wijesekera (Columbo: Kularatne and Co., 1976), pp. 196–202. Light symbolism also figures prominently in the names of the realms to which various levels of meditative absorption give access. See Mahāthera's *Buddhist Meditation in Theory and Practice,* p. 424; see also Frank Reynolds and Mani Reynolds, trans., *The Three Worlds according to King Ruang: A Thai Buddhist Cosmology* (Berkeley: University of California Press, 1982), pp. 263–69.

33. Mathieu Boisvert, *The Five Aggregates: Understanding Theravāda Psychology and Soteriology* (Waterloo, Canada: Wilfred Laurier University Press, 1995), pp. 36ff.

34. See Rhys Davids, *Visuddhimagga of Buddhaghosa,* pp. 175–76.

35. On the four material elements (*mahābhūtās* or *dhātus*) of the body and how they should be apprehended in meditation, see ibid., pp. 347–72.

36. See *Paramattha-Dīpanī-Theragāthā-aṭṭhakathā: The Commentary of Dhammapālācariya,* ed. F. L. Woodward, 3 vols. (London: Pali Text Society, Vols. 131, 143,

and 150; London: Oxford University Press, 1940–59), 1: 43. Since the sacrificial post or *yupa* was a central image of the method by which the Vedic sacrificer ascended into the other world for the duration of the sacrifice, the crematory post might therefore be taken similarly as an *axis mundi* or symbol of the upward passage linking subterranean, terrestrial, celestial, and supracelestial realms. "Post," therefore, is a moniker that carries with it much symbolic capital drawn from Vedic ritual theory and entitles the bearer to be seen as a Buddhist Agni, a pillar of fire linking this world to the unconditioned.

37. *Vinaya Pitaka*, ed. H. Oldenberg, 5 vols. (London: Pali Text Society, 1879–83), 2: 74–76. Dabba's use of a "digital" torch may be compared to that of the Buddha in a former life as Sarvada. *The Sūtra of the Wise and the Foolish* describes how Sarvada took pity on a group of wealthy merchants who had lost their way in the dark in a bandit-infested region. He illuminated their path by wrapping oil-soaked cloth around his arms and using them as torches to light the way. See M. W. de Visser, *The Arhats of China and Japan* (Berlin: Oesterheld and Co., 1923), pp. 27–28.

38. Ibid., p. 76.

39. *Sarīrassa jhāyamānassa ḍayhamānassa n'eva chārikā paññāyittha na masi. Udāna,* ed. P. Steinhal (London: Pali Text Society, 1885), pp. 92–93.

40. *Aṅguttara Nikāya*, eds. R. Morris and E. Hardy, 5 vols. (London: Pali Text Society, 1885-1900), 2: 165.

41. See Parry, n. 6.

42. Since as Parry has shown, the deceased "dies" only at the moment when the vital breath evacuates the body through the top of the skull as the corpse lies burning on the pyre, it is during the rite of cremation that there is a termination of life. Death and cremation, classified in Vedic literature as the final sacrifice *(antyeṣṭi)*, are coterminous. See Parry, *Death in Banaras,* pp. 178–84.

43. See Madeleine Biardeau, "Le sacrifice dans l'Hindousme," in Biardeau and C. Malamoud, *Le sacrifice dans l'Inde ancienne* (Paris: Presses Universitaires de France, 1976), p. 19.

44. Cited in Julian Sherrier, "Iconography of the *Mahāparinirvāṇa*," in *The Stūpa: Its Religious, Historical, and Architectural Significance*, eds. Anna Libera Dallapiccola and Stephanie Zingel-avé Lallemant (Wiesbaden, Germany: Franz Steiner Verlag, 1980), p. 212.

45. J. Przyluski, "Le Parinirvāṇa et les funérailles du Buddha," *Journal Asiatique* 15: 16 (1918–20): 485–529, 401–56, 5–54; Gregory Schopen, "Burial 'Ad Sanctos' and the Physical Presence of the Buddha in Early Indian Buddhism," *Religion* 17 (1987): 193–225.

46. On Mahākāśyapa's preeminence among the disciples of the Buddha and his assimilation to the Buddha as his legitimate heir, see Reginald Ray, *Buddhist Saints in India: A Study in Buddhist Values and Orientation* (New York: Oxford University Press, 1994), pp. 105–8. See also John Strong, *The Legend and Cult of Upagupta: Sanskrit Bud-*

dhism in North India and Southeast Asia (Princeton, N.J.: Princeton University Press, 1992), p. 60.

47. *Sayam eva Bhagavato citako pajjali. Mahāparinibbāna Sutta* 6.21–22; *Dīgha Nikāya,* 2: 163–64. A Burmese account of the Buddha's demise translated by Bigandet states that "all the while the pile was burning, streams of flames issued from the leaves and branches of the trees, shining forth with uncommon brightness, without burning the trees; insects of every description were seen flying in swarms on those trees, without receiving the least injury." See the Right Reverend P. Bigandet, *The Life and Legend of Guatama-Buddha of the Burmese*, 2 vols. (London: Trübner and Co., 1880), 2: 90.

48. The equivalence of father to son in Vedic-Hindu discourse is, as Paul Mus indicates, based on Brahmanic descriptions of the sacrifice of Prajāpati/Puruṣa and his reconstitution in his son Agni, the god of fire. Prajāpati/Puruṣa is reconstituted in the regenerative *tapas* of the sacrificial fire and lives on in Agni, just as the dead sacrificer (homologized to Prajāpati/Puruṣa) is reconstituted on the funeral pyre in the process being consumed and transformed in the radiant energy of Agni's *tapas*. See his preface to *Barabudur: Esquise d'une histoire du Bouddhisme fondée sur la critique archéologique des textes* (Hanoi: Ecole Française d'Extreme Orient, 1935; reprint Arno Press, 1978), pp. 51–55.

49. The *Mahāvastu*, ed. É. Senart, 3 vols. (Paris: Imprimerie Nationale, 1882–97), 3: 72–73.

50. Mus explains the equation of the Buddha as father and his monastic sons in his preface to *Barabudur* as follows:

> "In ancient India, one does not inherit *from* his father; one inherits his father, his person. To say that the disciples of the Buddha are heirs of the Dharma, and to attribute to the Buddha a 'body' of Dharma, is the same affirmation. . . . It is not an ontology but a theory of transmission, an identification of son and father, student and master (for to initiate a student is to engender him, and to engender him is to transmit the person of the master to him)."

See the preface to *Barabudur,* pp. 124–26.

51. On the spontaneous combustion of the pyres of *satīs* and other virtuous persons, see Parry, "The End of the Body," in *Fragments Toward a History of the Body*, 3 vols., ed. Michel Feher with Ramona Naddaff and Nadia Tazi (New York: Zone Press, 1989), 3: 505. By contrast to the highly combustible nature of the virtuous widow's body, the bodies of abject sinners are said to be highly incombustible. During his fieldwork, Parry was repeatedly told of the difficulties encountered in cremating the bodies of corrupt officials and other people tainted by their repeated failure to act virtuously. No matter how much ghee is applied to the pyres of such people, Parry's informants asserted, they do not burn properly. In contrast to the incombustible nature of such corpses, the virtuous person's body will not only go up in flames without any difficulty but will often require no special human agency in the release of the life force through the cranial suture as does the corpse of an ordinary person. Whereas ordinarily the chief mourner must release the soul of the deceased by crushing the skull after the body has burned, the skulls

of the virtuous are often said to explode by spontanous combustion without any assistance from the chief mourner.

52. A tale told in a contemporary guidebook for Hindu householders tells of a woman whose body becomes hot to the touch after she declares her intention to immolate herself at the death of her husband. When her uncle begs her not to immolate herself, she responds, "I don't do it but it happens," and procedes to demonstrate her igneous state by holding a flame to her finger until "her finger began to burn like a candle." She then threatens to burn the house down if she is not granted permission to follow after her husband and, finally, burns herself of her own accord when her relatives refuse to provide her with a proper pyre. See Swami Ramsukhdas, *How to Lead a Household Life: Performance of One's Duty and Protection of the Rights of Others* (Gorakpur: Govind Bhavan Karyalaya Gita Press, n.d.), pp. 43–44.

53. I am grateful to Paul Courtright (personal communication, July 1996) for pointing out to me how the rhetoric of spontaneous combustion serves to promote the image of *sati* as a voluntary act in which relatives do not play a coercive role.

54. On the controversies surrounding Roop Kanwar's death, see the contributions by Veena Talwar Oldenberg and Ashis Nandy to *Sati, The Blessing and the Curse: The Burning of Wives in India,* ed. John Stratton Hawley (New York: Oxford University Press, 1994); on the assertion that Kanwar's pyre spontaneously combusted, see Hawley's introduction to *Sati,* p. 7.

55. This monk is called "Upananda" in Sanskrit sources. Known as Subhadda in Pāli sources, this figure is to be distinguished from the the aged Subhadda who was the last person to be ordained by the Buddha and who, as we shall see in the next section, passed out of existence before *parinirvāṇa* of the Buddha.

56. See *The Life of the Buddha and the Early History of His Order,* trans. W. W. Rockhill (London: Routledge & Kegan Paul, 1884), p. 148.

57. Jean Przyluski includes a chapter on this Buddhist saint, who enjoys a strong cult following in Southeast Asia, in his *Concile de Rājagṛha: introduction a l'histoire des canons et des sectes Bouddhiques* (Paris: Paul Geunther, 1926), pp. 239–56.

58. Przyluski translates four Chinese accounts of the first council that refer to Gavāṃpati's *parinirvāna* in *Le concile de Rājagṛha;* see pp. 10, 31, 66, 97, 116. See also Bu-ston's Tibetan account: E. Obermiller, trans., Bu-ston Rin-chen-grub, *History of Buddhism* (Chos-hbyung), 2 vols. (Heidelberg, Germany: Harrassowitz, 1932), 2. 73–77.

59. By entering into meditation on fire *(tejokasiṇasamāpattivasena)*, the *Dhammapadāṭṭhakathā* explains, the Buddha was able to emit a ball of fire from his upper body; by entering into meditation on water *(āpokasiṇasamāpattivasena)*, he was able to emit a torrent of water from his lower body. The Buddha then proceeded to emit fire and water from various other parts of his body, including his eyes, ears, nostrils, shoulders, hands, fingers, and pores. See *Dhammapadāṭṭhakathā* (*The Commentary to the Dhammapada*), ed. H. C. Norman, 4 vols. (London: Pali Text Society, 1906–14), 3: 213-16. See also *Jātakāṭṭhakathā*

(*The Jātaka Together with Its Commentary*), V. Fausboll, 6 vols. (London: Pali Text Society, 1877–96; reprint London: Luzac and Co., 1962–64), 4: 139. For a discussion of representations of this scene in Indian Buddhist art, see Alfred Foucher, "La grande miracle du Bouddha á Shrāvastī," *Journal Asiatique* 1 (1909): 5–77.

60. "Before the Blessed One and his chief disciples have disappeared, I will enter into *nirvāṇa*." See *Sūtrālaṃkāra,* trans. Édouard Huber (Paris: Ernest Leroux, 1908), p. 387.

61. See *Sūtrālaṃkāra,* pp. 398–400.

62. T25.80c4-81a11 [fasc.3]. See also *Avadanaśataka,* ed. J. S. Speyer (St. Petersburg: Imperial Academy of Sciences, 1902–6) 2 vols., 1.228.3ff; trans. Leon Feer, *Avadana-śataka: Cent legends bouddhiques*, Annales du Musée Guimet, vol. 18 (Paris: E. Leroux, 1891), pp. 151–59.

63. John Strong, *The Legend and Cult of Upagupta: Sanskrit Buddhism in North India and Southeast Asia* (Princeton, N.J.: Princeton University Press, 1992), p. 308, n. 25.

64. Ibid., p. 62.

65. See Paul Griffiths, *On Being Buddha: The Classical Doctrine of Buddhahood* (Albany: State University of New York Press, 1994), pp. 125–26.

66. *Theragāthā* 3; see H. Oldenberg and R. Pischel, eds., *The Thera- and Therīgāthā* (London: Pali Text Society, 1883; 2d ed., K. R. Norman and L. Alsdorf, eds., London: Pali Text Society, 1966), p. 2.

67. For a study of *pratyekabuddha* that compares this figure to non-Buddhist counterparts, see Martin Wiltshire's *Ascetic Figures Before and in Early Buddhism: The Emergence of Gautama as the Buddha* (Berlin: Walter de Gryter, 1990); see also Ria Kloppenborg, *The Paccekabuddha: A Buddhist Ascetic* (Leiden, Netherlands: E. J. Brill, 1974), Reginald Ray, *Buddhist Saints in India: A Study in Buddhist Values and Orientation* (New York: Oxford University Press, 1994), chapter 7.

68. Ray, *Buddhist Saints in India,* p. 224.

69. See *Jātakāṭṭhakathā* (*The Jātaka Together with Its Commentary*), ed. V. Fausboll, 6 vols. (London: Pali Text Society, 1877–96; reprint London: Luzac and Co., 1962–64), 6: 41, 3: 381.

70. The epithet *tūṣṇīkaśobhana* is used to describe *pratyekabuddha*s at several points in the *Mahāvastu.* See É. Senart, ed., *Mahāvastu,* 3 vols. (Paris: Imprimerie Nationale, 1882–97), 1: 301, 3: 414.

71. Senart, ed., *Mahāvastu,* 3: 171, 1: 302.

72. Ibid., 1: 357. See Étienne Lamotte, "Le suicide religieux dans le Bouddhisme ancien," *Bulletin de la Classe des Lettres et des Sciences de l'Académie Royale de Belgique* 51 (1965): 159.

73. Pascal's recording of his mystical experience (a document he sewed into his clothes so that he could lay his hand on it and have immediate access to it for the rest of his life) begins: "Fire—God of Abraham, God of Isaac, God of Jacob, not of the philosophers and the scientists. Certitude. Certitude. Feeling. Joy. Peace. . . . " See *The Essential Pascal,* ed. Robert W. Gleason (New York: New American Library, 1966), pp. 205ff.

3

When a Wife Dies First: The *Mūsivāyanam* and a Female Brahman Ritualist in Coastal Andhra

David M. Knipe

On the virtues, powers, and capacities of the auspicious Hindu wife, much has been composed in the poetry and prose of antiquity, in the later literature of the *dharmaśāstras,* epics, *purāṇas,* and other genres, and in modern scholarly publications. She is as pivotal, generative, and positive a figure in familial and social life as the widow—the woman whose husband has died before her—is implicitly a figure of inauspiciousness, destabilization and dangerous negative force.[1] But relatively neglected in these genres of Indian literature, and in modern discussions inside and outside the subcontinent, is a third figure of considerable although unheralded significance in Hindu ritual and social life. She is the chaste and stainless wife *(pativratā)* who dies first, leaving behind a living husband, one who traditionally should credit her for her timely vows and purity of behavior that protected his person and their marriage throughout their life together. In much of coastal Andhra her funeral is concluded with a dramatic ritual that transforms her on the tenth or eleventh day after death into the goddess Gaurī, and propels her off to Gaurī-*loka,* the realm of the golden, brilliant goddess who because of her rigorous austerities in dogged devotion to her husband Śiva was transformed by Brahmā from inauspicious black (Kālī) to auspicious yellow (Gaurī). It is the only documented Hindu funerary ritual in which women are the principals, including the featured ritualist, a special Brahman who temporarily embodies the spirit of the deceased of any and all castes. It is one of the most distinctive of all mortuary rituals, recognizable on the riverside ritual grounds because women are the dominant, nearly exclusive participants. The performance serves as an imposing illustration of public women's rituals *(strīkarmāṇi)* of evocative power and symbolic presence.

The ritual is known in Telugu as the *mūsivāyanam.* Methodologically speaking, it is one of the most intriguing of funerary rituals because, although nontextual, it is pervasive among all castes and communities, including elite

Vaidika Brahmans. Structurally speaking, with regard to pan-Indian cultural notions of last rites of passage—known in Telugu as *aparam* (Vedic Sanskrit, literally, rites "for the future")—it is an elusive performance. It is sometimes called a *guptadāna*, a secret or hidden gift. Her death could be construed as *akālamṛtyu*, an untimely demise, the inauspicious death out of order, since the younger (often much younger) wife normally outlives her husband by a few or a great many years.[2] Then too it could be untimely and anachronistic if her parents, as well as her husband, are still living. And yet this death is auspicious, not inauspicious, and the *mūsivāyanam* is portrayed as a positive ceremony, not as a dark and baleful one. Concerns about *akālamṛtyu* are overridden by acceptance of the common belief that this death is somehow "timely." It is a grievous loss to the bereaved, yes, but it is also proper and exemplary—says tradition—for the wife to die first. What is perhaps most remarkable is Brahman acceptance of the *mūsivāyanam,* indeed, insistence upon it as ritually imperative, despite its lack of a Vedic or Sanskrit textual basis, despite the forcible presence of a priestess-surrogate for the deceased, and despite the sometimes strong display of possession phenomena that are generally dismissed by Brahmans as "non-Brahman" burdens and superstitions.

Fieldwork for this chapter began in 1980 with observations in Vijayawada on the Krishna River and Rajahmundry on the Godavari River, but initial interviews of ritualists and families did not begin until 1992 in East Godavari District, primarily in Rajahmundry. Observations of the *mūsivāyanam* and interviews continued during the pursuit of other Godavari Delta projects from 1995 to 2000.[3] Interviews were conducted with female Brahman ritualists routinely employed to perform the rite, relatives of wives for whom the *mūsivāyanam* was performed, and family *purohita*s. Also interviewed were three categories of Godavari Delta ritualists with whom research has continued on other projects since 1980: Vaidika Brahmans, including *āhitāgni*s in *agrahāram*s; *apara* Brahmans (funerary specialists); and *karmakāṇḍa* ritualists for the general range of *saṃskāra*s (life cycle rites).

The Mūsivāyanam

> "Who am I? Just a Brahman brat! Who are you? Nothing to me! But *because of this ritual* the one who died is equal to the goddess Gauri! So I receive veneration from everyone, no matter how grand they are!"—young Brahman *mūsivāyanam* ritualist with twelve years' experience

Although some spoke vaguely of the possibility that palm-leaf manuscripts might exist "somewhere," none of the professional and lay folk interviewed concerning the *mūsivāyanam* claims to have seen a text (*paddhati,* "ritual manual") detailing the rite. Two individuals said they had handwritten notes on the performance but neither was able (or willing) to locate them. The search for a text continues, but it should be noted at the outset that the following details have no textual backdrop and are based entirely on observation on one hand, and highly nuanced, surprisingly well-detailed articulations of professional ritualists and lay participants on the other. The basic problem encountered in this overview is that ritualists and participants—even when our study is limited to the confines of the Delta—come from so many communities and divisions within communities that no two of them agree on all significant details.[4] Following a brief account of one particular performance is a synthesis based largely on what has been witnessed and photographed and on the reports of those female ritualists who have considerable experience in performing the *mūsivāyanam* for both Brahman and non-Brahman communities.

The Name

of the rite is indeterminate but is said to come from paired baskets featured in the ritual gifting of certain items meant for the deceased on her journey to another world. These are typical woven fan-shaped baskets with curved bottoms used for winnowing rice paddy or for other newly threshed grain, the familiar *śūrpa* of Sanskrit reference. In Telugu it is a *cēṭa,* with the plural *cēṭalu* employed in the rite in the singular.[5] In this ritual one fan is turned upside down to cover the other, giving the appearance of a wicker clam shell and suggesting a closed-in-ness *(mūsivēta).* Via popular etymology *cēṭa,* pronounced with a flat first vowel in local dialect as *cāṭa*, may be stretched into a near homonym, *cāṭu*, something "hidden, secret, even mysterious." Not everyone is comfortable using the name *mūsivāyanam* and some ritualists simply say "that *vāyanam,*" just as they say "there" to avoid using the word *śmaśāna* for the burning and burial ground. Others may refer to it generically as a Gaurī *pūjā* or *suvāsinī pūjā.*

The second half of the ritual name, *vāyanam,* employs a common Sanskrit / Telugu word for the frequent ritual exchanges between auspicious married women, usually connected with vows (*vrata,* Telugu, *nōmu*) that may be the ritual preoccupation of a woman for part of a day or for a sequence of certain days stretching over several years. Just as entire villages or neighborhoods honor the goddess Gaurī in annual festivals that may last a week or a lunar month, so individual women or groups of women worship Gauri with vows that include fasts or *pūjā*s. One type of Gaurī-*vrata* or Gaurī-*nōmu* may serve as example of a routine *vāyanam* in which a woman may vow to perform *pūjā* on four successive Tuesdays in the month of Śrāvaṇa for five years. She must find five other auspicious married women each time she performs one of these twenty discrete events, and give to them in an open winnowing fan as *prasāda* from the *pūjā* special items such as betel leaves, bananas, Bengal grams, flowers, and sweets. In this example all six women have therefore worshiped Gaurī; all have received her grace to internalize and share with family members.[6] The event itself is in the category of the *pēraṇṭam* (Telugu), a married woman's formal call upon another married woman in her house. All those who participate in such ritualized reciprocity are recognized as *pēraṇṭālu*; thus, a *pēraṇṭālu* is a woman who attends a *pēraṇṭam.*[7]

The enormously rich symbols of the winnowing fans and their contents will be recalled later in this chapter. Here it is noted simply that the name *mūsivāyanam* situates the performance at once in the normative and auspicious realm of women's everyday ritual reinforcements of power, yet at the same time accords it, by means of the closed baskets, an air of the secret and hidden that adheres to a mystery rite. It concerns a ritualized giving of special items to one special woman en route to one special world. But it also concerns exchanges between numerous women whose ritual bonding serves crucial (and sometimes hidden) ends for the world of the living.

The Timing

of the *mūsivāyanam* in the sequence of funerary events discloses the Brahman / non-Brahman, or more precisely the twiceborn / Śūdra split that structures coastal Andhra society and religion. This division allies so-called Kṣatriya-*varṇa* and Vaiśya-*varṇa* castes with the Brahmans, at least in a blurred form of ritual solidarity if nothing more. Brahmans, and therefore Brahman-emulating castes such as Kōmatis (Merchants), perform the *mūsivāyanam* on the tenth day after death, and do it *vedokta,* "according to the Vedas," that is, with Vedic mantras, although no specific mantras are located in Brahmanic literature on funerals *(antyeṣṭi)* and ancestor rites *(śrāddha)*. The ritual has been squeezed uncomfortably into the end of the ten-day schedule of postcremation rites[8] where its purposes are decidedly at odds with the twelfth-day *sapiṇḍīkaraṇa* journey of the deceased into ancestral lineages. This disjuncture will be explored in further detail in this chapter.

For the great majority of the population, the non-Brahmans, the *mūsivāyanam* is a separate ritual in its own right and most frequently occurs on the "big day" (Telugu *peddadinam*) the eleventh day after death. Śūdras perform *purāṇokta,* "according to the *Purāṇas*," with Sanskrit *ślokas* (verses) in lieu of mantras. The eleventh is the first possible day subsequent to the obligatory ten days of postcremation observances, but *mūsivāyanam* may occur on days 13, 15, 17, 19, or 21 due to the *nakṣatra* (asterism) and *tithi* (lunar day) of the death date, or perhaps due to the fact that the eleventh is an inauspicious *tithi*. Some families place a notice in newspapers with a beribboned photo of the deceased, often as a bride or in her youth, and include the date, even hour of death, the entire schedule of funerary observances including the *mūsivāyanam,* and the names of all the closest family members who mourn her loss.

THE SACRED SPACE

elected for the *mūsivāyanam* is a standard ritual arena on the riverside (*ghaṭ,* Telugu, *rēvu*). Normally this will be in the village or town of the deceased's current residence, that is to say, in the home place of her mother-in-law and husband, where the cremation has taken place. A river or tank is essential for the ritual bath *(snāna)* plus a shampoo, both obligatory for this transition out of the pollution of death, cremation, and *preta*-hood, the condition of a disembodied spirit. It is not only an auspicious but also a popular place, one liable to be frequented by women for standard vows and for other morning rituals. Some of these women, perhaps unknown to the family of the deceased, may be recruited into the *mūsivāyanam* as participants, a striking example, at least among non-Brahmans, of a casteless communitas formed for the duration of the rite. These strangers, just like family members, will take away winnowing fans containing ritual offerings in the manner of *prasāda,* another illustration of contrariness to patterns, this being a funerary ritual that is not inauspicious.

Some Brahman and other high-caste families may choose to perform at home or in a secluded ritual arena, although others may go to the *rēvu* as do most Śūdra castes. The very few communities whose women are secluded and unseen in public may elect to have men give the *vāyanam* to the female ritualist. Such has not been witnessed by this writer, only learned from family *purohitas* (Telugu, *iṇṭipurōhita,* "house-priest").

THE RITUALISTS

for the *mūsivāyanam* include the indispensable *brahma-muttaiduva* ("Brahman married woman"), the ritual surrogate for the deceased, whose nature and function will be detailed later in this chapter. Here it is important to recognize that in the *brahma-muttaiduva* the deceased is understood to be actually present as the focal point of this rite of transformation. She arrives as an invisible but not as a silent presence in the form *(rūpa)* of the Brahman woman. The family Brahman *purōhita* is seated in the ritual arena for the invoking mantras or *ślokas* at the outset, but action quickly shifts to the assembled women, with a small number of them selected for primary ritual actions.

Strikingly absent as ritual participant in the *mūsivāyanam* proper is the deceased's husband. He is, however, usually on the *rēvu* at the periphery of the event. His day began abruptly in the early hours, about 2:00 A.M. when he was awakened by a Cākali (Washerman) and taken to the river in the dark to have his waist cord (Telugu, *molatāḍu*) forcefully broken.[9] Along with his *purōhita* he returns to the *rēvu* later in the morning for a series of rituals that occupy the tenth or eleventh day, according to the customs of his community. Again, according to the procedures of his community, he may be the designated chief mourner *(karta)* from the time of cremation nine or ten days earlier. On the other hand, that role may have gone to the eldest son, or in some cases to the youngest son if one or the other is married. But none has a role in the *mūsivāyanam.*

THE PARTICIPANTS

include two separate aggregates of women who meet together in the ritual arena. All those giving and receiving baskets in this *vāyanam* must be *punistrī,* "married women of experience" usually between thirty and sixty years of age.[10] A *punistrī* (colloquial form of Sanskrit, *puṇyastrī*), is a woman of "merit," *puṇya.* Three additional Sanskrit terms commonly employed with reference to an auspicious married woman are *pativrata,* the "wife who has vowed to protect her husband" *(pati), sumaṅgalī,* and *suvāsinī.* After the last term some ritualists speak of the *mūsivāyanam* as *suvāsinī-pūjā.* In addition to Telugu *peraṇṭālu,* referred to previously, another common Telugu word for a married woman is *muttaiduva.* Thus in the common vocabulary of all communities in the Delta there are at least six terms highlighting the valuable status of the auspicious married women participants.

The number of attendants could be as few as six, three on each side, or as many as two hundred. Although marriage and kinship systems in coastal Andhra are as varied as they are complex, one widespread pattern is a division between two "houses." Representatives of these two houses converge in a *mūsivāyanam* for one who lived sequentially in each, first her birth house, then her marital house. The critical transition for a female occurs at marriage when she goes as a bride from the house of her mother to the house of her husband's mother, from *puṭṭillu* to *attillu.* Along with her childhood she leaves behind the people of her mother's house *(puṭṭiṇṭivāllu)* in order to begin adult life with the people of her mother-in-law's house *(attiṇṭivāllu),* although lengthy visits to the natal home will occur with the birth of each child and at other times. The natal aggregate, the one that usually takes the lead in ritual procedures, includes the mother (provided that her husband is alive), older brothers' wives, younger brothers' wives, and sisters. The second group is that of affines, including the mother-in-law, husband's older brothers' wives, husband's younger brothers' wives, sons' wives and, on occasion, one or more sisters of the husband. The last, having married out, are no longer formally part of the *attiṇṭivāllu* aggregate, but may live within hailing distance and be invited to the ceremony.[11]

As noted, ordinarily no males of either natal or affinal houses have significant roles to play in the ritual other than a quick and silent contribution of cash from one individual to the *brahma-muttaiduva,* a moment ritualized as *dakṣiṇā.*

Nevertheless they are often there on the periphery of the rite with a close interest in procedures.

THE SEQUENCE

of events for those adhering to a more or less orthoprax ritual schedule begins with the cooking of rice, a *piṇḍapradānam* with rice balls on a leaf plate along with milk, curds, bananas, and incense, then a deliberate setting out of the offered *piṇḍa*s in the belief that the *preta* of the deceased, in the form of a crow, a common other-world representative, will arrive and express satisfaction by touching or eating the rice. The entire leaf plate of "eaten" food is then held in two hands and thrown back over the head into the river. This concludes what are known locally as *dharmōdaka*s, the ten days of essential "water" offerings to nourish a now fully constructed temporary and invisible body for the *preta* of the deceased. Tonsure and shaving of males concludes this sequence in which the *purohita*, husband/widower, sons, and other close male relatives are the principals, and usually only a few or no women are present.

The *mūsivāyanam* proper begins with the arrival of the featured *brahma-muttaiduva.* All of the attending women are by definition *muttaiduva*, "married women," but she alone is the *brahma*. She may have been hired well in advance or simply chosen from the group of ritualists available at dawn on the *rēvu.* The two "houses" of women, natal and affinal, arrive and seat themselves more or less formally in their respective ranks further up the steps. One or another may appear at times to be distressed, her grief barely under control. In one emotional outburst a middle-aged Kāpu woman broke down completely while braiding a dark fall into the old ritualist's gray hair, no doubt recalling the many times she had so dressed the hair of her deceased young relative. But for others there is a near festive air about the proceedings, and soon the women will all have bright fresh flowers in their braids. The winnowing baskets that will be presented to them are already partially filled, stacked, and awaiting distribution. It is not a typical atmosphere of mourning or solemnity.

The following synopsis with accompanying photos is of a *mūsivāyanam* for a Telaga (Śūdra cultivating caste) woman that took place on Pushkara *rēvu* in Rajahmundry beginning at 9:45 A.M. on February 15, 1992. About forty women participated. She belongs to a Telaga subsect that permits women to be in public. The Merikavīdhi subsect, by contrast, does not, and would have to do the *mūsivāyanam* by proxy.

Wetland seedbed earth *(maḍi)* brought by the women is placed directly on the concrete step in two chocolate-brown, wet heaps, rice flour is sprinkled across these two altar-like mounds, then the ubiquitous turmeric and vermilion powders (Telugu *pasupu-kunkum*[12]), and finally as the top layer, betel leaves. A brief *pūjā* to Vināyaka (Gaṇeśa) and *puṇyahavācana* are accomplished by the *purohita* facing north. A line of five women assembles before him. These include relatives of the deceased from both natal and affinal houses. Behind the *purohita,* to the south, stand close male members of the affinal house who occasionally step in as would-be stage directors.

The *brahma-muttaiduva,* a woman in her late sixties, is seated on two three-legged stools *(pīṭa),* her back to the river, her face to the east and the full assembly of women on the *rēvu.* Gaurī *pūjā* (or *suvāsinī pūjā)* now begins with ritual preparation for her to receive the spirit of the deceased. The five women quickly bend before her to wash and then daub her feet with turmeric and *kunkum* powders, and then in attitudes of worship smear her face, arms, and feet with turmeric paste and pour coconut oil into each of her ears as the *brahma-muttaiduva* bends her head to accept the substance. (See fig. 1.) Brahmans refer to this as *abhyaṅga-snāna,* an "ointment bath."

The women lead her into the river, carrying the two stools for her to be reseated in the shallows for the second procedure, *snāna,* a "ritual bath" that turns into a triple bath. The *brahma-muttaiduva,* again facing east, her knees up just above water, is bathed by the same five women who pour vessels of water over her clothed body. They continue into a second phase, a "head-bath" (Telugu, *talāntu*) or soap-nut shampoo, said to remove the *aśauca* (Telugu, *maila*) of death pollution.[13] The *brahma-muttaiduva* then stands and bathes herself, repeatedly pouring vessels of water down over her head and body. Drying her off, the five women give her a fresh *boṭṭu* (forehead mark) and bend down to mark the two stools with *kunkum* as well, five dots at the corners and center.

Now it is nine women who lead the *brahma-muttaiduva* back to the two earth altars and seat her once again on the two stools for presentation of *vāyanam*s, two pairs of closed winnowing baskets (again, *cēṭa*s in Telugu, *śūrpa*s for those using Sanskrit terms). (See fig. 2.) They place the fans on top of the earth mounds so that parts of them are also on her toes. Each double fan, when uncovered, contains a bed of raw rice grains, a bright red sari with an accompanying yellow blouse-piece, a green coconut, a large mirror, a comb, silver toe rings, bangles, and turmeric and *kunkum* powders plus collyrium for blackening eyelashes, in cosmetic boxes. (See fig. 3.) Only the natal *vāyanam* has a turmeric root on a new yellow cord. A stalk of bananas and a pumpkin accompany each fan. The first *vāyanam* is presented by the natal side, by the deceased's mother or a brother's wife. Perhaps as a balancing gesture, it is the new sari from the affinal side rather than from the birth-house that drapes the *brahma-muttaiduva.*[14] The second *vāyanam* is set down by the deceased's mother-in-law or by the husband's brother's wife.

Decorations (*alaṃkāra*s) of the *brahma-muttaiduva* to prepare for the arrival of the *preta* include, in addition to the *boṭṭu,* a renewed smearing with turmeric paste, sandalwood paste, green-gram (Telugu, *nalugu*) paste, eyetex (collyrium, Telugu, *kāṭuka*), bangles on her wrists, flowers in her hair, a necklace

1. At the beginning of the *mūsivāyanam* ritual five auspicious married women relatives of the deceased bathe the *brahma-muttaiduva* ritualist at the river's edge as she seats herself on two three-legged stools.

2. Reseated on the two stools on the riverbank, the *brahma-muttaiduva* is decorated and anointed in preparation for the arrival of the disembodied spirit *(preta)* of the deceased wife. Resting on her toes and on two altars of seedbed earth are two *vāyanam*s, "closed winnowing baskets of offerings." At *left* is the family *purōhita*.

3. The two sets of baskets are uncovered to reveal their contents on beds of rice: green coconut, pumpkin, new sari and blouse-piece, a packet containing turmeric and *kunkum* powders, sandal paste, mirror, comb, black beads, turmeric-root *tāḷi*, silver toe rings, bangles, and other items. In the foreground are the two altars with betel leaves and *akṣintulu* (reddened rice grains) on top.

of black beads (Telugu, *nallapūsa*), and the all-important tying of the marriage cord (*maṅgalasūtra,* Telugu, *tāḷi*) and slipping on of silver toe rings so that she is complete with all the signs of a bride. Instead of the gold disc emblem (Telugu, *śatamānum*) with its flanking gold tubes (Telugu, *mūsikas*) on the marriage cord tied by the mother or her substitute, a turmeric root is hung around her neck.

All is now ready for the *preta āvāhana,* "invocation of the spirit of the deceased," who was already recognized in the crow earlier in the day. The *purohita* recites what all describe as the intention *(saṃkalpa)* of the rite and the two women who have deposited the large *vāyanams* repeat a phrase in Sanskrit: "In order [for her] to achieve Gaurī's eternal (*śāśvata)* world *(loka),* I will give away a winnowing fan (*śūrpa)* of offerings *(vāyana)*."[15] Application of a small wad of turmeric paste (Telugu, *pasupu mudda*) on her forehead is, according to some ritualists, the critical moment of entry of the *preta* into the *brahma-muttaiduva.*[16] The family is anxious, and institutes a moment of ritual inquiry: "Who are you, Mother?" (Telugu, *evaravi amma nuvvu*?). All ears bend to hear the reply from the mouth of the *brahma-muttaiduva*. She should answer "Gaurī" or "Gaurī *dēvi,*" indicating that the ritual has proceeded correctly and the deceased has become a goddess. If the *brahma-muttaiduva* states her own name, for instance, "Laksmi," women laugh and say, "Yes, well, we know that, but who *are* you?" If she answers with the name of someone who died some time ago, consternation ensues in fear of *gāli-dhūli* (Telugu, evil spirits, ghosts, literally, "wind and dust") and the likelihood that some alien and opportunistic *preta* has jumped onto this Brahman ritualist. Perhaps a courageous older woman will step forth and demand that this intruder depart. Perhaps an exorcist will be sought. But there is a greater possibility that the correct *preta* will be demonstratively unhappy, full of anxiety, concerned perhaps that her children are not receiving proper care. In the voice of the *brahma-muttaiduva* she may make demands upon the family for twenty or thirty minutes until at last there are concessions from relatives for her every request. (See fig. 4.)

When all returns to normal[17] and Gaurī is identifed as the presence within the *brahma-muttaiduva,* worship of this goddess must now proceed to dismiss her properly to Gaurī-*loka.*[18] A large pan of uncooked rice (Telugu, *biyyam*) is emptied into the end (Telugu, *kongu*) of the *brahma-muttaiduva*'s sari, which she knots and holds out before her to contain the surfeit.[19] In addition to the rice and fruits she also receives raw food to take to her own home to prepare and eat as self-cooked food (*svayampāka*, also known as *pottarlu* in Telugu). A man steps in to provide rupee notes for her as her cash fee (Telugu *dakṣiṇā dabbulu*), usually an amount between twenty-five and fifty Rupees (about one to two dollars).

The *purohita* departs and action now shifts into a *prasāda* phase involving all of the women attending, including distribution of the many baskets stacked

4. The deceased has now become the goddess Gaurī. Each attending auspicious married woman *(muttaiduva, suvāsinī)* receives an open winnowing basket containing items similar to those given the deceased for her journey to Gaurī-*loka*. Despite the evident grief on the faces of these close relatives, no crying is indulged. An uncle of the deceased looks on.

up in heaps on the *rēvu*. (See fig. 4.) The core group of women who gave the rice goes up the steps to the assembled women and gives each a yellow *boṭṭu*. Then from a large flat pan a strong mix of turmeric paste is reciprocally applied to the feet of the nine women who in turn do the same to the assembled women onlookers. After the forehead mark and turmeric paste a third item is given to all attending, a bunch of threads of "forearm length" that each woman rubs with turmeric and then incorporates into her own marriage cord *(tāḷi)* without untying it, for the cord, once invested during her marriage rituals, must never be off the neck, or the husband dies.[20] Finally, each woman is given a bright red center dot on her *boṭṭu* as one of the nine principal family women presents an open winnowing fan, saying in Telugu, "I give this *vāyanam,*" the other replying, "I receive this *vāyanam*." Before acceptance each recipient bends to touch the feet of the offerer, then rises to take *kunkum*-reddened rice grains (Telugu, *akṣintulu*) from a tray and sprinkles them onto her own head.[21]

The *brahma-muttaiduva* returns from depositing her sari full of rice into a sack placed beside the bags of raw food. Again on her two stools (which she eventually receives), she is seen to have two huge *boṭṭu*s, one on top of the other, as is often the case with women possessed during goddess festivals. There is considerable emotion as the crowd of colorfully clad women presses together, perhaps in realization that the deceased is only now a departed one, and that the offerings she received for her celestial journey are now here in hand as her distributed grace. Before turning away, each woman takes the open basket (or baskets if she receives one from each side) into the fold of her sari, secretively, another expression of closure, like the covered baskets presented to the *brahma-muttaiduva*. Each fan contains whatever the bereaved families can afford to include, items in miniature such as a small mirror and comb, quantities of turmeric and *kunkum* powders, two or three bananas, flowers, betel leaves, incense, all the things that went into the two large *vāyanam*s for the *brahma-muttaiduva* except a *maṅgalasūtra,* toe rings, a pumpkin, rice, and other foodstuffs meant for the deceased wife's journey. In affluent circumstances the fans might include a new sari and cosmetics in silver boxes rather than newspaper or plastic parcels.

The women return to their homes and the duties of the day, the ritual having taken an hour and a half of their time. Their thoughts are on the departed and her family, but their prayers are to avoid the fate of an early death. As one woman who has attended numerous *mūsivāyanam*s puts it, one returns praying for long life, but not one that crosses that terrible threshold into widowhood. Once home, items in the winnowing fans each has received are either set aside or immediately given to service castes such as Washermen (Cākalis) and the empty *cēṭa*s are thrown up onto the roof where they may lie for a day or so before being pressed into routine household service. A high-caste Karaṇam woman reports, "I go home, enter through the back door, not the front, throw the empty *cēṭa*s on the roof. Next day I wash and use them. One day is enough, then they must be used up, not remain idle." But one should not use them on a Tuesday or a Friday, days of goddess worship. (See fig. 5.)

The Brahmamuttaiduva

> After the bath I am decorated like a bride with feet dyed red, bangles, flowers, sandalpaste, turmeric, *kunkum,* everything. New clothes are wrapped around me. The deceased's mother ties the *maṅgalasūtra* around my neck. Toe rings are slipped on. Everyone pays respects to me. Then they express goodbye and our relationship is finished. The debt *(ṛṇam)* is paid.
>
> —elderly *brahma-muttaiduva* with five years' experience
>
> Not everyone likes to do this job. No one should desire to be in this profession. To anticipate more rituals is to expect more death, and that is not a proper mind set.
>
> —young *brahma-muttaiduva*

THE RITUAL OBLIGATIONS of the *brahma-muttaiduva* are multiple. She is situated on one hand in the context of deep-rooted pan-Indian funerary traditions of final offerings *(antyeṣṭi)* at death and continuing offerings *(śrāddha)* to the recent and long-deceased ancestors. These traditions go back through the Gṛhya and Śrauta Sūtras and the Brāhmaṇa texts to origins in the Ṛgveda and Atharvaveda funerary hymns. On the other hand some of her roots appear to lie in equally deep-seated but nontextual traditions of spirit possession, divination, and the mysteries of agriculture, grain cultivation in particular. Essentially she is a surrogate for the deceased and her responsibilities include several significant tasks. First, her body serves as temporary container of the *preta* during its period of embarkation for another world, in this exceptional case, Gaurī-*loka*. Second, she is there as recipient and bearer of gifts *(vāyanam)* for that otherworldly journey. Third, the principal *dāna* she accepts is food, directly given from the living to the dead, and as the latter, as a *bhōkta,* an eater and enjoyer of food for the dead, she must consume what is given. Fourth, in a most important office, she expresses assurances to the living of her satisfaction with the entire course of the rituals, and blesses them before her departure. And fifth, in a symbolic distancing, she disappears abruptly and

5. The full assembly of forty women takes *prāsada* home from the offerings to the deceased.

has no further contact with the family of the deceased, vanishing from their sight in a fashion quite the opposite of the *purohita* who will continue to maintain routine ritual functions and responsibilities for all of the survivors.

Expanding briefly on each of these five responsibilities, her task of providing her body to be the temporary container of the *preta* comes first. A brief note on the Brahmanic funerary pattern may serve as useful background here.[22] According to the ancient *śrāddha* schedule the journey of the deceased required one year before his or her incorporation into the ancestors *(pitṛ*s*)*. Eventually, twelve months of offerings to sustain the *preta* were condensed to a symbolic year of twelve days, partly in fear that the *karta,* the chief mourner and ritual cornerstone, might himself die and leave the *preta* stranded short of ancestorhood. While family *purohita*s conducted the *navaśrāddha*s, the ten days of offerings after cremation, a special Brahman was obtained to observe closely all of the proceedings while performing no ritual actions, uttering no mantras. He was there as the deceased, watching the day-by-day construction of the invisible body that would carry him or her on to join the ancestors. On the eleventh day *dāna*s were bestowed on this special Brahman surrogate, all of the food, clothing, and other provisions for the long journey to the other world, ostensibly a year's worth of supplies that often included a bed, linens, utensils, gold, and personal items. On this day the daily and monthly offerings to the deceased for a full year were also crammed into the busy program, as well as a ritual feast for eleven Brahmans, kinsmen of the special *dāna*-Brahman. These chosen Brahmans came to be known as *mahāpātra*s, "great vessels," or *mahābrāhmaṇa*s, "great Brahmans." Despite their grandiose titles they were relegated to a degraded status because of their professional defilement by death. Although they go by many names and have varying roles to play in regional mortuary and planetary rituals, they are found all over India today and are universally described in formulaic terms as ignorant, without mantras, and greedy for money and materials. Of course the last scornful charge derives from their requisite function of looking out for the welfare of the deceased, an assignment accomplished not without self-interest as they repeatedly argue, ritually in medias res, for more and higher-quality items for the journey.[23] This ritualist is not as clearly defined in coastal Āndhra as in the north, but is nevertheless recognizable with the lore of all his negative features intact. In Southeast India he also frequently doubles as one who receives the *dāna*s that unload malevolent effects *(doṣa*s*)* from such planets as Śani (Saturn), Kuja (Mars), and the demons of eclipses, Rāhu and Ketu.[24]

It is the *mahāpātra*'s role that appears to serve as a partial model for the *brahma-muttaiduva* of coastal Āndhra in matters of ritual functions and social degradation. The remarkable fact is that there are no known female *mahāpātra*s in ethnographies north or south. Brahman males in modern accounts serve both genders. But here in the Godavari Delta the *brahma-muttaiduva* presents her body to accommodate the *preta* of the deceased wife, just as the *mahāpātra* of

North or Central India today serves as a "vessel" for the *preta* in its twelve-day transit. Worthy of attention here is the fact that the *brahma-muttaiduva* is decorated as a bride and, as two of these quotes indicate, this is a positive, even rewarding role for her to play. Far from being degraded by offering her own form *(rūpa)* to the *preta,* she takes delight in the respect and favor she garners as a bride. And then she becomes not an ancestor *(pitṛ)* but a goddess, Gaurī (Pārvatī), the spouse-lover of Lord Śiva.

The second task of the the *brahma-muttaiduva* is to accept "ritual gifts," *dāna*s, the two *vāyanam*s that have been offered by the two aggregates of women in her life. All that is presented in the closed winnowing fans is meant for her journey to Gaurī-*loka*. Not always successfully, women ritualists try to cut out the middlemen (and they are always males) who schedule the *mūsivāyanam*, for they may appropriate more than half the fee as well as many items meant for the deceased. As just noted there is an extraordinary range in the amount of *dakṣiṇā,* according to family means and intentions. But in *mūsivāyanam*s one does not see gold or other lavish items such as electronic appliances, wristwatches, and expensive beds that are frequently bestowed on male *dāna*-Brahmans, particularly in the northern and western regions of India. The *dāna*s consist of food, the symbolic paraphernalia of a bride, cosmetics for decoration, and a small cash *dakṣiṇā.*

As just revealed, the greater part of the ritual is devoted to the washing and decorating of the *brahma-muttaiduva.* The obligatory inclusion of two large mirrors along with the combs and supplies of *pasupu-kunkum,* sandalwood paste, collyrium, and other items for her journey suggests that the deceased will continue to prepare herself as an "auspicious woman," a *suvāsinī.* Her repeated toilet and costuming (sari, blouse-piece, necklaces, bangles, toe rings, and *tāḷi* thread) are obviously more important than being provisioned with books, newspapers, a radio, or an electric fan. And there are no cooking pots! Her routine work is over, but she must be properly attired and decorated.

The aggressive argumentation for more food and necessities on the part of the *mahāpātra* is paralleled by the moment of ritual inquiry in the *mūsivāyanam* when the *preta* sometimes expresses her anxieties about events and relationships at home. But contrary to the protesting *mahāpātra,* she voices no comment on the *vāyanam*, no complaints about things. Her concerns appear to be directed more toward her loss of control over family members and family affairs.

The third task of the *brahma-muttaiduva* is to serve as *bhōkta*, "an eater and enjoyer of food." The *dāna*-Brahmans of both genders are often referred to simply as *bhōkta*s. In this role they participate in a time-honored tradition of the funerary feast. Brahmans must be feasted on the eleventh day, but because no "clean" Brahman would take food in a house polluted by death, or from those who live in such a house, the task devolves to the degraded Brahmans for hire. The previous section discussed the moment in the ritual when the *brahma-muttaiduva* receives into the fold of her sari a great quantity, ten to twenty kilos in all, of uncooked rice (*biyyam,* sometimes replaced by soaked or "half-cooked" rice, Telugu, *nānubrālu*). The rice is basic and is complemented by bundles of leaves in which uncooked vegetables, tamarind, spices, and all the raw stuff for cooking a meal are contained. These bundles are for *svayampāka,* literally "self-cooking."[25] The *brahma-muttaiduva,* contrary to the male *dāna*-Brahmans eating cooked food on the ritual arena, accepts provisions for the journey to Gaurī-*loka* only in the form of raw food to take home, cook, and eat. Nor does she accept later offers of food in the homes of clients. "If I have a long distance to travel home," conceded one *brahma-muttaiduva,* "I will sometimes accept a cup of coffee. But that's all."[26]

The fourth responsibility of the *brahma-muttaiduva* is to provide assurances to the living that she, the deceased, is satisfied with the ritual procedures and all that has been said and done for her in the ten or eleven days since her demise. "This is for your satisfaction" and "Are you satisfied?" constantly recur as addresses to the deceased through the history of *śrāddha* texts in Hinduism. Vedic *tṛpti* (satisfaction, contentment) is perpetuated in modern Telugu with the same meaning, and justification for performing the *mūsivāyanam* always includes the statement, "It is for her satisfaction *(tṛpti).*" The fullness, completeness, and adequacy of the ritual should be hers to enjoy. Interestingly, several ritualists maintain that it is the mother-in-law's and husband's side, the affinal house, which sometimes engages in cost-cutting and abbreviating, so that the natal side, in their desire thoroughly to satisfy the deceased, will make up the difference. It is recalled that in extreme cases a husband refused to contribute and the natal side bore all of the expenses. Or worse, some remember situations in which no one attended from the affinal side and natal relatives were forced to act out both roles in the performance. One ritualist put it graphically: "That son-of-a-bitch [husband of the deceased] renigged on his promise, so the *suvāsinī*'s parents had to bring all the *vāyanams* for both sides!"

Satisfaction should be declared by the deceased before she departs from the world of the living. Thus the phase of ritual inquiry to the *preta* manifest in the *brahma-muttaiduva.* Once it is established that she is indeed the *preta* of the woman who died a week and a half ago, she is given voice for outstanding grievances of past and present as well as apprehensions for the future. It is a mechanism for knowing the health or disease of relationships before a journey separates forever one world from another. When she declares herself to be the goddess Gaurī, closure is then established, her contentment with her lot is known by her survivors, her blessings on them have been secured, and she is—to borrow a phrase—cleared for takeoff.

Finally, the fifth task of the *brahma-muttaiduva,* her brusque, silent departure and maintenance of a symbolic distancing, is also multisided. Self-described "clean" Brahmans, even if they must work only centimeters away, must never be touched by *dāna*-Brahmans and there is to be no social intercourse with them. When the *purohita* for the ritual that was just described was subsequently asked about the *brahma-muttaiduva* who sat beside him, he replied that he had no knowledge of her name or residence. She lives within sight of the *rēvu* and is there every day. He said that she had been brought by a middleman, whose name he also could not recall. Regarding *brahma-muttaiduva*s in general he added: "We keep them at a distance; we *purohita*s do not interact with such Brahmans." This is typical ostracization of all of those Brahmans, male or female, who receive *dāna*s for the dead or for the unloading of malevolent planetary *doṣa*s. They are sometimes known as "faceless" Brahmans because no one should remember or see them again.[27] They are as inauspicious as those dreadful bearers of naked corpses to the *śmaśāna,* the *śavavāhaka*s.

And the *brahma-muttaiduva*, for her part, keeps her clients at a distance for they are by definition from a polluted house of death. An elderly *brahma-muttaiduva* was asked about the caste of the family she had served that day in a village twenty kilometers from her home. She could not say, then commented:

> Normally I don't know anything about [client] families and their background. I carry along an extra sari, keep it safe in a bag in an out-of-the-way place so nobody in that family will touch it. When the whole ritual is over I bathe again, rinse the *vāyanam* sari, change into the fresh sari I brought, pick up the food and stuff and take off. I have nothing to do with that family any more. I do not know anything about them before or after.

An additional distancing is declared by the fact that some married women are unwilling to attend a *mūsivāyanam* and others who do attend sometimes decide not to take winnowing baskets home. There is some consternation when *vāyanam*s are still remaining after everyone has gone. It is an inauspicious sign to have *prasāda* remain unaccepted. Despite all declarations that this is an auspicious, affirmative ceremony, the *brahma-muttaiduva* sits at the juncture of opposing *loka*s, the horizontal world of beings caught in the disjointed flux of *saṃsāra* and the vertical world of migrating spirits and permanent celestial divinities. It is a hazardous place to be, these two unwieldy three-legged stools.

Thus the *brahma-muttaiduva* is multivocal, serving as body and voice for the *preta,* taking the substances intended for the dangerous and polluting dead, eating the food, assuring survivors that she is content and that they have her continuing blessings, and finally fading from sight as quickly as the deceased has departed for a distant and invisible domain .

The Background of Women who Serve

as *brahma-muttaiduva* is somewhat different from Brahman men who act as surrogates for the deceased and accept funerary *dānas*. There are fewer than a dozen of these women in the town of Rajahmundry. One or two others may be found in nearby towns such as Tanuku, Bhimavaram, and Ravulapallem. Those in Rajahmundry with a good reputation for promptness and expertise may be sought from as far away as Visakhapatnam, five hours by train, and be paid as much as Rs.1,116 ($45) in addition to travel costs. But such windfalls are rare and the usual fee is quite sparse, whether in the town or in an outlying village. The scarcity of Brahman women *dāna* recipients in remote village areas is sometimes met by *purōhita*s who send their wives to serve, a practice seeming to undercut the strict separation stressed by other *purōhita*s. Funerary choultries (pavilions next to temples) in Rajahmundry "guarantee" the authenticity of the Brahman women they recommend, but several *purōhita*s admitted that there can be no such guarantee because of frequent changes in the pool of available ritualists and the immediacy of need for someone's services. In fact, one "Brahman" married pair interviewed for this research provided a distressing case. She worked as a *brahma-muttaiduva* and he accepted funerary *dāna*s of any and every kind. The day he suddenly died she was widowed and therefore by definition unemployable as a *brahma-muttaiduva.* Evicted from the house they had lived in together for twenty-five years, hassled by the police for bribes to allow her to sleep on the ground in the scavenger colony, the penniless and dying woman gave up pretense and revealed herself to be not a Brahman but a Kōmati who had lived with an "authentic" Brahman for all those years.

Like male *bhōkta*s, the *brahma-muttaiduva*s work out of necessity, out of a lack of any other livelihood, and are not usually following a hereditary tradition as are many of the *apara* Brahmans, the upper-class funerary priests who were trained in mantras by their fathers, uncles, or older brothers. But because they must be married in order to serve as *brahma-muttaiduva,* and most have children and/or grandchildren at home, their families anchor them in particular neighborhoods and on the whole they are less vagrant than their male counterparts. The outsiderhood status of male *dāna* recipients, who are not required to be married, is declared in one description of them as "kites with severed strings."

But both men and women are always protecting their reputations. Defensive posturings in interviews, constant unsolicited remarks ("Ours is not a harmful profession," "We are not bad or immoral people") reveal something of the pain in those who routinely suffer common gossip, that the men are all alcoholics and the women all promiscuous.

Another comparative aspect concerning male and female *dāna* recipients has to do with transferring or unloading the negative effects of harboring *preta*s and accepting substances intended for them. It is a common tactic for some male *bhōkta*s, even when they are said to be "ignorant" of mantras, to use mantras such as repeated *japa*s of the Gāyatrī in order to shed the effects of death pollution or, in the case of those who accept sesame seed for Śani, the effects of planetary malevolence. But no *brahma-muttaiduva* mentioned attempting this, no doubt because none had any mantra training. Some *purohitas* mentioned the possibility of women going to a *purohita* for *prāyaścittas* (expiations), but this may be no more than an ad hoc explanation.

A singular departure from traditions of the male surrogate for the deceased lies in the respect and veneration accorded the *brahma-muttaiduva*. She is worshiped by the women participants and nowhere in the ritual arena is there insulting language to declare her ignorant and greedy. Nor does she become cantankerous and argumentative over the inadequacy of the gifts for her journey. Negative comment on her social status is reserved for occasions away from the ritual ground and argumentation over the amount and value of gifts occurs between the two houses prior to the ritual, often opportunistically exercising grievances of long-standing.

Thus in nature and function the *brahma-muttaiduva* diverges from her masculine prototype in as many ways as she parallels him. Intriguingly, this female role has either been perpetuated from a deep past or has been invented in recent centuries to fill a need. At this point in our knowledge, the *brahma-muttaiduva* is perhaps best understood as a figure in keeping with a South Indian predilection for possession phenomena and for strong ritual roles for female mediums and diviners trading in possession ritualism.[28]

Interpretations

> The performance of all our rituals *(karmakāṇḍa)* is like throwing a stone out into the darkness. But they have to be done. We are doing *karmakāṇḍa* to help the deceased escape whatever *piśāca rūpa* (demonic form) he or she happens to be in.
>
> —Brahman *purōhita,* discussing the *mūsivāyanam*

The first part of this chapter was a step-by-step overview of the ritual, while the second part was a closer look at the ritualist, the *brahma-muttaiduva*. This final part focuses on the deceased wife herself, with attention drawn to additional meanings of the *mūsivāyanam* tradition as a whole. Of course, "interpretation," not initiated in the present paragraph, has been here all along in shaping and articulating the material. For example, already included was a description of five discrete responsibilities of the *brahma-muttaiduva,* beginning with the ritualist as "a temporary container of the *preta*." No lay or professional participant has thus far expressed the role of the *brahma-muttaiduva* precisely this way. But insiders' voices are themselves multilayered and often conflicted in remarks about how the *brahma-muttaiduva* arrives at the river as a Brahman woman, takes (or offers) the form *(rūpa)* for the *preta,* and then takes (or is given) the form of the goddess Gaurī. As in a description of the drama of the Shī'a *taziyah* or Christian Eucharist, there is no innocent or single way to describe a sacred, transformative event. Now in this overview of the fate of the deceased various interpretative remarks will be added to the inside perspectives proffered by layfolk and professional Brahmans, with attention drawn to a few selected symbols and actions. In other words, in an attempt to uncover meanings, the historian of religions, anthropologist, or cultural historian may annotate, expand upon, or diverge from views of coastal Āndhra culture regarding the *mūsivāyanam.*

One set of explanations that proves instructive at this point comes from Bruce E. Tapper's detailed study of Yatapalem village, a community dominated by the Gavara (Śūdra) farmer caste in Visakhapatnam District, about two hundred kilometers northeast of the Godavari Delta. In this, the only other regional ethnographic example of a special ritual for a wife who dies first, a Jangam woman brought by the husband takes the role of the deceased in a rite known as *mūṣānam* on the eleventh day after death.[29] This ritualist receives an immense wad of turmeric paste that covers her forehead and much of her hair. A rough anthropomorphic image *(bomma)* of mud from a tank is created to represent the deceased and then decorated with items to signify married status, including black beads representing a *maṅgalasūtra,* toe rings, bangles, turmeric, a tiny box *(bariṇi)* for *kunkum,* and flowers. Then,

> relatives ask her if she accepts the offerings they have brought her. Three women lift and lower a rice winnow of offerings covered with their sari ends and say, "if you do not accept it tell us, don't turn into a ghost *(dayam)*". She acts reluctant at first but finally agrees. Then the mud image, the items on it, other offerings brought in the rice winnows, and the turmeric wad on the forehead of the Jangam woman are removed and taken out and immersed in the tank. The new rice winnows that were used in the ceremony are distributed to the *pēraṇṭālu* who have attended. Also distributed to the *pēraṇṭālu* is *prasādam* of fruits and liberal quantities of turmeric and vermillion which they apply to their foreheads in the hope that they will also live their lives without ever becoming widows.

Aside from the name *mūṣānam,* which suggests that the connection between this ritual and other standard women's *vāyanams* may have been lost, there are many significant differences between the Godavari and Yatapalem rituals. In the latter the ritualist is non-Brahman; she is not transformed into Gaurī, with Gaurī-*loka* as her destination; there is no indication that separate but cooperative natal and affinal houses make the offerings to her; there are no three-legged stools or ritual inquiry. In the Yatapalem *mūṣānam* emphasis appears to be on the graphic dissolution of a mud image of the deceased along with her bridal decorations and symbols and the huge turmeric wad from the forehead of the Jangam woman. Elemental dispersion in water seems more the point than establishment in a secure celestial residence.[30]

Despite their differences these rituals obviously illuminate one another, and Tapper's observations as well as those of Yatapalem residents provide pertinent insights. A major point made by Gavaras performing the *mūṣānam* is that the husband is "released from his marriage vow and free to remarry."[31] The Jangam woman "is implored to give a statement that she releases her husband from his marital obligations to her. (One man explicitly described the ritual as being like getting a divorce paper from the deceased woman)."[32] Tapper sees in the *mūṣānam* not only "the obvious glorification of the auspicious wifehood of the *pēraṇṭālu*" but also an attempt to appease her vengeful nature since she died without a complete life. Women "are believed to have more attachment, *āśa*, to their loved ones and be more emotional and less under control than men. For these reasons, a woman who dies before her husband is believed to be motivated to return as a ghost and cause harm to people, despite her meritorious death as a *pēraṇṭālu*."[33]

Most of the Godavari funerary ritualists interviewed with regard to the *mūsivāyanam* were shown a striking photo of a seated Jangam woman with her head covered by a turmeric-paste wad the size of a flattened grapefruit, and the mud image dressed with turmeric, bangles, and other items at her feet (Tapper's *Rivalry and Tribute*, plate 13).[34] None had ever seen such a massive wad or such a mud image, and all denied that the rite had to do with releasing the husband to remarry since, as several remarked, he is free to do so without the deceased wife's sanction. But there are numerous subtle connections here, to be noted in remarks in the next section.

To return to the evidence from the Godavari Delta, the deceased wife may be regarded from different vantage points. Among her guises, in the same order as she appears in the *mūsivāyanam* ritual, are the deceased as spirit sojourner, as a bride again, and as a divine emigré and otherworldly goddess. A closer examination of each of these three now follows.

A Spirit Sojourner

is one characterization of the *preta* in transit, en route to another world, a sheltered realm more substantial than the world of *saṃsāra* now abandoned by the female body. A striking feature of the *mūsivāyanam* is that the exact location of the deceased is declared by the ritual for the first time since cremation. For ten or eleven days subsequent to release through the broken cranium of her skull on the funeral pyre she has been scudding about, declaring her presence obliquely and momentarily in various symbolic entities. Now she is here, pinpointed in the visible, tangible body of the *brahma-muttaiduva*. The indefinite multilocality of the disembodied spirit ends with the invocation *(preta-āvāhana)*, as long as the *preta* accepts the *rūpa* of the woman ritualist, and therefore the agenda of conversion into Gaurī.

Out of a universe of *preta*s the correct one must be captured for a successful ritual. Proper identification of the *preta,* as just noted in the phase of ritual inquiry, is a necessary challenge. One *purohita,* perhaps thinking along the lines of one-size-fits-all, observed that "the rice *piṇḍa*s are balls because the *rūpa* of a *preta* is so difficult to distinguish." But attention is drawn to another evocative item, the winnowing fan (*śūrpa*, Telugu, *cēṭa*). Featured in the ritual bone-collection *(asthisancayana)* out of the ashes of the pyre, when the *preta* is notably vigilant, the winnow is now again a focus of attention for the tenth- or eleventh-day *mūsivāyanam*. It appears as one of those natural objects "disengaged from its mere actuality and used to impose meaning upon experience."[35] The basket may serve as a powerful aid in the ritual process of apprehending the *preta,* although its history is so complex, its origins so multiform and obscure, that no ritualist today articulates its symbolism.[36] Shaking the fan and tossing threshed paddy is an everyday task that separates edible rice grains from inedible husks. In a funerary context, the separation of an immutable soul or life-force from a mutable, dispensable body may be signified. The *śūrpa* gained a vivid history in both Vedic and regional non-Vedic traditions as a potent symbol combining agrarian symbolism with mortuary rituals and beliefs, including the all-important journey of the life-principle to another form or another world. Perhaps of equal antiquity in South Asia is ritual use of the winnow with rice as an instrument for triggering possession states and for purposes of divination, parallel to the classic shamanic drum.[37] Capturing a particular disembodied person from the entire company of spirits is an obvious advantage for the rite under investigation. In the *mūsivāyanam* it is to be noted that the mysteriously closed pairs of *cēṭa*s are not employed for winnowing but for prestations, including a quantity of already winnowed and cleaned rice grains. Perhaps the presence of the paired fans on the two earth altars is enough to command the attention of the desired spirit. In any event, with all of its ambiguities,[38] this winnow that can signify both life and death is not only the central symbol in this auspicious transformation of a *suvāsinī* into a goddess, but also one worthy of multiplication into *prasāda* carriers for each of the attending married women so as to disburse the deified *suvāsinī*'s grace.

A key factor in unraveling the general mysteries of Hindu conceptions of death and regeneration is retention, on its own terms, of the ancient notion of *antyeṣṭi*, "final sacrifice" of the body. A sacrifice, in its primary form in Vedic-Hindu tradition, involves ritual killing in which transformation takes place, never annihilation. There is ritual killing, but no being dies. This is exactly the case with *antyeṣṭi* and with subsequent *śrāddha*s in which the primary emphasis is not upon "the deceased" but upon the living *preta*. Secondary emphasis is upon a series of destructions of temporary containers of the preta-in-transit, toward *pitṛ*-hood in the standard Brahmanic *śrāddha*s, toward Gaurī-hood in the *mūsivāyanam* tradition. Certain properties, that is, ritualized embodiments for the living *preta,* are retained or ritually constructed, endowed with worship, then eliminated to effect the difficult, ongoing passage of this being. Every action (karma) points toward a recognition of the *preta* as sojourner spirit that first, does not die; second, inhabits multiple spaces in simultaneity; third, undergoes numerous transitions while exiting this elemental world and; fourth, if all goes well ritually, becomes an immigrant being. This means that after exiting the smashed skull the *preta* can be in the charred bones of its former body; in the tree at the burning/burial ground; in the crow hovering in wait for a rice-*piṇḍa;* in the rice *piṇḍa*s themselves; in the stone *(pretaśila)*; in the *kuśa* (grass) effigies planted in the ground; in the *navadhānya* sprouts watered in a basket; and in the *bhōkta* who may also be the presence of Yama himself as death is returned to Death in the form of the funerary feast. There are even indications that the *preta* may light upon the chief mourner.[39] All of this is in simultaneity and / or succession. It is not a problem for the spirit to be multilocal or multivalent.

Ritual disposition of each of the entities that temporarily houses the *preta* often suggests ritual killing. The body no longer needed is "killed." The fire that has eaten the body is no longer needed, and is itself ritually immolated by the smashed water pot at the head of the burning pyre. The rice *piṇḍa*s are "eaten" by the crow, then merged with the river, and the *preta*-stone is also cast into the river when it has served its purpose. The *navadhānya* basket in which dripping water has brought nine different seed grains to healthy green sprouts in ten days of careful nurturance is thrown into the river, short of fruition, a garden of the *preta* parallel to the garden of Adonis in the Greek Adonia festival.[40] Here perhaps is an opportunity to understand the wad of turmeric paste on the forehead of the *brahma-muttaiduva,* a small one at the moment of the invocation of the *preta* in the Godavari Delta, a massive one in Yatapalem. As just noted, a turmeric paste lump is pressed onto the forehead of a corpse before either burial or cremation.[41] This is possibly an act of cooling, half of the customary bracketing of the heat of cremation / transition.[42] Perhaps purification is intended as well. But this procedure is possibly a seal of elimination on the forehead, in keeping with the ritual disposition of all of the other temporary entities that have served the sojourner *preta.* In such an interpretation the Brahman ritualist is declared by a turmeric seal to be a corpse, no longer needed as the wife who died first moves on to goddess status.

A Bride Again

is another distinguishing role for this *preta* in transit. It is well known that in both North and South India the bride is elevated to goddess status, the groom to that of a god, and that anointing with turmeric, oil, and other substances may be considered acts of worship, as in *pūjā* for images of deities.[43] Certainly understandable is the concentration of turmeric paste and powder as auspicious substances with cooling and purifying effects and other properties associated with marriage preliminaries.[44] But the *mūsivāyanam* raises the question of why the deceased should depart this world in the middle of what appears to be a marriage sans groom. Her one-time groom is alive and well, free this very morning (with the replacement of his *molatāḍu*) to marry another, living woman if and when he chooses. He may be observing the scene from a distance, but he is not ritually present. There is no suggestion here of marital vows renewed by the *mūsivāyanam* for eternity, and the turmeric-root *maṅgalasūtra* tied by the deceased's mother is not the original one tied by the husband.

The *brahma-muttaiduva*/"bride" sits on her two stools in and out of the river, a liminal space of flowing water. When the ritual is concluded no trace remains of the makeshift seat for a *preta*-cum-goddess. This lonely figure provides sharp contrast with actual marriage preliminaries in which the bride and her co-bride (Telugu, *tōṭipeḷḷikūturu*) do everything in tandem. The co-bride, a ritual double or alter ego rather than a mere "bride's maid" or attendant, goes through all of the seated and standing preliminaries inside and outside the bride's mother's home during the "planting" of a freshly cut tree in a posthole, washing and rubbing the household mortar stone with turmeric, and holding a sprouting green coconut and then the pestle belonging to the mortar. But here in the *mūsivāyanam* the bride performs her entire departure scene alone.

An inverted hourglass is one image to carry away from this scene of two flanking lines of women that converge upon the bride, as if the ritual pours the sand grains of her life back into the funnel from which they came, until action freezes on the day of her marriage. A woman split in two by a wedding has been returned to one person. Two houses—the two halves of her life cooperating—have taken her back in time to a predivisive threshold. It could be understood as recovery of an age of innocence and maximum presexual *śakti* with which to start life in the realm of Gaurī. Her marital life with all of its consequences has been poured back. It could also be construed, as declared so directly in the Yatapalem *mūṣānam,* as removal of a now useless, no longer fruitful spouse to clear the way for a new wife.

Ritual restitution of the nuptial ceremony raises an interesting question that understandably confounds Brahman ritualists. Manu 9:22 states that a woman assumes the qualities of her husband. Contemporary ethnographers,[45] proceeding from various fieldwork regions, debate the degree to which bodily substances are transformed by marriage. If her blood changes, for example, when a woman enters her husband's lineage, one wonders if it changes back to natal blood for the *mūsivāyanam* migration during ritual ministrations from her original family.

Is it remarkable for a woman to return to bridal status and depart this world as a bride? These are separate questions. Regarding the first question, Holly Reynolds observes that a married woman goes back to the status of a bride every day, and with every annual thread change:

> Just as daily care of the *tāḷi* suggests a return to beginnings, conceived of as the marriage day, so too does the yearly changing of the thread indicate a return to the beginning. . . . A woman, in changing her thread, seeks not to be married again, but rather to return to the time when she was first married, when she was a new bride.[46]

Again, however, in the *mūsivāyanam* the marriage thread is not given routine anointment with turmeric or augmentation with new thread but is replaced altogether by a turmeric root on a cord tied by the mother or female substitute.

As to the second question, departure from the living as a bride, there are examples worthy of consideration. For one, there is the *satī.* A *satī,* although a "virtuous wife" like the deceased *suvāsinī* with a husband still alive, would appear to be antithetical to the latter for she is the momentary widow who accompanies the body of her husband onto the funeral pyre. And yet because she is *sahagamanī,* "one who goes with" her husband, she is not considered a widow and burns with all of her ornaments still upon her.[47] She may even be dressed as a bride on the pyre, as in the bizarre case of Bāḷāsatīmātā who died a natural death at age sixty-seven, some forty-three years after *intending* to commit *satī* while dressed as a bride in the funeral fire. She was dissuaded from doing so but nevertheless became, in the eyes of devotees, a *satīmātā.* And the pyre was not that of her husband, who died while she was still a child, but that of her nephew-in-law, Man Singh, whose daughter-in-law also intended to burn herself on his pyre in the garb and ornaments of a bride.[48] More recently, in 1987 in Deorala, Rajasthan, there was the famous and controversial case of Roop Kanwar, an eighteen-year-old woman married for eight months until her twenty-four-year-old husband died and both were cremated. According to a news report she was in bright red bridal clothes.[49] After the willing or forced immolation this goddess *(devī)* was worshiped as a seated bride in her *satī-sthala* and commemorated with a souvenir photo montage showing her in bridal attire surrounded by flames, her husband's head on her lap.[50]

None of these scholars investigating *satī* examines the significance of bridal attire, even in the cases when the *satī* was never married to the deceased man on the pyre. This ritual return to bridal status is shared on one hand by the *satī* wife (or would-be wife) whose husband (or would-be husband) has died first, and on the other hand by the *mūsivāyanam* wife who dies before her husband.[51] Each is endowed with high status as a supremely virtuous woman who leaves the world of the living to become a goddess. Each has returned to the nuptial ceremony in which a powerful embodiment of *śakti* is recovered. Perhaps it is regarded as her maximum, and defining moment of *śakti,* her transit from virgin to wife now recovered for her transit from human to deity. The difference, of course, is that one has received death, the other—as tradition would like to believe—has reached out for it.

A second example provides a situation of reverse traffic between ancestral and living worlds across this threshold of bridal status. It is a Tamil ritual of interest by way of contrast. Observed by Isabelle Nabokov in her fieldwork in South Arcot District is a non-Brahman ritual performed a day or two prior to the marriage of a firstborn son whose mother, father, or both are deceased.[52] In this *pūjā* the deceased parent or parents are joined by a host of other ancestors invited in collectivity as an incoming bride, "the woman who wears flowers"; this is accomplished by successive stages of possessions. Why must the dead return as a bride and not simply as ancestors invited to a wedding preliminary, is the puzzle Nabokov attempts to solve. Her solution: the "woman who wears flowers" is "invested with attributes distinctive of the ideal married woman *[sumaṅgalī]* at 'her' installation in the family sanctuary . . . which unfolds as a wedding ceremony."[53] "The symbolic dimensions of this 'marriage' have then been expanded into a sacramentalized union between the living and the dead, for a Tamil household intent on preserving its genealogical integrity over the generations."[54] The Tamil rite provides instructive counterpoint for understanding the *mūsivāyanam.* In the latter there is no need to transform the dead into a *sumaṅgalī,* for her status sanctioned this ritual. Rather than entering the house for installation as a household deity, a necessary outsider daughter-in-law who introduces "the missing ingredient that would allow for generational continuity", the wife who dies first is being escorted out the door, a daughter-in-law-bride going the other way, one for whom generational continuity can no longer be relevant. But at the same time she is a daughter-bride being worshiped at the threshold before departure. Instead of crossing that threshold into the ritually accessible "world of the ancestors," *pitṛloka,* she is entering an exceptional celestial realm. Her ritual is concealed *(mūsivāyanam),* gifts to her are hidden *(guptadāna),* and her destiny is discreet (Gaurī-*loka*).[55]

Finally, a third example brings discussion back to an identity of the transiting deceased wife with the goddess Gaurī in the context of bridal symbolism. In Tapper's presentation of the Gairamma (Gaurī Mother) festival in Yatapalem, the major annual event of the village and one that may last as long as seventeen or twenty-four days, a papier-mâché image of Gaurī and a Gaurī pot with live rice plants and a turmeric root are placed beside each other.[56] As in the *mūṣānam,* a Jangam *pūjāri,* but a male priest in this case, performs *pūjā* and offers the wooden cosmetic box *(bariṇi), pasupukunkum,* mirror, bangles, flowers, and *tulasī* leaves. At the conclusion of the festival the image of Gaurī, with her pot alongside, exits the village in a bridal palanquin, accompanied by wedding songs, to be immersed in the village tank. The moment the image and pot enter the water all fireworks and drumming cease and the festival is over. Gaurī (Pārvatī) has returned to her husband Śiva.

A Divine Emigré and Otherworldly Goddess

are two more roles to reexamine for the wife who dies first. At the close of the ritual an observer may ask, "Where is [name of the deceased] now?" and receive different replies from ritualists and family members. Here the Brahman / non-Brahman split is most disjunctive. Brahman funerary *(apara)* specialists adamantly go by the book for orthoprax clients and insist that eleventh- and twelfth-day *śrāddha*s subsequent to the *mūsivāyanam* be observed in detail. Even though the *suvāsinī-preta* has just been transformed into Gaurī and sent to Gaurī-*loka,* she is now said to remain a *preta* until dismissal *(preta-visarjana)* on the twelfth day. At that point "she wears the Vasu *rūpa,*" the form of the Vasu or nearest of the three levels of immediate ancestors, joining them via the *sapiṇḍīkaraṇa* through her mother-in-law's lineage. This means that when the long rice *piṇḍa* is cut and she is blended into the Vasu level of ancestors, she joins her mother-in-law (if deceased), that woman's mother-in-law, and again to the next level of that woman's mother-in-law.[57] The incongruity of having the deceased simultaneously in Gaurī-*loka* and in the company of her husband's ancestors who return to receive regular feeding in *śrāddha*s is one quite apparent to *purohita*s.[58] Brahman lay folk, however, can easily erase metaphysical discrepancies with the reply that the deceased wife is "up above," in *ūrdhva-loka,* covering both Gaurī-*loka* and a generalized *pitṛloka.*

In popular beliefs of the non-Brahman majority there is little concern for continuing *śrāddha*s or any other routine ritual attention to the deceased. Some families observe an anniversary rite, the *samvatsarīkam* being a standard procedure for the dead in general. Others perform a ritual without a Brahman *purohita* at some point before a year has passed, a *dāna* of a new sari and blouse-piece to a *brahma-muttaiduva* from the affinal house. Still others have no ceremony subsequent to the eleventh-day *mūsivāyanam.* For them the deceased is a goddess, a nonreturner, gone to a just reward.[59] Seldom mentioned by bereaved families is her formal establishment in the household shrine[60] of deities, in the fashion, for example, of a *pīṭha* that incorporates for daily worship the *vīrabhadra*s and *vīrakanyakā*s of deceased male and female children.[61] A photograph with *pasupu-kunkum boṭṭu* may suffice. There is, however, a potentially powerful "presence" to be reckoned with in the case of the husband's remarriage, if the new wife wears on her *tāḷi* thread one or more gold emblems (e.g., a *śatamānum*) from the *tāḷi* thread of the deceased wife.[62] Possession *(pūnakam)* of a living wife by a preceding deceased wife is not uncommon. As the Yatapalem evidence and the citation at the head of this part of the chapter suggest, those who perform the *mūsivāyanam* have every concern that the deceased remain satisfied and inflict no misfortune on the living.

Already encountered were several signals that the deceased wife is a non-returner. The brief Sanskrit *saṃkalpa* (intention) of the ritual stresses her fixed, permanent, "eternal" residence in Gaurī-*loka* by employing not one but two terms, *nitya* and *śāśvata,* both common in Telugu speech and understood by all. There is the sandalwood-paste image of Gaurī dissolved in the Godavari River, reminiscent of the Yatapalem dissolution of the mud image of the deceased. Another indication is the restraint placed by the *brahma-muttaiduva* upon overt signs of grief during the ritual. "I won't let anybody cry when I do the ritual," says one. "No offering should be made in tears if what is given is to reach her." When an attending woman begins to sob she may be assigned a distracting task to perform with one or another ritual item. The concern is for the deceased wife's clinging to this world, an attachment that must be weakened, not fostered by displays of grief.[63] Yet another sign of distancing is omission of sesame seeds in the *mūsivāyanam.* From the period of the Atharvaveda (e.g., 18.3.69) to the present day, offerings to the dead have featured sesame (*tila,* Telugu, *nuvvulu*) as a third necessity, along with rice and water, for nourishing a *pitṛ* and for preventing ancestral dissolution. But sesame seeds are pointedly excluded from the *mūsivāyanam,* a ritual deprivation seemingly testifying to the remote self-sufficiency of this nonreturning deceased wife.

The divine emigré belongs only to herself now. In Gaurī-*loka* she is in a goddess-controlled heaven, not in a realm governed by Viṣṇu (Vaikuṇṭha), Śiva (Kailāsa), Rudra (Rudra-*loka*), Kṛṣṇa (Kṛṣṇa-*loka*), or Rāma. For the first time in her existence she abandons male control. She departs as a "bride" but not one going toward a male for consummation of the marriage and the opening of her sexual life. From the initial moments of the *mūsivāyanam* women dominate her ritual send-off. Other than financial contributions, her father or husband have no part, and even in the unfortunate situation in which her husband refuses to contribute, women go right ahead, take his side, and accomplish dismissal. Males cannot direct her earthly departure nor otherworldly arrival.

A defining aspect of this ritual is the choice of Gaurī, an alternative name for Pārvatī, consort of Śiva. In the Godavari Delta people of all communities routinely consult possession ritualists, both male and female, concerning major and minor problems. Many of these mediums relate the basic narrative of their initial, paradigmatic possession states in the structure of a shamanic death-and-rebirth sequence. Bharani, a fifty-five-year-old Kāpu woman, provides a typical narrative from her middle years. Suddenly a goddess meant for a woman ritualist at a goat sacrifice jumped onto her and Bharani took lighted camphor in the palm of her hand and began to spout possession-speech:

> For five days that Jaganmātā was on me. She placed my body in a sitting posture like a corpse. . . . My real body she took to *svarga*, to Kailāsa, as *nitya* (eternal) Pārvatī. . . . Everyone came and offered *pūjā* to my dead body. I was offered turmeric-paste wads like those on a dead body. . . . But every half of a split second I was Pārvatī off taking a bath in the Krishna and Godavari Rivers.[64]

There are scores of possession ritualists like Bharani who daily tell their stories of being caught and taken up by a goddess, their "dead" bodies remaining at home for three, five, or nine days while their training takes place as or with a powerful goddess in her *loka*. And everyone is familiar with the story of Polamma's ascension into heaven, thence to become a popular neighborhood goddess. All of this creates a narrative backdrop for the deceased wife's journey and allows for easy familiarity with the fact that special women in the neighborhood, unaccompanied by men, have been to heaven.

Pārvatī has been described as the keystone of the South Indian pantheon. Brenda Beck portrays the married woman as nucleus of the Tamil kinship system, just as Pārvatī is the bonding link for the family of deities, holding together Brahmā (protofather), Viṣṇu (brother), Śiva (husband), Gaṇeśa (and Murugan in Tamilnadu) as sons.[65] Routine women's worship and vows are directed to the harmony and stability of this masculine framework centered on a powerful female. As a case in point, Gaurī *pūjā*s and *vrata*s are rituals in support of masculine well-being, the prosperity of the husband in particular, or as ritual means by which girls obtain husbands. The wife who dies first receives as accolade the *mūsivāyanam* because of her success in this enterprise. Śiva and Pārvatī are projected as "a paradigmatic model for all human couples."[66] But considering their celebrated, highly emotional separations and reunions, a stormier, more problematized paradigm could not be found. Gaurī, the Brilliant, receives her name and golden color following a prolonged absence in anger and austerity after Śiva called her Kālī, "Black One." In this paradigm harmony and stability are an ideal, not a reality.[67]

The unmarried girl or bride who worships Gaurī identifies with her and then, as the auspicious wife, becomes a participant herself in sequential separations from, and reunions with, her spouse, transiting between affinal and natal homes in shifts that are often accompanied by the *vāyanam* type of ritual exchanges described at the outset of this chapter. In the language of myth and body symbolism she extracts her body from that of her spouse, then adds it back upon return. And Gaurī herself, like other village deities, undergoes journeys for her festivals in villages, moving from "outside" to human habitation and back. Already noted is the Yatapalem Gaurī festival, including the goddess's departure as a bride back into the water. Similarly, for her festival in Hassan District, Karnataka, Suzanne Hanchett describes Gaurī being carried from the river to the village and then returned for immersion in the river three or five days later.[68] The journey is understood to be from her affinal home (the river) to her natal home (the village), her worshipers therefore being a collective mother welcoming, then sending off, an auspicious married daughter. In Hanchett's description, Gaurī is not an image *(mūrti)* but a ball of sand taken up from the riverbed or, as a variant, a pot *(kalaśa)* of river water.

Several disparate aspects of the Godavari *mūsivāyanam* now begin to come together when the narratives and rituals of women worshipers of Gaurī are balanced. First, there is the creation-dissolution of a representation of the wife who dies first. In the Godavari *mūsivāyanam* the basic altars are a pair of wet seedbed-earth mounds that are merged with the river at the close of the rite. A variant just noted is the creation of a sandalwood-paste image of Gaurī (like the turmeric-paste image of Gaurī in the *atlanōmu*) that is merged with the river. In the Yatapalem *mūṣānam* mud from the tank bottom is used to fashion an image of the deceased wife. It is dissolved back into the same tank that serves as destination for Gaurī after her festival. In Hassan District a ball of sand from the riverbed is Gaurī obtained and then dissolved. Evidently Gaurī's world *(loka)* is riverine,[69] watery for some, while for others it remains profoundly celestial, "up above." After proper worship, her elemental form (mud, seedbed earth, sand, turmeric paste, and the body of the *brahma-muttaiduva*), simply disappears.

Second, there is in the divine/human Gaurī ensemble, an evident counterpoise of structural movements. There are outside/inside manifestations, affinal/natal residences, and separations from/unisons with the spouse and birth family. In their twenty-one-day performances of Gaurī vows (Telugu, *nōmu*s, Tamil, *nōṉpu*s) Telugu Brahman and some Tamil non-Brahman women in Madurai District tell supporting narratives of Gaurī extracting her body from that of her husband.[70] Without her *śakti* Śiva becomes a useless corpse *(śava)*. On the other hand, the women tell narratives of Pārvatī demanding half of Śiva's body. An acquiescent spouse then becomes Ardhanārī *īśvara,* the god who is half female. In the case of the wife who dies first, the woman who has identified with Gaurī throughout her life of *nōmu*s has subtracted her body from that of her spouse for a final passage from her conjugal home to Gaurī-*loka,* a journey in bridal guise sponsored in the presence of her birth family. There is every opportunity here for the deceased to be declared Gaurī the symbolic bride, about to rejoin Śiva and to furnish the great god with the female half of his body. But no ritualist or layperson suggests this. The mirrored tensions of myth and ritual are retained. Gaurī the extractor of her self from Śiva, creator of his lifeless body, is Gaurī the virgin-bride-returnee to the elements of water and sky. The *suvāsinī* Gaurī, protector of her husband, eulogized and deified, is the *suvāsinī* eternally isolated, a nonreturning resident of Gaurī-*loka*.

In conclusion, death rituals in India are frequently stunning in their candid capacity to state existential issues that doctrinal and legal discourse seldom articulate. For example, the Vīrabhadra cult of deceased children who continue to live with their families as centers of ritual, social, and emotional attention is capable of saying, "Look! Our child is not erased! She is here, she speaks and appears before our eyes, and is the true source of our household harmony and prosperity!" As noted, the *mūsivāyanam* says many things. It celebrates the passing of an esteemed *suvāsinī* in the context of myths, rituals, and symbols of a powerful goddess. It draws together and marks with ritual and social solidarity not only a wider set of relatives that contributed to this marital union, but also a large company of nonrelated auspicious married women, often in a casteless sisterhood, temporary but meaningful. And, as with all death rituals, it serves a primary aim in assuring that the deceased is not abandoned unsatisfied. Who could not be satisfied with deification and residence in Gaurī-*loka,* be it a sacred river or a special heaven?

Under the surface of the ritual's declared intentions, however, lurk other expressions. The deceased child *vīrabhadra* or *vīrakanyakā* is part of the household, worshiped daily, celebrated in annual processions, and capable of speaking through loved ones, a returner, in spirit often stronger than in life. By contrast, the *suvāsinī* is a nonreturner. After the death anniversary ritual there may be nothing for her. In the *mūsivāyanam* her second life as a married woman, the one that should serve as crown for her first life, childhood, has been unraveled. She has ritually been reverted to virginal bride, child of her mother, then dismissed. Her *preta* has been caught, transformed, and exiled. In direct opposition to the *vīrakanyakā,* perpetuated as virgin household goddess, the *suvāsinī* has been erased from the household and society. The husband has no ritual obligations toward her and if young or middle-aged is expected to remarry.

Is the *mūsivāyanam* unique to coastal Andhra? Does it have current unrecognized parallels elsewhere? Was it once practiced more widely and then became extinct except for coastal Āndhra? The history of the *śila pratiṣṭhā,* "ritual establishment of a small stone" to represent the deceased, provides an example of shifting values in recent centuries in what sometimes appear to be immutable Hindu funerary traditions. It is a textually authorized procedure that now has disappeared from much of India although it remains an obligatory practice in Āndhra and is the occasion when the *preta* is most likely to possess living relatives. The *mūsivāyanam,* never textually sanctioned, is also expressive of a South Indian predilection for possession ritualism. It may indeed be something quite ancient or, on the other hand, a ritual emergent only in recent centuries to honor as well as dismiss the wife who dies first.

Notes

1. So powerful a word is Telugu *vedhava* (or *vidhava*, from Sanskrit, *vidhavā*; cognate: English, "widow"), that it has been withdrawn from polite discourse lest it be

taken as an insult or obscenity. Note: In this chapter all technical terms are Sanskrit unless identified as Telugu or as another language.

2. Manu 9:94, for example, prescribes an 8-year-old girl for a man of 24, a 12-year-old for a man of 30. Vaidika Brahmans of the Godāvari Delta today have formal betrothals for girls at the ages of 8 to 11, before puberty, with 5-day *vivāha* performed soon thereafter. Their husbands are usually 5 to 10 years older. The marriage is consummated according to the length of time young men require to complete their Veda studies and (nowadays) public education; see David Knipe, "Becoming a veda in the Godāvari Delta," *in India and Beyond. Aspects of Literature, Meaning, Ritual and Thought. Essays in Honour of Frits Staal,* ed. Dick van der Meij (London-New York: Kegan Paul International, 1997), pp. 320 ff. Śūdra and Scheduled Caste girls in the last generation were often married off as soon after menarche *(samarta)* as possible, schooling being curtailed at sixth- to eighth-class levels at most, their husbands being considerably older and usually better educated. With increasing family affluence today many communities keep daughters in school and college longer and marry them later, thus shrinking the age differential with marriage partners.

3. My gratitude is extended to the American Institute of Indian Studies, New Delhi, for a Senior Research Fellowship, 1991–92; Dr. V. Rama Rao, Atlanta, Georgia, for his enthusiastic encouragement; my longtime research associate, Prof. M. V. Krishnayya of Andhra University, Waltair, for his detailed knowledge of the area and its many dialects; Bruce Tapper, Washington, D.C.; and the many women and men of Rajahmundry, Amalapuram, Sriramapuram, Nedunuru, and elsewhere who gave so generously time and insight.

4. Brahmans automatically discount non-Brahman rituals as inauthentic and inferior, and portray them as vague but dense with accretions in the form of local practices *(ācāras)*. Non-Brahmans, with the exception of a very few Brahman-imitators, have little firsthand experience of Brahman ceremonies, funerary ones in particular. In preparing this chapter I am aware that I have not been able to witness the full range of communities performing *mūsivāyanam,* including those few who, I am told, must secure proxies for families whose women do not go out of the house. By definition, the *mūsivāyanam* is a rare performance, and as with all death rituals, an outsider's observation is limited strictly to chance and to the gracious consent of a bereaved family and the professional ritualists.

5. According to Suzanne Hanchett, *Colored Rice: Symbolic Structure in Hindu Family Festivals* (Delhi: Hindustan, 1988), p. 142 in villages of Karnataka one does not buy one winnowing fan but two and, "for Gaurī offerings to new brides [i]t must be a pair of pairs," a significant observation in light of the Godāvari ritual under discussion.

6. Hanchett succinctly highlights the special relationship an auspicious married woman entertains with a benign goddess such as Gaurī or Laksmī in *Colored Rice*, pp. 73–74: "An important part of many married women's vows is the offering of gifts to other married women, who are thought to represent both auspiciousness and the protection of the benign goddess herself."

7. In regional terminology the word *pēraṇṭālu* may also sometimes specify the woman who dies while her husband still lives, that is, one for whom the *mūsivāyanam*

should be performed. A *bālapērantālu,* similarly, is either a prepubescent girl who attends a *pērantam,* or in some regional speech, a girl who dies before marriage.

8. These ten days are the ritual gestation and delivery of a temporary, invisible new body for the spirit *(preta)* of the deceased. Āndhra Brahmans have generated their own funerary terminology and the classical Sanskrit set of *navaśrāddhas* (ten days of rites for the "new," i.e. the recently deceased) is known as *dharmodakas*. Mixed *(miśra) śrāddhas* begin on the eleventh day and on the twelfth the *sapiṇḍīkaraṇa* dramatizes incorporation of the deceased into the world of ancestors *(pitṛs)*. See Knipe, "*Sapiṇḍīkaraṇa*: The Hindu Rite of Entry into Heaven," in *Religious Encounters with Death: Insights from the History and Anthropology of Religion,* eds. Frank Reynolds and Earle Waugh (University Park: Pennsylvania State University Press, 1977), pp. 111ff.

9. This ritualized severance is parallel to the breaking of a widow's marriage thread and bangles by a group of other widows at the *rēvu,* also in the early morning hours of the eleventh day. The difference is that the widow will remain without her thread and seldom remarry, even if her community permits such, whereas the widower will have a new *molatāḍu* tied immediately by the Cākali with the words, "Now you are free to marry again." The *molatāḍu* represents male power and virility and is invested in infancy, not as part of the marriage ritual like the *tāḷi* or *maṅgalasūtra* for a bride.

10. Sometimes widows may be seen in attendance as apparently they bring no threat to this ritual. But they are spectators only, not actual participants, and should not receive a *cēṭa* at the end of the rite.

11. The complexities of different marriage and kinship systems make a considerable difference in interrelationships of the women involved in a *mūsivāyanam,* and in each woman's multiple kinship connections with the deceased, as for example, in the difference between a family in which the husband of the deceased is her mother's brother and a family in which the husband is her father's sister's son. Karin Kapadia, in *Śiva and her Sisters: Gender, Caste and Class in Rural South India* (Boulder: Westview, 1995), provides a useful analysis of marriage and kinship in rural Tamilnadu that is to a degree applicable to the Godāvari Delta.

12. *Pasupu-kunkum* is a conventional compound for these two indispensable and complementary ritual substances, the first a natural one from the turmeric root, the second a manufactured red obtained (among several methods) by adding fresh lime juice to turmeric powder and wood ashes. On *haldi-kunkum* as the appropriate offering to female deities and married or marriageable unwidowed women in Maharashtra see Anne Feldhaus, *Water and Womanhood: Religious Meanings of Rivers in Maharashtra* (New York: Oxford University Press, 1995), p. 43. On the colors yellow and red in Karnataka see Hanchett, *Colored Rice* (pp. 283–89) as well as "turmeric" and "vermilion" in the index.

13. The *talāntu* similarly removes *maila* at the conclusion of every menstrual cycle.

14. Usually the new sari is worn on the ritual arena directly after the bath. Contrarily, in the rite described here, the *brahma-muttaiduva.* quietly slipped away while *vāyanams* were being distributed to all of the *muttaiduvas*, then entered a small temple to change out of her wet sari, and disappeared toward her home.

15. Recorded as pronounced in rough grammar: *śāśvata Gauri loke prāptyartham śūrpa vāyana dānam kariṣye.* A variant was recorded: "In order [for her] to reside *(nivāsārtham)* permanently *(nitya)* in Gaurī's eternal *(śāśvata)* world, I will give away a *śūrpa-vāyana.*" This second version doubles the emphasis on the deceased's permanent residence by employing Sanskrit synonyms for "eternal," *śāśvata* and *nitya,* both of them common in Telugu. At times women may speak without prompting, saying in Telugu "For this *pūja* I offer this *dāna* to you," while using a metal vessel in the left hand to pour water over the right hand that offers *akṣintalu* (rice with red powder) to effect the *dāna.*

16. Along with a *kunkum boṭṭu,* the *pasupu mudda* is also placed on the forehead of a corpse immediately after death. In his *Rivalry and Tribute: Society and Ritual in a Telugu Village in South India* (Delhi: Hindustan Publishing Corporation, 1987), p. 145, Tapper notes that in Yatapalem a widow's funeral involves no turmeric anywhere on the body. Cf. also David Sopher, "Indigenous Uses of Turmeric *(Curcuma domestica)* in Asia and Oceania," *Anthropos* 59 (1964) p. 103.

17. In the particular ritual documented here there was no indication of erroneous possession or expression of dissatisfaction from the deceased. If it occurs at all, possession *(pūnakam)* of a living person attending a postcremation ritual is most likely to occur during the *śilapratiṣṭhā,* seating of the small stone used to break the water pot at the cremation ground, and in this invocation of the *preta* for *mūsivāyanam.*

18. In one town in the interior of the delta the local *mūsivāyanam* practice among the three twice-born classes includes creation of a small sandalwood-paste image (Telugu, *bomma*) of Gaurī that remains on a betel leaf throughout the worship of the *brahmamuttaiduva* and then is "merged" into the river. It may also be noted that in Rajahmundry two special *nōmus*, one month apart, performed by virgin girls before marriage or newly married women, feature paste images of Gaurī. The first is *uṇḍrallataddi,* the second *aṭlataddi,* on the dark third (*tadiya,* colloquial Telugu, "*taddi*") of Śrāvaṇa and Bhādrapadam, respectively. For her first *aṭlataddi* after marriage a new bride will return to her natal home, invite an odd number of auspicious married women, go the the river at 3:00 A.M. to create Gaurī from turmeric paste in a vertical wad on a betel leaf that is then merged into the Godāvari. Special sweet cakes (Telugu, *aṭlu,* pl. of *aṭṭu*) are presented in winnowing fans with the same Telugu words of exchange as in the *mūsivāyanam,* "I give this *vāyanam*" and "I receive this *vāyanam.*"

On images of mud representing the deceased and merged into the water in Visakhapatnam District, see the next section.

19. The sari end is *kongu* in Telugu. R. S. Khare remarks on the North Indian custom of *konca* in which raw rice, sweets, turmeric, and rupees are dropped from a winnowing pan into her sari end (Hindi *konca*). Intriguing here in our attempt to understand the *mūsivāyanam* is that this winnowing pan is ritually employed when a wife is in transit between her natal and affinal houses, after childbirth, for example. In the *musivayanam* the wife who dies first is making this transit for the last time, at least to its midpoint, and receives into her sari for the ongoing journey these same items. See Khare, *The Hindu Hearth and Home* (Durham: Carolina Academic Press, 1976), p. 196 and n. 13.

20. See Holly Baker Reynolds, "To Keep the tāḷi Strong": Women's Rituals in Tamilnad, India (Ph.D. diss., University of Wisconsin, 1978), p. 217. This is a thoroughgoing, well-documented study of the *tāḷi* and its rich mythic, folkloric, ritual, and symbolic background, structured on women's ritual vows (Tamil, *nōṉpu;* Telugu, *nōmu*). Although the fieldwork was carried out in the village of Vadapalanji, Madurai District, Tamilnadu, there is significant influence from Telugu women's rituals, as in the case of the Gaurī *nōṉpu* observed by Telugu Brahman and Tamil non-Brahman women.

21. In other *mūsivāyanam* performances it is the *brahma-muttaiduva* who sprinkles *akṣintulu* on the heads of all the donating women. In some performances a pancake-like mass of turmeric is pressed on top of the head of the *brahma-muttaiduva* instead of onto her forehead.

22. For more detailed observations from varying perspectives see Knipe, "*Sapiṇḍikārana*; Knipe, "Softening the Cruelty of God: Folklore, Ritual, and the Planet Śani (Saturn) in Southeast India," in *Syllables of Sky: Studies in South Indian Civilization*, ed. David Shulman (New York-Delhi: Oxford University Press, 1995); Jonathan Parry, *Death in Banaras* (Cambridge: Cambridge University Press, 1994); Pandurang Vaman Kane, *History of Dharmaśāstra*, vol. 4 (Poona: Bhandarkar Oriental Research Institute, 1953); Dakshina Ranjan Shastri, *Origin and Development of the Rituals of Ancestor Worship in India* (Calcutta: Bookland, 1963).

23. Press reports indicate that King Birendra and Queen Aishwarya of Nepal were gunned down in patricide-matricide by Crown Prince Dipendra, along with seven other members of the royal family attending a dinner party June 1, 2001. One Brahman ritualist represented Birendra as *mahāpātra* for the eleventh-day ritual. Required to eat marrow from a royal bone gathered in the *asthisancayana* after cremation, he is said to have consumed a substitute animal marrow because the rite, known as *katto,* is now "symbolic." In a bizarre repetition, a second Brahman ritualist, Devi Prasad Acharya, then represented the assassin himself, because Dipendra lived as king for a few hours after a self-inflicted gunshot wound subsequent to the death of his father. In Dipendra's eleventh-day ritual the priest took his momentary kingship at face value and demanded a "palace" and the murdered king's furniture in addition to opulent traditional *dāna*s. A dwelling appropriate for one harboring the *preta* of a king for a year, even though a murderer-suicide, seemed to suit the logic of the ritual. Reports from p. 1 of *The Hindu* June 12 and 15, 2001.

24. See Knipe, "Softening the Cruelty of God," pp. 206–48.

25. Also known in Telugu as *pottarlu.* Since the provisions are for a year, an additional Sanskit/Telugu designation is *samvatsara-grāsa,* "food for a year."

26. Funerary feasting, it may be noted, is a complicated, many-sided feature of Hindu mortuary schedules, and different communities provide quite disparate examples. Viśvabrahmans (Goldsmiths), for example, who consider themselves higher than Brahmans, bury their dead seated upright with hands in their laps to receive a complete dinner and beverages poured into a hole in the grave mound directly over the hands on the day following interment. Several communities have full family meals seated in circles on the *śmaśāna* itself. Some Vaiṣṇavas, including those who perform the *mūsivāyanam,* bring

in a non-Brahman Sātāni *pūjāri* to join relatives of the deceased with the same family name (Telugu, *iṇṭipēru*) and, on the eleventh day, consume a meal reminiscent of the tantrika *pañcamakāra,* with meat, fish, and liquor as well as rice and other ingredients. It should be noted, from the perspective of adherence to ancient practice, that this Sātāni Vaiṣṇava consumption of meat in a funeral feast is neither esoteric nor transgressive.

27. See Knipe, "Softening the Cruelty of God," pp. 234ff.

28. See Knipe, "Balancing *raudra* and *śānti:* Rage and Repose in States of Possession," in *Vidyārṇavavandanam. Essays in Honour of Asko Parpola,* eds. Klaus Karttunen and Petteri Koskikallio (Helsinki: Finnish Oriental Society 2001), pp. 342–57 and references; Knipe, "Ritual Subversion: Reliable Enemies and Suspect Allies," in *The Vedas: Texts, Language, and Ritual,* Proceedings of the Third International Vedic Workshop, eds. Arlo Griffiths and Jan E. M. Houben (Leiden: Intternational Instutute for Asian Studies, 2003).

29. Tapper, *Rivalry and Tribute,* pp. 155ff, cf. pp. 145ff.

30. Some qualifications are in order here. The Yatapalem account reflects the homogeneity of a village's dominant caste, the Gavaras, whereas the Godāvari ritual, theoretically available for all castes, has been described for an entire region. Significantly, the Gavaras' name is said to derive from Gaurī, known locally as Gairamma, the goddess featured in their major annual festival. They are split into two funerary clans for death rites in general. One employs Jangam *pūjāri*s who aid in sending the deceased to Śiva's heaven, Kailāsa; it is only this clan division that performs *mūṣānam.* The other clan division employs Vaiṣṭapodu *pūjāri*s who conduct rituals to send the deceased to Viṣṇu's heaven, Vaikuṇṭha. See Tapper, *Rivalry and Tribute,* pp. 153f. The latter *pūjāri*s recall the Sātāni Vaiṣṇavas of the Godāvari Delta.

31. Ibid., p. 156.

32. Ibid., p. 147.

33. Ibid., p. 156.

34. I thank Bruce Tapper for providing me in January 1998 with an additional twenty-six photos of the Yatapalem *mūṣānam.*

35. Clifford Geertz, *The Interpretation of Cultures* (New York: Basic, 1973), p. 45.

36. Among other compelling insights into the winnowing fan, Hanchett (*Colored Rice,* pp. 141f.) calls attention to the symbolism of separating the daughter from her family at marriage, as well as the infant placed in a winnow at birth. On the other hand, in her highly nuanced analysis of North Indian rituals Gloria Goodwin Raheja situates winnowing in company with husking and churning as "the disarticulation of negative qualities and substances" in order to separate "chaff" from that which is auspicious. See Raheja, *The Poison in the Gift: Ritual, Prestation, and the Dominant Caste in a North Indian Village* (Chicago: University of Chicago Press, 1988), pp, 87, 123ff. On associations between goddesses and winnows, see Don Handelman, "The Guises of the Goddess and the Transformation of the Male: Gangamma's Visit to Tirupati and the Continuum of

Gender," in *Syllables of Sky: Studies in South Indian Civilization,* ed. David Shulman (New York-Delhi: Oxford University Press, 1995), pp. 295ff., 303, 326f.; David Kinsley, *Tantric Visions of the Divine Feminine: The Ten Mahāvidyās* (Berkeley: University of California Press, 1997), pp. 11, 176, figs. 5, 28; Alf Hiltebeitel, *The Cult of Draupadī.* 2 vols. (Chicago: University of Chicago Press, 1991), 2: 324; Eveline Meyer, *Aṅkālaparamēcuvari: A Goddess of Tamilnadu, Her Myths and Cult* (Wiesbaden, Germany: Franz Steiner, 1986), cited and discussed by Hiltebeitel, *Cult of Draupadī.* References within and without South Asia, burdened with nineteenth-century issues of magic, totemism, and fetishism, are in William Crooke, *The Popular Religion and Folk-lore of North India,* 2d ed., 2 vols. (Delhi: Munshiram Manoharlal [1896] 1968): 2: 187ff., 308ff. But apropos of the *mūsivāyanam*'s upside-down winnows and the *brahma-muttaiduva* on her three-legged stools, an 1867 report from C. A. Elliott in Hoshangabad is cited by Crooke: a cultivator, in the solemn ritual of first winnowing in which his family and the village priest are present, must stand on a three-legged stool to winnow. "[T]he basket must never be set down on its bottom, but always upside down . . . [lest] spirits use the basket to carry off the grain." John Abbott has a contrary note, *The Keys of Power* (London: Methuen and Co., 1932), p. 383.

37. Mircea Eliade, *Shamanism: Archaic Techniques of Ecstasy* (New York: Bollingen, 1964), pp. 425f.; Dorothy Spencer, "The Recruitment of Shamans among the Mundas," *History of Religions* 10 (1970), pp. 7f., n. 15.

38. In the left hand of Dhūmāvatī, the old and ugly North Indian hag-goddess who rides a crow and dresses in widow's garb, the winnow is anything but auspicious unless it is construed as a balancing symbol of regeneration. Hanchett's emphasis is on the auspicious winnow, sometimes known as "wealth-producing" in Kannada, and she reports no association with death rituals or symbols.

39. In *Death in Banaras,* p. 157, Parry remarks: "It is tempting to suggest that the chief mourner's stoicism should be seen in the light of the fact that he is a kind of living counterpart of the deceased." Actually there are overt ritual events in this direction, such as the wearing of a shroud piece by the *karta* from the moment of cremation.

40. Cf. Marcel Detienne, *The Gardens of Adonis,* trans. Janet Lloyd [1977, from 1972 French] and Froma Zeitlin [1994: Afterword, from 1985 French] (Princeton, N.J.: Princeton University Press, 1994). My suggestion here, without detailing further the Āndhra *navadhānya* funerary ritual, is that this basket of sprouts is deliberately killed in the ritual, its purpose as temporary ten-day container having been fulfilled, as the garden of Adonis is set out to wither in the heat of July, exactly the contrary, as Detienne maintained, of a rite of fertility and regeneration.

41. Two individuals, one a *mūsivāyanam* ritualist, claimed the lump to be *śeṣa* (the cosmic serpent of Viṣnu) with no further elucidation. Introduction of serpent symbolism in a context of bodily death and *preta*-continuity adds another dimension.

42. Knipe, *In the Image of Fire. Vedic Experiences of Heat* (Delhi: Motilal Banarsidass, 1975), pp. 134ff; cf. Brenda Beck, "Colour and Heat in South Indian Ritual," *Man* n.s. 4: (1969): 553–72; Piers Vitebsky, *Dialogues with the Dead: The Discussion of Mortality among the Sora of Eastern India* (Cambridge: Cambridge University Press, 1993), p. 49.

43. Lawrence Babb, *The Divine Hierarchy: Popular Hinduism in Central India* (New York: Columbia University Press, 1975), pp. 84, 89.

44. Beck, "Colour and Heat in South Indian Ritual"; Sopher, "Indigenous Uses of Turmeric."

45. In *The Sacred Marriage of a Hindu Goddess* (Bloomington: Indiana University Press, 1989), p. 134, William Harman cites the Manu passage and eight contemporary writers on this contested notion of physiological transformation of the bride. Cf. Heli Uusikylä, "The Seeds in the Container: Metaphors of Conception and Kinship in Rural Bangladesh," in *Changing Patterns of Family and Kinship in South Asia,* eds. Asko Parpola and Sirpa Tenhunen (Helsinki: Finnish Oriental Society; *Studia Orientalia,* vol. 84, 1998), p. 58, for parallels among Bengali Muslims where transmitted blood, as well as male and female semen are concerned: "After marriage women join the husband's line, but still carry their fathers' blood *(rokto)*" even though they will not pass their fathers' blood to their children. Cf. also Lina Fruzzetti, *The Gift of a Virgin* (New Brunswick: Rutgers University Press, 1982).

46. Reynolds, *"To Keep the tāḷi Strong,"* p. 223.

47. Lindsey Harlan, "Satī, the Story of Godavari," in *Devi: Goddesses of India,* eds. John Hawley and Donna Wulff (Berkeley: University of California Press, 1996), p. 236; but cf. Harlan, *Religion and Rajput Women: The Ethic of Protection in Contemporary Narratives* (Berkeley: University of California Press, 1992), pp. 150ff; cf. Julia Leslie, "Suttee or Satī: Victim or Victor?" in *Roles and Rituals for Hindu Women,* ed. J. Leslie (Delhi: Motilal Banarsidass, 1992), p. 189.

48. Man Singh died in 1943; see Paul Courtright, "*Satī*, Sacrifice and Marriage: The Modernity of Tradition," in *From the Margins of Hindu Marriage: Essays on Gender, Religion and Culture,* eds. Harlan and Courtright (New York: Oxford University Press, 1995), pp. 196f.; cf. Courtright, "The Iconographies of Satī," in *Sati: The Blessing and the Curse. The Burning of Wives in India,* ed. John Hawley (New York: Oxford University Press, 1994), p. 46.

49. Leslie, "Suttee or Satī," p. 181.

50. V. N. Datta, *Sati: A Historical, Social and Philosophical Enquiry into the Hindu Rite of Widow Burning* (Riverdale, MD: Riverdale, 1988) xi.f; Leslie, "Suttee or Satī," p. 191, plate 15.

51. This is a hypothetical comparison, there being few trustworthy reports of *satī* in the historical record for coastal Andhra.

52. Isabelle Nabokov, "When the Dead Become Brides, Gods and Gold: Marriage Symbolism in a Tamil Household Ritual," *Journal of Ritual Studies* 10 (1996): 113–33.

53. Ibid., p. 130, n. 18.

54. Ibid., p. 127.

55. Intriguingly, elsewhere Nabokov reports from the same fieldwork period that a particular non-Brahman widow was decorated as a bride in rituals on both the seventh

and sixteenth days after her husband's death. On the latter she was then stripped of her new sari and all decorations, including the extra-large forehead daub of vermilion, her bangles were broken, and her *tāḷi* was cut, rendering her formally a widow. See Nabokov, *Religion against the Self: An Ethnography of Tamil Rituals* (New York: Oxford University Press, 2000), pp. 103–5.

56. Tapper, *Rivalry and Tribute,* pp. 198ff.

57. See my video, "Death and Rebirth in Hinduism," Program 15 in *Exploring the Religions of South Asia* (Madison: WHA-TV. University of Wisconsin, South Asian Studies Department, 1974) and the analysis in my "*Sapiṇḍīkaraṇa*."

58. Dualities in the fate of the deceased are a study in themselves. Consider the investigations of Vitebsky into the Sora, an aboriginal "tribe" living on the border of northern Andhra and Orissa. Exogamous patrilineage reveals the cryptic pose of a deceased married woman. Most men and unmarried women receive only one "stone planting," establishment of an upright memorial stone subsequent to cremation, a rite accompanied by a buffalo sacrifice. A married woman, however, receives two stone plantings after two separate funerals conducted first by her husband at his lineage cremation ground and then by her brothers' lineage at their cremation site. By these rituals she is consolidated into two different sets of ancestors, a scenario somewhat different from the Godavari wife who is incorporated into Gaurī-*loka* and her husband's lineage. See Vitebsky, *Dialogues with the Dead.*

59. It was mentioned that there are newspaper notices of the death date and program of rituals including the *mūsivāyanam*. It is not unheard of that death notices deliberately publicize grievances, including charges tantamount to murder. In one recent vituperative example a natal family served notice under a photo of the deceased wife: "leaving us in an ocean of sorrow, we have come to know that you departed this world on 6/2/1996 by becoming a sacrificial animal *(balipaśuvu)* in your husband's hands." The date for eleventh-day rituals "in our own house" was then provided and the notice signed by the deceased's father, mother, father's father, mother's mother, six older brothers, an older sister, and a brother-in-law. I thank M. V. Krishnayya for this clipping.

60. However, cf. Tapper, "Widows and Goddesses: Female Roles in Deity Symbolism in a South Indian Village," *Contributions to Indian Sociology* (NS) 13 (1979): 1–31, p. 16; Tapper, *Rivalry and Tribute*, p. 157.

61. See Knipe, "Night of the Growing Dead: A Cult of Vīrabhadra in Coastal Andhra," In *Criminal Gods and Demon Devotees*, ed. Alf Hiltebeitel (Albany: State University of New York Press, 1989), pp. 123–56; "Balancing *raudra* and *śānti,*" pp. 352–56.

62. For a North Indian tradition of worship and appeasement of a deceased first wife (in the form of a gold image) by the second wife, see Jack Planalp, "Religious Life and Values in a North Indian Village," 2 vols. (Ph.D. diss., Cornell University, 1956), pp. 563ff.

63. This is an ancient concern. The oldest literary reference to burial in the subcontinent is the famous hymn, Ṛgveda 10.18. Verse 7 calls attention to the prominent presence of an assembly of women with good living husbands, healthy, well dressed,

eyes anointed with butter, and *without tears*. This is a prescription for the women attending the *mūsivāyanam,* although of course this hymn reverses roles and portrays the death and burial of a man with a living wife.

64. Knipe, "Rivalries Inside Out: Possession Ritualism in Coastal Andhra," (Seminar: The Dynamics of Rituals and Narratives in Indian Folk Culture, Centre for Folk Culture Studies, University of Hyderabad, 1997), pp. 14f. For more on Bharani and her colleagues see Knipe, "Balancing *raudra* and *śānti,*" pp. 345–52, and "Ritual Subversion."

65. Brenda Beck, "The Kin Nucleus in Tamil Folklore," in *Kinship and History in South Asia,* ed. Thomas Trautman (Ann Arbor: Michigan Papers on South and Southeast Asia, no. 7, 1974), pp. 7ff.

66. Reynolds, *"To Keep the tāḷi Strong,"* p. 329.

67. For commentary on Skanda Purāṇa 1.2.27–29 and Padma Purāṇa 1.46.1ff. versions of this myth see Wendy Doniger O'Flaherty, *Hindu Myths* (Baltimore: Penguin, 1975), pp. 251–61; Wendy Doniger, *Splitting the Difference: Gender and Myth in Ancient Greece and India* (Chicago: University of Chicago Press, 1999), p. 233; and Wendy Doniger, *The Bedtrick: Tales of Sex and Masquerade* (Chicago: University of Chicago Press, 2000), pp. 70-74. Cf. Matsya Purāṇa 154.520–158.28 in Don Handelman and David Shulman, *God Inside Out: Siva's Game of Dice* (New York: Oxford University Press, 1997), pp. 155f.

68. Hanchett, *Colored Rice,* pp. 128ff.

69. There are important connections between Gaurī, rivers, and other goddesses that cannot be pursued here. Gaṅgāmma, for example, highly visible in the Godavari Delta, is associated with Gaurī and with the rivers as in the Karnataka ethnography of Hanchett.

70. Reynolds, *"To Keep the tāḷi Strong,"* pp. 329–50.

4

Return to Tears: Musical Mourning, Emotion, and Religious Reform in Two South Asian Minority Communities

Richard K. Wolf

A recurring theme in cross-cultural discussions of mortuary rituals is the complexity of affect or emotion, elements of happiness mixed with sadness, varieties of "celebration" in contexts of mourning.[1] This chapter is concerned with such complexity, its articulation through ritual, music, and discourse, and its constraints. My intentions are threefold: (1) to extend my project of documenting and explaining the ways in which music creates and supports meaning in South Asian ritual contexts; (2) to address a special methodological problem: how to think about two historically and culturally unrelated field projects in a larger interpretive frame; and (3) to offer a hypothesis, namely, that there has been a narrowing of emotional spectrum in *public* displays of mourning, especially in urban areas of the Indian subcontinent, over the last one hundred and fifty years or so, and to suggest how this narrowing is registered musically.[2]

The chapter is based on two fieldwork projects conducted over four years. The first case is a study of the mortuary rituals of a "tribal" minority community, the Kotas of the Nilgiri hills in Tamilnadu. The second is a multisited study of public Muḥarram observances in India and Pakistan. The first part of this chapter is devoted to explicating the affective diversity of selected rituals, especially as they relate to music. One of the important implications of such diversity, in both case studies, is that it draws attention to nuances in the ways in which the living might relate to the dead. This is not only significant in mortuary ceremonies (where the deceased are remembered friends and relatives), but in Shī'ī memorial practices as well. Music sometimes highlights the ways in which agents articulate a sense of loss; sometimes it also provides a means for celebrating the life of the deceased, or in the Shī'ī case, for celebrating the empowerment Husain's martyrdom ultimately conferred upon the Muslim community.

The second part of this chapter outlines the kinds of historical factors, primarily reformist ideologies, which would seem to have placed constraints on affective diversity in connection with public ritual. In attempting to cover a great deal of ground in a limited space, I cannot, unfortunately, provide a fine-grained exegesis of how participants experience emotion, music, and ritual, and how they communicated that experience to me, nor can I elaborate on the dynamics of reform movements.[3] My hope is that these case studies—because they are unrelated in many ways—will stimulate the reader to envision a process of change occurring on a scale that transcends the specific examples, and that involves affectivity or emotionality as one of its many parameters.

A Few Notes on Fieldwork

I became interested in learning about the music of Nilgiri tribal peoples (my first case study) after having spent a decade studying South Indian classical music on the *mridangam* drum and on the stringed instrument, the *vīṇā,* in Madurai and Madras. As an ethnomusicologist, I wanted to study a type of music that was embedded both in standardized ritual forms and in everyday life; Indian classical music was alive for me aesthetically, but I yearned to study a music that was more vital in the religious lives of a particular community. This objective led me to the Kotas, who maintain a lively and complex ritual culture that is articulated strongly by music.

I traveled to the Nilgiri hills in 1990 and stayed there for two years, learning the Kota language (a Dravidian language without a script), and living in a Kota household for fourteen months. There I observed and participated in funerals, marriages, temple festivals, and virtually all formal and informal aspects of Kota life. I engaged in numerous conversations about the meanings of rituals and musical pieces, gathering information from young and old in all of the seven villages. After sifting through my data, I returned to the Nilgiris to ask further questions, present Kota associates with my publications, and discuss ideas.[4]

After completing my work, I wished to broaden my methodological horizons, addressing systematic questions of how music functions in ritual in several parts of South Asia rather than in one particular society. This led me to initiate a more geographically diffuse project on ritual in Islamic contexts (1996–99), one in which I could not wholly rely on my intuitions from my experiences with south Indian Hindus and tribals. I lived in the city of Lahore, Pakistan, for the first year, and for the second I lived with a Shīʻī family in the Ghazi Mandi neighborhood of old Lucknow. One focus of research was the public aspect of performance during Muḥarram, the Shīʻī observance in honor of Imam Hussain, the martyred grandson of the Prophet Muhammad. My insights into the place of emotion in this observance, and by extension into music, pageantry, poetry, architecture, and other domains, have emerged from interviews with members of all communities who participate in it, not just Shī'ahs.

Music and Mourning, Case 1: The Kotas

The Kotas number about fifteen hundred by their own estimates and are classified by the government as a Scheduled Tribe. Although Kota culture exhibits cultural and linguistic features distinct enough, perhaps, to have warranted a separate administrative classification, Kota religion shares features with the Hinduism of the majority population—the notion of divinity inhering in fire and objects, the importance of "visual interaction,"[5] and the spiritual significance of sound.[6] Many Kotas participate in popular South Indian Hindu worship and some call themselves "Hindus." Until about midcentury Kotas served as musicians, carpenters, iron and precious metalworkers, basketmakers, and potters for other communities in the Nilgiris.[7] Although this has changed for complex economic, cultural, and demographic reasons, the Kotas continue to maintain a lively and complex ritual culture in which artisanship plays an important symbolic and performative role. The most elaborate rituals are organized according to a dual classification system of "god" and "death"; the system is articulated strongly by the names of musical pieces, the genres in which they are classified, and the principle of musical nonmixing—that is keeping contextually defined pieces melodically distinct.

The focus here is on Kota mortuary ceremonies, of which there are two types: the green funeral *(pac tāv)*, in which the corpse is cremated and bone relics preserved in a special crevice located in the "green" cremation ground; and the dry funeral *(varldāv)*, in which the bone relics from all those who have died over a specified number of years are placed on colorfully decorated biers and once again incinerated in a "dry" cremation ground. The green funeral is so named because the corpse is wet and fresh, and symbols of life such as green plant stalks are used to decorate the funeral bier. The dry funeral is named after the dried bone fragments preserved from the initial cremation. The rituals are highly complex and can be analyzed in many ways. Two aspects should be emphasized here: (1) the soteriological: it is believed that the spirits of the dead are somehow appeased and their journey to the land of the dead assisted by the proper performance of both funerals; and (2) the social: the period of mourning is formally concluded so that spouses of the deceased may remarry and the village may celebrate its yearly cycle of festivals.[8]

As the successive stages of Kota green and dry funerals unfold, a variety of emotional and aesthetic textures emerge. Grief is seldom unmitigated. Kotas explain that as the green and dry funerals proceed there is a general progression from sadness to happiness, distance from the divine to proximity to the divine, and defilement to purity. In its general outlines, this progression is a cross-culturally common one.[9]

Kotas divide their musical world into contextually defined genres: music for god *(devr koḷ, devr pāṭ)*, music for death *(dukt koḷ)*, and music for dancing *(āṭ koḷ)*. There are separate repertoires of vocal and instrumental music and these are used for different purposes. Outdoor instrumental music, the focus for this discussion, is performed on shawms called *koḷ*, and cylinder and frame drums. Special instrumental tunes accompany most important funerary rituals; one of the implicit functions of instrumental music is to effect the process of moving the deceased out of the village. The process is physical as well as metaphysical, so as the deceased leaves the village, death is also made to leave. Along the way, individual pieces and subgenres within the funeral repertoire help to define the subtly changing emotional character of the proceedings.[10]

The rituals composing the green and dry funerals are intrinsically interesting and extraordinarily complicated. Here I focus on a few of the rituals that are both accompanied by special musical pieces and evocative of emotions that are not merely sad, but of a mixed or multilayered character. Kotas explain that tunes carry context-specific resonances, bearing an affective imprint of the accompanying event. The problem is in isolating what a musical piece, apart from its context, makes people feel. Perhaps we can accept the thesis that a piece tends to support the emotional tenor of a ritual moment. If an unsuitable piece is inadvertently played at the wrong time there is public outcry; and much of this outcry is based on the way in which Kota instrumental music makes Kotas feel.

A few examples will help illustrate this idea. At the beginning of the dry funeral, musicians perform an emotive melody for a ritual of pouring millet *(vatm)* in front of the house of the deceased. This tune is said to be very moving and in practice appears to bring copious tears to the eyes of widows and female relatives—although one must always keep in mind that the public display of grief and the inner experience of grief are not necessarily convergent. The ritual as a whole, and the music specifically, are said to draw the souls of the dead into the village from the cremation ground and to substantialize their spirit in the form of millet. Then, musicians perform what they describe as relatively more cheerful pieces, dance tunes, for the processions between each site of millet-pouring. It is a conscious technique on their part; Kotas are communicating musically that the sad moment is over once the millet is poured and that the soul has begun the next stage of its journey to the other world.[11] For several nights following the millet-pouring, men and women dance in a special dancing area *(āṭ kavāl)* in front of certain village houses.

The dancing on these nights is lighthearted; in some villages, men drink heavily and stumble through the dances. Such behavior, while tolerated, is not considered part of the ritual. By the time the dry funeral is celebrated, the immediate feeling of loss has subsided—signs of intense grief are manifested only at ritually specified times. For most participants in the dry funeral it is neither difficult nor contradictory to dance with abandon. In contrast, participants still feel the pain acutely when dancing around the corpse during the green funeral. Although many describe this dance as constituting a sort of farewell party for the deceased, it tends to be far more sober in the green funeral than in the dry funeral.

On the eighth day, male volunteers close to the deceased collect bone relics from the initial cremation, place them on highly decorated biers, and carry these biers in procession along with a number of symbolic objects to be recremated. Kotas perform songs and dances, eat communally, and spend the night in an area reserved for this ceremony. Men used to compete with one another to subdue and sacrifice large semiwild buffalo in honor of the deceased.[12] Tunes that Kotas recognize to be in a separate, somewhat jubilant, emotional category *(kēṛ koḷ)* were performed for this sacrifice fifty years ago when it was still common. Finally, early in the morning when the planet Venus is sighted, the musicians perform a special melody to send the souls of the dead off to the land of the dead. This tune belongs to the class known as the gathering at the land of the dead tunes *(nāṛgūc koḷ)*; they are considered to be the most emotive and important of the Kota mourning tunes, and are also generally the longest.

One might wish to ask at this juncture, "What does it mean for a Kota instrumental tune to be sad?"—or the related question, "What does it mean for a piece to belong to the funeral genre as opposed to the genres of god tunes or dance tunes?" To summarize a complex issue, Kotas believe that funeral tunes are sad either because they are themselves conventionally associated with sadness, or because they resemble other conventionally sad tunes; these tunes are also sad because Kotas feel they iconically resemble crying, and because they possess a slow, lethargic quality that in Kota culture, like the segment of American culture in which I was raised, tends to be associated with sadness and mourning.[13] But not all the tunes performed during funerals are meant to be mournful; various subrepertoires and isolated pieces emphasize for Kotas such funerary themes as respect, individual and communal memory, love and loss, and excitement and competition. Such themes, far from being limited to the Kotas, are typical of mourning rituals in many cultures, including rituals of mournful commemoration, such as those in Muḥarram, which are not funerals at all.

Case 2: Shīʿahs , Muḥarram, and Music in South Asia

Shīʿī Muslims make up about 10–15% of the Muslim population in the Indian subcontinent (Muslims comprise a total of 25% of the total population). A minority in most Muslim countries (except Iraq and Iran), Shīʿahs, like other

Muslims, believe the Qur'ān was God-given, that Muhammad was the last Prophet of God, and that God, Allah, is unitary. They differ in their allegiance to particular members of Muhammad's family, whom they believe were his legal and spiritual successors.

Muḥarram, the specific concern of this part of this chapter, commemorates the pitched battle of Karbala, Iraq, in 680 C.E., in which the army of the Ummayad ruler Yazid slaughtered Muhammad's grandson, Husain, and his followers, after Husain refused to abdicate his position of political and spiritual leadership of the Muslim community. To show their allegiance to the slain martyrs, and to the principle of successorship that Husain embodied, Shī'ahs retell the story of Husain's martyrdom. They recall scenes from the battle using a variety of dramatic verbal genres, and participate in processions, carrying battle standards, tomb replicas, and other icons of the Karbala story.[14] In rural areas Shī'ahs play drums but in cities it is generally Hindus and Sunnis who play drums and other musical instruments during Muḥarram.

That which is called *mūsīqī*, "music," is frequently criticized in Islamic scriptures (except those of certain Sufi orders), because, to put it very simply, it distracts one's mind and senses from thoughts of God. But what constitutes "music" often turns on shifting definitions; frequently music means instrumental music or vocal music accompanied by musical instruments. In South Asian Muḥarram observances, poetic recitations, set to melodies, may be perfectly acceptable if they are not accompanied by musical instruments and if their texts relate to the theme of Muḥarram (judgments vary from region to region). Performing such texts is considered "reading" or "reciting," not "singing."

South Asian Muslims, like Kotas, sometimes represented their range of ritual observances to me in terms of two categories sad occasions *(g͟ham ke mauq'e)* and joyous occasions *(k͟hushī ke mauq'e)*. The former consist of funerals and Muḥarram; the latter include the birth anniversary of the Prophet, weddings, and the celebration at the end of the month of fasting. Although "sad" and "happy" is the macroclassification scheme for most occasions, there are areas in which the distinctions are blurred. Just as a spirit of excitement prevails in the Kota buffalo sacrifice, so too does an atmosphere of frenzy and passion prevail in certain Muḥarram observances. Whether in the form of Shī'ī preachers who verbally whip their audiences into a frenzy, musical performances that tunefully coax mourners into extended states of excitement, or guilds of *nauhah* poetry reciters and breast beaters who accelerate their own fervor, the enactment of Muḥarram produces a state of zealous passion *(josh)*.

Participants distinguish feelings of passion from feelings of sadness, though both can exist simultaneously; the degree to which one or the other of these emotional complexes is emphasized depends upon religious community, family practice, location, and particular event in the sequence of Muḥarram rituals. The slaying of Husain and his supporters is considered tragic, but many South Asian

Muslims feel that through this tragedy Islam attained a higher victory. The passion with which they observe Muḥarram reflects both Islam's victory and participants' attempts to empathize with Karbala's martyrs. Outside of Muḥarram as well, devout Shī'ahs live and interpret their lives today largely within the moral and social implications of the Karbala narrative.

In addition to passion and sadness, episodes of the Karbala narrative evoke secondary emotions—emotions that by themselves are distinct from sadness, but that in the context of the Karbala tale tend, sometimes ironically, to amplify the theme of tragedy. For example, the intensity of a mother's love for her child, mixed with the unthinkable experience of loss, is created in the women's mourning assembly as participants sing lullabies to Husain's infant-son, Ali Asghar, in the persona of Husain's wife. Husain's brother's son, Qasim, was quickly married before he died in battle (so the story goes; it is not historically verifiable). On the seventh day of Muḥarram, South Asian Shī'ahs sometimes sing special songs and hire a brass band to "celebrate" his wedding.[15] Participants explain that this celebration does not connote pure joy, but a paradoxical joy that intensifies the effect of tragedy.

Over Muḥarram's sixty-eight days, the principal contexts during which participants perform musical instruments are processions. Processions are arenas for aesthetic elaboration not only of sound, but also of visual and sometimes martial arts. Depending on locality, Shī'ahs, Sunnis, and even Hindus parade *ta'ziyahs,* multistory structures representing the tomb of Imam Husain. "Some processions also feature horses symbolizing Husain's steed, *Zuljina,* and replicas of Ali Asghar's cradle, Qasim's marriage palanquin, and other paraphernalia.[16] Participants also parade "standards," called *'alam,* representing characters in the Karbala tragedy.

An important mode of Muḥarram religious performance is mimetic. Muḥarram's dramatic narrative is that of Karbala, on the battlefield of which participants wish to place themselves. In the Shī'ī style of embodied remembrance, individuals vow, in the name of Imam Husain, to offer their children, or themselves, as beggars, soldiers, or water carriers in the procession; in this way they viscerally participate in the "battle." In similar spirit, just as drummers would have participated in the battle of Karbala, so also do mourners assume the role of drummers to place themselves meaningfully and realistically on the battlefield. The kettledrums, cylinder drums, and double reed aerophones used in these procession are also symbols of royal power throughout the Muslim world.[17]

As already noted, Shī'ī communities in the subcontinent differ in the degree to which they find drums and musical instruments appropriate or inappropriate. One reason for this is that in cities and among modern families there is a feeling that "respectable" or high-status communities in India should not beat drums, play musical instruments, and participate in parades when they are ostensibly in mourning. Since the overall theme of Muḥarram is one of sadness, *gham*, Shī'ahs in urban areas have become increasingly uncomfortable with musical practices that appear to be celebratory. This does not mean that processions, drumming, and instrumental performances no longer exist during Muḥarram, just that in cities, devout Shī'ahs are trying very hard to disassociate themselves from these practices. Note, however, that some of the same urban Shī'ahs who disassociate themselves from musical performances still embrace the practice of *mātam* (literally, mourning)—breast-beating with the hands at least, but sometimes with razor blades and swords. Urban attitudes do not reflect a simple process of communities becoming bourgeois, as some colleagues have suggested upon hearing an oral version of this chapter.

Possible reasons for these apparent changes in attitude will be cited in the next section, including some of the arguments Sunni clerics have leveled against Shī'ī practices in general as well as against musical performances in particular. In preparation for the critiques, it would be useful to consider the possible rationales for musical instruments during Muḥarram processions. The following are among the most important: (1) Textual surrogates: The melodies and rhythms performed on musical instruments assiduously match meters and melodies of Muḥarram poetic forms; thus some instrumental pieces are considered less as music than as vehicles for propagating religious messages. (2) Mimesis: Drums mimic sounds of galloping horses, marching platoons, and the peace of a battlefield at the end of a battle; bands also create a festive atmosphere in the symbolic marriage of Qasim. (3) Affect: The tonal and rhythmic quality of the music sounds mournful to some Muḥarram participants. (4) Functionality: Drum rhythms both announce starting, stopping, and intermediate points in processions and act as sorts of musical ushers or conductors, not unlike the rhythms of Western marching bands. (5) Creation of beauty: Decorated battle standards, tomb replicas, and other processional floats; and music and agile martial displays of sword fighting serve as forms of aesthetic entertainment for the spiritually present martyrs.[18]

In fact, music and drumming could very well support the emotional and thematic contours of Muḥarram, and one might imagine that, in another political climate, pious Shī'ahs could use these rationales to explain away Islamic injunctions against music. Professional and amateur drummers and performers of other instruments have professed that what they play during Muḥarram is not really "music" after all—but many professional musicians have privately confessed that they regard their performances as musical; it is simply not politic to openly use the word *music* to describe what they perform during Muḥarram.

Still, there has been a gradual decline in the degree of musical performances and the diversity of musical repertoire associated with Muḥarram in South Asia, and this decline is attributable to a variety of historical factors, particularly religious reforms.

Recent Movements toward Reform

Here I wish to focus on what appear to be some of the musical consequences of religious revival and reform in South Asia beginning late in the eighteenth century. Specific cause-and-effect relationships between reforms and musical practices are difficult to trace, and would in any case be of limited utility in assessing the larger phenomena; my discussion emphasizes only the ideological thrust of the reforms. I summarize the kinds of changes that have taken place (or are supposed to have taken place) and consider what I was led to regard as the impetus for these changes. I start with the late eighteenth century because it coincides with the rise of British power in the subcontinent and because descriptions of ritual musical practices before this period are scant. Important to note for our period is not only British political influence but the moral influence bestowed by temporal power.

Both Muslims and Hindus felt challenged by Christian religious ideals and by modern Western rationalist thought and sought to respond—although in different ways at different times.[19] Early Hindu responses were "defensive": reformers laid emphasis on religious precepts that did not conflict with missionary criticisms of Hinduism; such criticisms were leveled, for example, at polytheism, widow-burning, female infanticide, untouchability, and local ecstatic practices involving sex and spirit possession.[20] Nineteenth-century reformers in such societies as the Brahmo Samaj and the Arya Samaj did not usually target music per se, but they did affect larger institutions of which music was a part.

The historian of nineteenth-century Bengal may find my treatment of reform rather scant; indeed movements toward social and religious change varied both historically and geographically. My interest here is in the broad contours of these movements in the subcontinent; few would dispute that there were congeries of related ideas "in the air." To get a better sense of these ideas, it might be worthwhile to provide a bit of background on the Brahmo Samaj, for it evidently "played a crucial role in the genesis and development of every major religious, social, and political movement in India from 1820 to 1930."[21]

The Brahmo Samaj was founded in 1843 by Debendranath Tagore, building on the Unitarian Committee and later on the Brahmo Sabha of Rammohun Roy. The reforms were initially set in Bengal, drawing upon the unitarianism of England and the United States, and involving an elite minority in Calcutta. There were "links" between the Calcutta-based initiative and the Unitarians, according to the historian David Kopf: (1) an emphasis on "rational" religion, emancipating human beings from "meaningless superstitions, and other-worldly beliefs and values"; (2) social elevation of economically and culturally downtrodden men and women; and (3) a universal movement toward the perfection of humanity.[22]

The Brahmo Samaj was not, and did not always remain, a single "movement." There was a great deal of internal variation, infighting, and change. In the early twentieth century, Rabindranath Tagore defended an earlier form of Brahmoism as against the "emotionalism" that Bijoy Krishna Goswami had infused into the movement. The following quote from Rabindranath's letter of 1910 will serve as an example of how music registers in reformist discourse, that is, not as a pointed target of attack in its own right, but as part of a series of activities, a class of behavior that is undesirable:

> The last goal of Shaktism and Vaishnavism is emotionalism. . . . We can achieve nothing lasting by drinking wine or playing on the *khol* (a drum) or by smoking *ganja*. When we try to create an excitement in ourselves by disregarding the outer world completely, then we can imagine ourselves anything or anyone such as Krishna. To avoid the rightful protest of the outer world, we declare such religious outbursts as meaningless. . . . Instead we should try our best to spiritualize the outer world.[23]

Neither musical performance as a ritual act, nor the inner spiritual effect of music as a religious goal, are regarded as legitimate. More broadly, early Hindu reformers in the subcontinent labeled many local practices as *superstitious*. Some searched for a more pure form of religion captured in a source that transcended locality, namely, the Vedas. Low-caste funeral practices such as vibrant drumming to call gods and spirits, to entertain the souls of the dead, or to drive away evil spirits would not have been encouraged in these early movements; indeed, drumming was also one of the first activities that the early missionaries banned. Hindu reformers, concerned with social uplift, also fought against what they considered to be unnecessary expenditures of time and money on elaborate rituals, be these marriages or funerals. Later, of course, Gandhian principles of nonviolence further affected the ritual treatment of animals—especially among tribes and castes who performed bloody animal sacrifices. These downtrodden communities began to modify or abandon rituals organized around animal sacrifice, and along with them associated musical practices.

The rise of British power in the late eighteenth century was also a harbinger of the Mughal empire's final demise. The social and political problems Muslims faced as an increasingly powerless minority during the nineteenth century were, in the minds of some leaders, attributable not only to the vagaries of world political and economic change, but also to individual moral corruption. By returning to scriptural Islam and eschewing customary practices that were, after all, Indian, or worse, Hindu, Muslims of a certain ilk felt that they would, with the help of god, return to a state of grace.

Religious decrees, and responses to them, provide a trace of public Islamic debates of the past century and a half. For the present purposes it will be useful to focus on the debates concerning Shīʻī sm, and in doing so I will mention only a few representative criticisms leveled against Shīʻahs by the prominent theologian, Shah Abdul Aziz. Aziz led a circle of influential reformist thinking in Delhi from 1763 to 1824 and published an extensive, if somewhat vicious and ill-informed diatribe against Shīʻīsm that was completed in about 1790.

Aziz, it should be kept in mind, was among the most outspoken and extreme of the critics of Shīʻīsm; he considered both Shīʻahs and Sufis (at least those who supported the use of music such as Qawwali) to be infidels. He branded Shīʻahs "childish" for their mimetic performances and for their belief in the martyr's spiritual presence.[24] He also criticized the mournful affective dimension of Shīʻī piety, the redemptive value of "weeping, making images and playing instruments as acts of worship." Here Aziz drew attention to the fact that Shīʻī clerics did not commit their support of these popular practices to writing.[25] Aziz compared Shīʻī regard for their Imāms as embodied in their treatment of *ta'ziyahs* with Hindu worship of images. This is a strong condemnation in a religion that not only forbids iconic representations of God, but also of human beings (and sometimes of almost anything at all). Furthering this critique of iconicity, he targeted the ritual commemoration of Qasim's wedding, which, being "exactly like a that of a living being" was disturbingly representational. Leveling the ultimate insult in the subcontinental context, he accused them of being "more superstitious than the Hindus."[26]

Shīʻī *'ulema* responded promptly and thoroughly to these vicious attacks; but notably, they did not defend local "superstitious" practices, ascribing them, rather, to ignorant village people who were not fully conversant with true Islam.[27] Like the early, defensive, Hindu reformers, Shīʻī leaders of the nineteenth century concentrated on (non-place-specific) validating practices that could be justified in the Qur'ān or in the sayings of the prophet. Music during Muḥarram did not fall into this category, despite the fact that rationales for musical performance followed a more general cultural logic that was accepted. In an Urdu translation of Aziz's *fatwas* (religious decrees) in Arabic, Aziz repeatedly addressed the issue of music. In a brief treatise on singing *(ghina)*, Aziz drew upon sayings of the Prophet, primarily in the Hanafi legal tradition, and appears to have concluded that singing—Aziz localized the notion of singing to the singing of *rāgas*—is forbidden *(harām)* even in the absence of musical instruments.[28] In a different *fatwa*, he cited *'ulema* who support singing, either alone or accompanied by the frame drum, in sanctioned contexts of joy, so long as such singing was not frivolous (involving *lahv*) and did not contain prohibited texts (e.g., praising men, beautiful women, or the effects of liquor). Aziz adopted the position that under no circumstances would it be acceptable to sing or listen to singing at graves—a clear jab at Sufis and Shīʻahs.[29]

These decrees and their responses contributed to the polarization of Shīʻī and Sunni communities, which gained momentum in the late nineteenth century.

Religious leaders used such controversies to pit their respective constituencies against one another. Early in the nineteenth century and increasingly in the late nineteenth and early twentieth centuries, riots began breaking out during Muḥarram in Lucknow city, a Shī'ī stronghold known for elaborate Muḥarram processions. Gradually, Shī'ahs and Sunnis began emphasizing their differences, reinforcing if not creating new religious boundaries.[30]

The musical consequences of these changes, to put it simply, were that musical instruments and drumming came increasingly to be regarded by Shī'ahs as cheerful and celebratory. This evidently led Shī'ahs to abandon drumming in many cities—even during the ritual commemoration of Qasim's wedding. Sunnis and Hindus, to some extent, continued to maintain traditions of Muḥarram drumming. Conversely, self-mortification *(mātam)* and crying became even more strongly paradigmatic of Shī'ī Islam.[31] Shī'ahs in urban areas frequently told me that Sunnis play drums during Muḥarram because they inappropriately celebrate the occasion; they are happy, or at least not suitably mournful. In fact, South Asian Sunnis generally do not express happiness that Husain was slaughtered, but they do emphasize the positive aftermath of the battle in which the values of Islam were restored. Processions in Lucknow used to include Shī'ahs, Sunnis, and Hindus; as communities and values became polarized, these communities began organizing their own processions. When these antagonistic processions crossed paths, fights broke out. And it was not uncommon for the immediate cause of these fights to be discord, both rhythmic and moral, between Sunni drumming and Shī'ī breast-beating.

With the division of Shī'ahs and Sunnis, and the gradual polarization of perceived sad-versus-happy observances of Muḥarram, we find that the public displays among Shī'ahs in cities have become increasingly oriented toward the visible embodiment of mournful sentiments. Some one hundred years ago, Muḥarram's rather splendorous affective texture was registered in the public sphere—Abdul Halim Sharar's (1860-1926) accounts in *Lucknow: The last phase of an oriental culture* bear eloquent testimony to the lavish Muḥarram observances in the time of Wajid Ali Shah, and those of Mrs. Meer Ali Hassan do so for the earlier part of the century.[32] Now it appears as if this emotional spectrum has narrowed in Shī'ī discourse and in public display. Shī'ī drumming—taken as a public sign of celebration—has been almost completely obliterated in major Indian cities, and almost all Shī'ahs I spoke with found it impossible to believe that a Shi'ah could ever consider drumming during Muḥarram. But in small towns and minor principalities in Uttar Pradesh, it is still possible to find continuity in these drumming practices (although Shī'ī drummers consider drumming sad in these places). Sunnis, of course, continue to observe their own forms of Muḥarram, but they too were affected by reforms; some of them intimated that they were instructed by their religious leaders to abandon practices of drumming and making tomb replicas.

Kota practices were also affected by Victorian morality and religious reform, and as among Muslims, the actual changes in practice lagged some fifty to seventy-five years behind the movements themselves. Critiques in Kota society were leveled at the dry funeral and bore the unmistakable stamp of national social and religious reformist ideologies: (1) the dry funeral was considered wasteful because it required an enormous expenditure of time and money; (2) central rituals in this funeral were disgraceful because they required cow and buffalo sacrifices; and (3) the behavior characteristic of this ceremony included licentiousness and intoxication, in the twentieth century considered indecorous in light of high-caste Hindu and Christian funerary practices. Although the dry funeral was completely abandoned in only one of the seven Kota villages, general effects of reform permeated the entire population.[33]

Their overall affective impact was a "hardening of the categories." In times past, rituals and pieces associated with divinity and death, and worshipfulness, joy, sadness, and somber respect, were juxtaposed and interwoven in complex and not always easily explainable ways. The rituals are still complicated, but there has been a clear attempt to rationalize the Kota religion—rationalism being a key reformist concept.[34] So, for example, in the same village where the dry funeral was abandoned, the practice of dancing around the corpse during the green funeral has also been dropped—too cheerful for a ritual that has crystallized into something more narrowly somber. In another village, on the understanding that there is a clear progression from sadness to happiness, the practice of performing the "gathering at the land of the dead tune" has been discontinued; it is the saddest tune in the Kota repertoire, and by the end of the dry funeral people feel that all that sadness is supposed to have been eliminated. There are other changes as well: special repertoires for buffalo sacrifice and for other discontinued rituals are gradually being forgotten; one result is that the tunes are being recontextualized, serving as reminders—albeit ambivalent ones—of these bygone practices.

Again, this is not a matter of simply mimicking high-caste or bourgeois values, nor is it a matter of imbibing directly the ideals of any one major reform movement: funeral music has not been abandoned, only dancing (in one case) and competitive, public animal sacrifice; the reasons behind each individual change in practice are tied to specific cultural and historical issues, but they are also clearly related to subcontinental trends. There are many ways in which one can represent the end results of the changes in Kota funerals and Muḥarram rituals; I have chosen to use emotion and affect because it seems to me that the rituals that were stripped away in both cases are those which, in the view of the participants, appear to increasingly critical onlookers as affectively inappropriate to the occasion—too happy, frivolous, sensuous or permissive for an occasion morally "defined" by sadness.

Concluding Reflections

In discussing reformist impacts on musical practice I am afraid I may have painted a grim picture, but I should emphasize that these changes in size of repertoire are most pronounced in urban or urbanizing areas. Remarkably, a great deal of variation continues to be generated as people from cities and villages interact with one another and as peoples of different communities alternately fuse and polarize in response to political and economic exigencies. Although some repertoires are indeed becoming impoverished, others are not. In either case, the epistemological data about the role of music and the place of emotions in mourning rituals remains astoundingly rich and diverse.

Moving beyond the immediate field data presented here, I would suggest that it will be fruitful in further research projects to examine ritual contexts that exhibit rich textures of sentiments. Mourning rituals make good case studies because they involve remarkable concatenations of diverse emotions, such as grief, wistfulness, triumph, and tribute, and these emotions are registered in multiple kinds of behavior. I was surprised that in a recent volume on the meanings of death in South Asia, although several authors cited Peter Metcalf and Richard Huntington's *Celebrations of Death,* none elaborated much on the affective complexity of mortuary rituals, nor on its spatiotemporal contingencies.[35]

I have found that peoples' aesthetic responses to musical mourning repertoires vary widely, and eliciting these responses was a serious methodological problem. Still, a number of Muslims, Hindus, and tribals were able to describe to me the musical features that they felt held the power to move them emotionally. Some felt, for instance, that sadness was communicated by muted timbres, lethargic tempi, and deep pitches—musical features that resonate with doleful attributes in my own culture. But the problem was that in practice so-called sad music did not always exhibit these stylistic features; this may be one of the reasons why music is considered so problematic in Muḥarram—the overall occasion is supposed to be sad, but in modern times for urban Shī'ahs the traditional music associated with it is not sad enough. And to further complicate matters, aesthetic statements applying to one instrument did not necessarily apply to another. In the end, I found that the ways in which people connected musical sound to emotional attributes were extremely idiosyncratic and tied to specific contexts in particular political climates. For these reasons I have focused on general principles of classification and not on the relationship between emotional attributes and musical styles.

At the risk of overgeneralizing, I think it worthwhile to adopt (tentatively, at least) a subcontinental view of music in mourning, and to observe that the more culturally distant are communities from high-caste Hindus, the more variegated, marked, and pronounced are their musical repertoires of mourning. Whereas, at one extreme, one may observe that Brahmins (except in rare cases) avoid using instrumental music in their funerals, at the other extreme, there is a concentration of primarily Scheduled castes whose musicians perform, or once performed, distinctly funerary instrumental repertoires, defined largely by rhythm. Moving down the caste scale (not a continuum, necessarily), there are not only funerary repertoires of increasing distinctiveness but also public displays of increasing pomp, occasionally bordering on the comical. In parts of Tamilnadu and Andhra Pradesh, corpses are at times carried in sitting rather than prone positions, and decorated with colorful powders and flower garlands, coins and shiny objects, mirrors, and fancy clothes. Drummers in some South Indian funeral processions clown around and dance, playing their instruments artfully or acrobatically, and collect money from appreciative onlookers using their teeth. I would suggest that it is in these displays, and in urban funeral processions that employ Western marching band instruments, that we find the most significant continuities between *dalit* and tribal funerary practices and Muḥarram as it is practiced in many parts of South Asia. It is useful to think about the recent history of ritual mourning in urban South Asia metaphorically in terms of a narrowed emotional spectrum; but affective diversity and difference has by no means disappeared. What has been particularly interesting to me is how the variety of musics and the variety of emotions characteristic of mourning rituals have been reshaped according to patterns that are both regional-cultural and national, both intricately interwoven with issues of local religion and panreligious, and both characteristic of South Asia and applicable to the study of music in mourning anywhere in the world.

Notes

1. See, for instance, discussions and references in Peter Metcalf and Richard Huntington, *Celebrations of Death: The Anthropology of Mortuary Ritual,* 2d ed. (Cambridge: Cambridge University Press, 1991); Klaus-Peter Köpping, "Death as Experience and Institution in Anthropological Theory," in *Ways of Dying*, eds. Elisabeth Schömbucher and Claus Peter Zoller (New Delhi: Manohar, 1999), pp. 36-46; Robert Hertz, *Death and the Right Hand,* trans. Rodney Needham and Claudia Needham (Aberdeen, Scotland: Cohen and West, 1960).

2. See Richard K. Wolf, "Of God and Death: Music in Ritual and Everyday Life. A Musical Ethnography of the Kotas of South India" (Ph.D. diss. Ethnomusicology), School of Music, University of Illinois at Urbana-Champaign, 1997; "Rain, God and Unity among the Kotas," in *Blue Mountains Revisited: Cultural Studies on the Nilgiri Hills,* ed. Paul Hockings (Delhi: Oxford University Press, 1997), pp. 231–92; "Embodiment and Ambivalence: Emotion in South Asia Muḥarram Drumming," *Yearbook for Traditional Music* 32 (2000): 81–116; "Music in Seasonal and Life-cycle Rituals," in "South Asia: The Indian Subcontinent," *The Garland Encyclopedia of World Music*, ed. Alison Arnold (New York: Garland Publishing Co., 2000), 5: 272–87; "Three Perspectives on

Music and the Idea of Tribe in India," *Asian Music* 32 (1:2000/2001): 5–34; "Mourning Songs and Human Pasts among the Kotas of South India," *Asian Music* 32 (1: 2000/2001): 141–83. "Emotional Dimensions of Ritual Music among the Kotas, a South Indian Tribe," *Ethnomusicology* 45 (3): 379–422 Fall 2001.

3. I discuss these issues at greater length in "Embodiment and Ambivalence" and in "Emotional Dimensions of Ritual Music among the Kotas."

4. These visits of one to three months each occurred between 1996 and 1999, and between 2000 and 2001.

5. Cf. Lawrence A. Babb, "Glancing: Visual Interaction in Hinduism," *Journal of Anthropological Research* 37: 4 (1981): 387–401; Diana Eck, *Darsan: Seeing the Divine Image in India* (Chambersburg, PA: Anima Books, 1981).

6. Cf. Guy L. Beck, *Sonic Theology: Hinduism and Sacred Sound* (Columbia: University of South Carolina Press, 1993).

7. David G. Mandelbaum, "The Kotas in Their Social Setting," in *Blue Mountains: The Ethnography and Biogeography of a South Indian Region,* ed. Paul Hockings (Delhi: Oxford University Press, 1989), pp. 144–85.

8. Mandelbaum, "Form, Variation, and Meaning of a Ceremony," in *Method and Perspective in Anthropology: Papers in Honor of Wilson D. Wallis,* ed. Robert F. Spencer (Minneapolis: University of Minnesota Press, 1954), pp. 60–102; Wolf, "Mourning Songs and Human Pasts among the Kotas of South India."

9. Cf. Maurice Bloch and Jonathan Parry, eds., *Death and the Regeneration of Life* (Cambridge: Cambridge University Press, 1982).

10. Wolf, "Of God and Death"; "Mourning Songs and Human Pasts among the Kotas of South India"; "Emotional Dimensions of Ritual Music among the Kotas."

11. Wolf, "Emotional Dimensions of Ritual Music among the Kotas."

12. For a discussion of a song addressed to one such buffalo, see Wolf, "Mourning Songs and Human Pasts among the Kotas of South India," p. 158.

13. See Wolf, "Emotional Dimensions of Ritual Music among the Kotas."

14. Compare Peter Chelkowski, ed., *Taziyeh, Ritual and Drama in Iran*, New York University Studies in Near Eastern Civilization, no. 7 (New York: New York University Press, 1979).

15. The appearance of a symbolic marriage in South Asian Muḥarram observances accrues significance when viewed in the context of mortuary rituals in the subcontinent. It is not uncommon for some sort of ritual "marriage," or at the least a rite affirming the importance of affinal bonds (at least in South India), to be performed in connection with a funeral or memorial observance. Such is the case with several of the Nilgiri hill communities, including the Kotas. See Wolf, "Of God and Death," pp. 214–15. See also Nabokov's discussion of marriage symbolism in Tamil rituals of transforming deceased

relatives into household deities in "When the Dead Become Brides, Gods and Gold: Marriage Symbolism in a Tamil Household Ritual," *Journal of Ritual Studies* 10:1 (1996): 113–33.

16. See, for example, David Pinault, *The Shiites: Ritual and Popular Piety in a Muslim Community* (New York: St. Martin's, 1992); *The Horse of Karbala: Muslim Devotional Life in India* (New York: Palgrave, 2001).

17. For a discussion of how the meanings of such ensembles have been transformed, see Reis Flora, "Styles of the Śahnāī in Recent Decades: From Naubat to Gāyaki Ang," *Yearbook for Traditional Music* 27 (1995): 52–75.

18. Rationales 1–3 are discussed at some length in Wolf, "Embodiment and Ambivalence."

19. Aghendanda Bharati and Francis Robinson, "Religious Revival in Times," "Hinduism," and "Islam," in *The Cambridge Encyclopedia of India, Pakistan, Bangladesh, Sri Lanka, Nepal, Bhutan, and the Maldives*, ed. Francis Robinson (Cambridge: Cambridge University Press, 1989), pp. 345–50, 352–55.

20. Ibid., p. 345.

21. David Kopf, *The Brahmo Samaj and the Shaping of the Modern Indian Mind*, (Princeton, N.J.: Princeton University Press, 1979), p. xiii.

22. Ibid, p. 3.

23. Quoted in ibid., p. 77.

24. Saiyid Athar Abbas Rizvi, *Shāh 'Abd Al-'Azīz: Puritanism, Sectarian Polemics and Jihād* (Canberra, Australia: Marifat Publishing House, 1982), pp. 337–38.

25. Ibid., pp. 340–41.

26. Ibid., pp. 340–351.

27. Some of these passages on Shah Abdul Aziz are adapted from Wolf, "Embodiment and Ambivalence," p. 102 n.47.

28. Shah Abdul Aziz, *Fatāwa-e Azīzī,* vol 1. Translated into Urdu by Haji Muhammed Said (Calcutta (?), 1926), pp. 139–43.

29. I am indebted to Amera Raza for translating Aziz's *fatwa*s for me from Urdu to English and discussing with me their implications. See ibid., p. 78.

30. Mushirul Hasan, "Traditional Rites and Contested Meanings: Sectarian Strife in Colonial Lucknow," in *Lucknow: Memories of a City*, ed. Violette Graf (Delhi: Oxford University Press, 1997), pp. 114–35.

31. For more on the argument that *mātam* is a ritual behavior that is distinctively Shī'ī, see Pinault, *Horse of Karbala*; for more on the Shī'ah-Sunni divide and their positions on drumming, see Wolf, "Embodiment and Ambivalence."

32. Abdul Halim Sharar, *Lucknow: The Last Phase of an Oriental Culture*, trans. and eds. E. S. Harcourt and Fakhir Hussain (Translation of *guzishtah lakhnau*; reprinted Delhi: Oxford University Press, 1994); Mrs. Meer Hassan Ali, *Observations on the Mussulmauns of India: Descriptions of Their Manners, Customs, Habits and Religious Opinions Made during a Twelve Years' Residence in their Immediate Society,* 2 vols. (London: Parbury, Allen, and Co.,1832).

33. For the soteriological implications of these ritual changes, see Wolf, "Mourning Songs and Human Pasts among the Kotas of South India."

34. See, e.g., Kopf, *Brahmo Samaj and the Shaping of the Modern Indian Mind,* pp. 42–85.

35. Schömbucher and Zoller, *Ways of Dying.*

5

Deanimating and Reanimating the Dead in Rural Sri Lanka

Jonathan S. Walters

As an historian I regularly deal with people who are dead, but I do not usually deal with them *as* dead; I think about them as though they were alive, living in the historical contexts I create in my own mind. When I deal with some long-dead Sri Lankan king, he is doing something in Sri Lanka a thousand years ago, and he is doing it to, or with, or for only people who are, like him, dead. But in at least this sense—"people who *are* dead"—*every* historian practices a sort of necromancy, however different it may be from the necromancies studied by historians of religions. Paraphrasing the philosopher of history R. G. Collingwood, perhaps in a way he would like, the dead *exist* insofar as they are encapsulated within the present, enjoying in the minds of historians a certain "life" that could be said to defeat the grave. However much we might eschew the reality of medieval conceptions of the afterlife we at least cannot escape from having some *construct* of deadness, some *idea* about the state of the dead that is not itself dead.

I think it productive—and Collingwood *would* like this application of his theories—to see the difference between this historiographical necromancy and "traditional" or "premodern" or "religious" necromancy as not merely a difference of kind, but additionally as a difference of degree. The actions of an American historian reconstructing medieval Anurādhapura to finish a conference paper and an Anurādhapuran healer resurrecting Grandma to haunt a rival into repaying a debt are not so unrelated as might at first glance appear: both employ culturally current "necrotechnologies" (methods for dealing with the dead made "real" or "believable" or "appropriate" through accordance with culturally current presuppositions about what death is), and both do so for some particular purpose. The question then becomes, "in degrees and kind of *what* do modern and premodern, or "scientific" and "religious," necromancy differ?" My own answer would be that *we discern differences in the degree and kind of agency ascribed to the dead.*

The historian insists that dead people are agentive only in an imaginary sense, only in the past reconstructed in the historian's own imagination, though he or she might still confess (as did Collingwood) to imaginary conversations with them, and might even feel haunted by them as particular deadlines approach. The Sinhala healer *(Veda-mahātmaya)*,[1] at the other end of this spectrum, insists that dead people can be powerfully agentive in the world of workaday reality: agentive enough to cause madness, death, and disease; to steal, to spit betel, to terrorize with words, and even to be witty. Yet he too (never she) often slips toward the middle: he counts much of his success on convincing his patients or victims that he does indeed have the power to empower the dead in these ways; he recognizes that the dead communicate with the living more often through dreams and signs than they do face-to-face; he tries to allow them no agency beyond acting out the healer's own intentions.

As suggested, underlying these different degrees and kind of agency assigned the present dead are different sets of culturally current presuppositions about what death is. The shifts in perspective and occasional inconsistencies within our imaginary historian's necromancy become more complex if he or she happens to be religious: a Christian will likely believe that at least one dead person, if not a whole pantheon of saints, can be agentive in the "real" world; a Muslim will allow that the dead are at least agentive *somewhere,* if not actively emanating power from their corpses here and now; a Confucianist will not deny the agency of dead ancestors and culture heroes; even the hardened postreligious historian might occasionally act differently with an eerie sense that a dead parent or teacher is watching. The same inconsistency is no less true of a Sinhala Vedamahātmaya, whose views embody not one but many sets of presuppositions about the dead, as a result both of the coalescence of different strands in the historical development of Sinhala tradition, and of individual experience, belief, and fancy. These many differences of kind and degree, both between and within our historian and healer, produce (and reflect), of course, variation in the necrotechnologies at hand (thinking historically, praying, honoring, binding with spells and thorns, resurrecting as a zombie, and so forth) as well as variation with regard to the choice to employ one or more of these, or not, in some particular situation.

In studying any particular necromancy we should therefore pay attention to the agency ascribed the dead, expecting in both kind and degree of agency considerable variation across cultures and even within the same individual, but recognizing that in context, and if done correctly, resurrecting Grandma to frighten a rival is no less "real" to the healer and the rival than is a good piece of historical writing that is "real" to the historian and to his or her audience.

This perspective helps me appreciate the reality that the Buddhists whom I discuss in this chapter accord the idea that the dead, in certain cases, can be very much present and active in "the real world" of day-to-day experience. In the process of fieldwork I have been conducting on the history of medicine and religious healing in rural Sri Lanka, on and off for the last decade, I *often* have had to deal with the dead *as* dead, reckoning with forms of necromancy—ways of interacting with the dead—that assign both more and different agency to the dead than I myself ordinarily ascribe them. In this chapter I provide a brief sketch of the different sets of presuppositions about the dead that inform the Sinhala healers I know, and the different sorts of necrotechnologies that produce and are produced by these presuppositions; this allows me to speculate at the end about some changes that are emerging in contemporary Sri Lanka in tandem with Westernization and civil violence.

The dead, of course, reside primarily in the cemetery (*sohompiṭiya,* "place of graves")[2] and the funeral is the primary venue for the exercise of necrotechnologies. Although neither the dead nor my comments *always* stay confined to the cemetery, more often than not it remains their focus. So the cemetery and the funeral constitute the proper place for me to start.

In the village where I did my research, in Sri Lanka's North Central Province (NCP), *sohompiṭiya* is no Euro-American necropolis; it is landscaped only by the shovels of generations of peasants, marked only by the scattered remains of pyres or diggings (which quickly disappear forgotten into the earth), and visited in broad daylight only when the next villager dies (or when a persistent American ethnographer is being humored). The cemetery here is a nearly triangular parcel of land—less than an acre in extent—situated at a crossroads on the southern outskirts of the village. Numerous villagers told me that in precolonial times, "the time of the kings," it was set apart for this purpose, and that it therefore has no owner *(ayiti näta)*; no one farms it, harvests it for wood or fruits or wild honey, builds on it or maintains it. It consists of remarkably thick dry thorn jungle, with a current clearing about twenty feet by twenty feet and evidence of other clearings from the not-too-distant past. When the current clearing is "full"—nowhere left to dig graves, or too big a pile of bone-studded crematory refuse—a new one will be made and the current one will not be touched again until it is the thickest jungle within *sohompiṭiya*. Even so, I am told that it is not at all uncommon for villagers to encounter the skeletons of former villagers when they are digging graves; six feet of earth on an acre is not much space for the dead of the last thousand-odd years.[3] *Sohompiṭiya* is literally the place of corpses (hence the synonym *minipiṭiya*); it grounds the corpses of an entire history.

The villagers here consider themselves Theravāda Buddhists, so it is not surprising that a large set of presuppositions about death and resultant necrotechnologies here are distinctly Buddhist in flavor. Though most religious people invent comfortable fictions that death somehow is not really death, the Buddha is known to have been almost modern in his frank acceptance of death's reality. The village's *sohompiṭiya* perfectly illustrates the Buddhist view of death as inevitable, interminable, final, repetitive, natural, and meaningless; the graves upon graves of ancestors and past lives, the pieces of bone and ash littering every inch of *sohompiṭiya,* the evidence of wild boar and rodent burrowings in search of human carrion, the decaying banners and arches of obsequies past, and the nonidentity attending the residents of unmarked plots[4] all serve to make the cemetery a fitting—if underemployed—site for Buddhist meditations on the nature of death and impermanence (*asubhabhāvanā, maranānusati,* etc.),[5] reminiscent of the charnel fields of ancient India where monks and nuns gathered robes from putrid corpses or sat to contemplate their decay.

This Buddhist strand is reinforced in the funeral proper. Ideally, at least, the role of monks at the funeral is limited to droning home the essential Buddhist teaching that "all things born are born to die; in flux indeed is all that is." Monks are expected not to grieve or mourn—a genuine social faux pas—and the only consolation they offer is the recognition that this dead person exhibits the universal end of human life. The monk is thus responsible for deanimating the dead: cutting their ties to the world by reinforcing the peculiarly Buddhist construct of just what death is. Of course "deanimation" is itself perhaps inappropriate terminology for the practices of people who deny that there is an "anima"—*ātman*—in the first place, but it conveys the goals after which monastic participation in a funeral strives: affirmation of the dead person's deadness, of the emptiness of the corpse over which the mourners nevertheless now mourn. Whatever terminology we choose, monks push the karmic heap called "the person" on to the next plane of *saṃsāra;* while they preach their sermons about the three marks of existence—impermanence, essencelessness, and dissatisfactoriness—the mourners pour water into a teacup until it flows over. This is not the "cup runneth over" of Christian beatitude but a symbolic representation of the running over of the dead person's karmically alotted life span. Like the water, the karmic force of the dead kinsperson flows beyond its former container. The monk continues to hammer home the notion that the dead person is gone for good at almsgiving rituals performed to mark the first week after death, then at first month, third month, first year, and henceforth annual almsgivings in his or her memory, held as long as family members actively mourn. The substance of the sermon is always the same; the kinsfolk transfer the merit of almsgiving to whatever the dead person has become—and whatever it is, it is not here and now; dead is gone. Thus we might portray Buddhism as a necrotechnology of deanimation through insight. The absence of grave-marking[6] reflects this deanimation: there is nothing to mark; the corpse is just a corpse, if it is not already rat-food or worm-food or dust.

But this is not the end of the story. These are South Asians (something all-too-often forgotten by ethnographers and historians of Sinhala culture), and Buddhist ideas represent at best one layer within a much wider set of presuppositions about death and resultant necrotechnologies. Separating out the strands of these non-Buddhist necrotechnologies gets rather dicey,[7] but in the most general sense they are all Theist (Hindu). Some of them may be very ancient, going right back to the sources of South Asian civilization (e.g., the practice of reserving cremation for those who die of natural causes after their own parents have long-since died, burying anyone who dies unnaturally or young, reminiscent of contemporary Hindu practices based upon genuinely Vedic assumptions about Agni). Others of these non-Buddhist necrotechnologies may be considerably more recent (e.g., Śaiva necromancy *mantra*s in eighteenth-century colloquial Tamil).

It is these later non-Buddhist, that is, Theist, necrotechnologies that particularly interest me, not only because they dominate the practices of the healers with whom I studied but also because their integration into "the tradition" is recent enough that I can take a pretty good stab at reconstructing the context in which it occurred. As mentioned, the language of the texts that enact these necrotechnologies—*mantra*s and *yantra*s both to afflict rivals with the dead and to undo the rivals' own use of the dead against oneself and one's patients—can be dated quite precisely to the eighteenth century, a time when this village was at least nominally ruled by the later kings of highland Kandy, Nāyakkars from South India who, though ostensibly champions of the Buddha, were often in personal practice Śaiva. The language of the court in Kandy, and of a sizable number of influential merchants who came with their kinsmen and carried on a lucrative trade with India (much to the consternation of the Dutch overlords of the coastal regions of the island)[8] was oftentimes Tamil; though the nationalists who now claim Kandy as the last bastion of untainted Sinhala Buddhist culture might not want to admit it, during the Kandyan period things Tamil were, not surprisingly, highly prestigious. Earlier Sinhala tradition—itself already long since dialogically interactive with South Indian traditions—quickly absorbed Tamil words, gods, styles of dress and ornamentation, medicines, music, medical and religious philosophies, and magico-religious practices, including of course necrotechnologies. There is even evidence that this was enforced from Kandy; the rituals to the gods who empower Sinhala *vedakama* in this region—mostly minor forms of Śiva such as Ayyanār and Ilandāri, or of Kālī, such as Pattrakālī and Bhadrakālī, all arranged hierarchically within villages, among villages, across regions, and ultimately nationally—are still called *rājakāriya,* that is, "obligations to the king."

This integration of, and adjustment to, the then-vanguard cultural technologies of Kandy, among which necrotechnologies represented a sizable proportion, required no small effort. It involved elaborate mobilization of resources, much more than the sheer transcription of this material onto palm leaves. Learning the range of medical and magical sciences—*vedakama* and *gurukama*—that constitute the domain of the *Vedamahātmaya*, not to mention cognate sciences such as astrology *(nakśāstrakama)* and liturgical priesthood *(kappuwakama)*, requires a lifetime of study. And while we can assume that some educated proportion of the current healers' eighteenth-century ancestors and predecessors understood Tamil, the modern healers with whom I studied know at best a smattering. The literal meaning of the *mantras* and *yantras* is largely unknown—at best one or two words are familiar enough to be recognizable as Tamil at all[9]—but this seems to make no difference: the language is said to be *devabhāṣāva,* "the language of the gods," and the villagers' own theologies of the gods who empower the *mantra*s are conveyed through a huge genre of Sinhala theological poems *(devakīma, devakavi)* composed to fill the gap. In addition to composing this Sinhala literature *about* the gods being imported to empower the new necrotechnologies *(gurukama)* of the eighteenth and nineteenth centuries, the ancestors or predecessors of the modern healers also had to compose detailed *nighaṇḍu* (bilingual Tamil-Sinhala dictionaries of terms for diseases, herbs and other ingredients, medical and pharmaceutical techniques and equipment, and so on), because it matters very much indeed that one understand the literal meaning of the medical recipes *(vedakama).* Even this literary output proved to be insufficient, and it is notoriously true that the written *śāstras* of these healers remain virtually useless in the absence of the Sinhala oral traditions through which the healers learned these arts.

At the same time, these new technologies were not received entirely passively. Even rural Anurādhapura—not to mention Kandy—was already the possessor of proud and ancient traditions that adjusted and responded to the influx of Tamil, and largely Theist, culture; this too represented industry of no small proportion. These were Buddhist traditions, but were themselves representative of a particular sort of Theravāda Buddhist thought and practice that was already highly conversant with earlier Theist (and Mahāyāna and Vajrayāna Buddhist) traditions from the mainland. Corpses were only available to the newly trained necromancers in the first place because these Buddhists already respected Agni enough not to feed him those who die unnaturally. Likewise, pre-Kandyan Buddhist medical treatises already had a basis in the *Cārakasaṃhita*, and Buddhists had developed a uniquely Buddhist alternative, in liturgical Pāli, to the recitation of *mantras*, which is called *pirit* in Sinhala (Pāli, *paritta*). Scholar-monks in Kandy revised earlier medical treatises, such as *Bhesajjamañjusa,* to incorporate the new Tamil technologies. Likewise, in about the eighteenth century two entirely new genres of *pirit* were appended to the liturgy: *dähänas* (Pāli-Sinhala *mantra*s, complete with *Oṃ namo* and *svāha* but based on famous arahants and previous Buddhas) and *yantras* (which rearrange *pirit* texts—including verses from the early Pāli canon—in magical diagrams whose origin is as obvious as it is startling). Thus "the tradition"—already the product of Buddhist-Theist interaction—both absorbed and adapted to a new layer of Theist technology to produce a new "tradition" (still officially Theravāda Buddhist) which is "the tradition" that later absorbed and adapted to "Westernization," the other moment of technological imperialism in Sinhala history that I discuss in this chapter.

But before I turn to the British and their aftermath, let me say a few more words about "the tradition" that confronted them, "the tradition" that emerged in the eighteenth and nineteenth centuries as a result of the influx of Tamil Śaiva culture under the Nāyakkars of Kandy. The adaptation of Buddhist to Śaiva necrotechnologies proliferated in all sorts of forms. Among those that I have encountered in my studies are Pāli *suttas* interspersed verse-by-verse with Sinhala instructions obviously based upon those affixed to Tamil *mantra*s ("mantraize [*maturanna*] a 7-knotted thread with this verse [*gāthā*] 108 times; necromantic nastiness [*angan* and *suniyam*] will not befall you"); hybrid Tamil *mantras* that incorporate Pāli verses directly into them to similarly eliminate or cause some *gurukamic* nastiness (e.g., a Tamil *mantra* combined with the *iti pi so gāthā* to make a woman's menses ceaseless); Pāli *pirits* with slight modifications that will kill some enemy's cow; there is a widespread oral tradition that *Oṃ namo* means "praise to the Buddha" even in Tamil *mantras* that follow the invocation with *Śivāya* and that animate a dead skull to kill or bewitch; and oral theologies that transform Ayyanār, Pulleyār, Pattrakālī, Bhairava, and other South Indian Śaiva deities into *bodhisattvas* (*budu ena deyyo,* usually enumerated as 10).

"The tradition" I study—including the specific South Indian imports as well as the variety of Buddhist responses to them — has transformed the cemetery *(sohompiṭiya)* and funeral in distinct ways. Appended to the Buddhist layer of associations with the cemetery and with its main inhabitants, the dead, is a Theist layer symbolized by Sohon *deviyo*, the "god of graves" (whose *mantras* identify him with no less a figure than Nārāyaṇa/Viṣṇu!). He lives in the cemetery, ostensibly to protect corpses from wild animals and necromancers but just as often as not to assist necromancers in their evil doings. Conflated with the demon Kaḍavara and with the demonic Śiva Bhairava, also considered permanent loiterers in the cemetery, Sohon *deviyo* is known to reanimate *(jīvan karanna)* corpses to frighten villagers to death *(holman karanna)*.[10] He will reanimate crematory ash into a weapon that thrown into the lap of an enemy renders him unable to urinate until his bladder bursts; he will reanimate skulls to enslave cows or women.

In this Theist layer the residence of the dead becomes a center of fear, danger, and pollution. Animated not only by the dead themselves but also by the gods-demons who eat and use them and by the necromancers who sneak in there at night to employ the dead—as well as the demons—to do their bidding by chanting *mantras* and by performing animal sacrifice (a loathsome activity from the Buddhist perspective), the cemetery is transformed from a Buddhist meditation hall into an arena where the gods and demons continue their endless battle using human beings, both dead and alive, as their pawns. Not surprisingly, the fear, danger, and pollution associated with the cemetery is even greater at the funeral, where the corpse, unburied or uncremated, lies in state with the assembled villagers. The death house (*marana ge*, the site where the corpse lies in state) counteracts both strict medicine *(vedakama)* and white magic (*sudu gurukama,* e.g., protective amulets), and hence remains off-limits to those suffering from illness or recovering from a necromantic attack, and by extension to those who are in intimate contact with them (at the very least, after visiting a death house one should first bathe and change clothing before practicing medicine or white magic or interacting with a patient or practitioner of one of those arts).

Thus when the monks arrive at the funeral to deanimate the corpse, they address a situation charged with the belief that contrary forces are trying to reanimate it. The chanting of Buddhist philosophy does not simply express universal opinion; it simultaneously battles necromantic representations of the dead as not really dead, as at least potentially active and agentive in the world conjured up by wicked gurus. Of course the sides in this battle between deanimation and reanimation are more complex than monks against healers, for the healers themselves also employ counternecromantic technologies both Buddhist *(pirit*s, *dähänas,* and other Buddhist "*mantra*s") and Theist (Tamil *mantra*s, countersacrifices, amulets containing magical oils, and Tamil *yantras*) in order to protect themselves and their patients from the power of rival necromancers, while in the NCP the practice of *gurukama,* and especially *vedakama,* often overlaps with the more strictly Buddhist vocations of the monk.[11]

I reconstruct this rich tradition of religious deanimation and reanimation as one of the eighteenth and nineteenth centuries because in modern Sri Lanka it is quickly disappearing. Though British medicine, and attendant extramedical practices and presuppositions, began infiltrating this region of Sri Lanka during the late nineteenth century, with the opening of Anurādhapura to gentleman-archaeologists and civil servants,[12] its real impact has been in the present generation. Ironically enough, this has occurred since independence, when nationalist politicians—though ostensibly championing traditional cultures—propagated British medical imperialism through the proliferation of state-controlled "dispensaries" and "hospitals" that foisted Western medicine (*ingirisi behet,* contrasted to "Sinhala" medicine [*Sinhala behet*, i.e., "the tradition," Sinhala-Tamil/ Buddhist-Theist hybrid]) upon the general populace.[13]

It is not only in the realm of necrotechnology that "Westernization" is eradicating this hybrid tradition ("ancient Sinhala Theravāda Buddhism") which absolutely dominated life in this region even in the living memories of the older villagers. The secret medical and magical traditions for which my gurus fought tooth and nail with other pupils of their gurus are laughed off as archaic by their sons, who study chemistry or economics at the university or work in the local bank or post office; it was sadly the case that only I willingly submitted to the discipline of apprenticeship/pupilship under many of the gurus with whom I studied. The destruction of the wild jungle for resettlement and irrigation and electrification schemes forces them to turn to government ayurvedic (traditional South Asian medical) suppliers for medicinal ingredients, priced beyond the capability of men who traditionally accepted a handful of betel leaves in exchange for their medical services, and communalist ethnic policies aimed at securing votes in national elections for London-trained Colombo elites have denigrated things Tamil to such an extent that even those who know Tamil no longer brag about their skills (a change that I have witnessed in the last decade).

But it is the necrotechnological change that most interests us here. And in the realm of necrotechnology the effects of Westernization, propagated by post-independence nationalist politicians, is felt most strongly. In the early 1960s Mrs. Sirima Bandaranaike's first government enacted stringent legislation regarding the disposal of the dead. In addition to police investigations of deaths and the requirement of coroners' examinations/death certificates, Mrs. Bandaranaike's government legislated the "flower shop" (*mal śālāwa*-funeral parlor) business, requiring modest embalming and the use of regulation coffins (which put a serious dent in the economic base of village carpenters). As a result, the primary issue surrounding funerals suddenly shifted from pollution/danger to cost: a store-bought coffin and related services from the "flower shop" is beyond the means of most of the villagers in this region. In response Mrs. Bandaranaike's government instituted the "funeral assistance committee" (*maranādhāra sammītiya*) that collects funds from each home in the village annually, supplemented by a death-tax levied on every household when a villager dies; currently (2002) the villagers jointly contribute seven thousand rupees (about $70) whenever someone dies, to help cover the costs of coffins and associated funeral accoutrements, and the funeral committee helps organize volunteers to assist in providing food, drink, and betel to the crowds that always assemble at death houses. Maintaining the largest concentration of loanable capital in the village the funeral committee functions as the most important village political institution. By law it must keep elaborate bureaucratic records, which are periodically audited; as far as I can determine this is the first necrological tradition to emerge in the long history of Sri Lankan Buddhist culture. Through the funeral committee and the government for which it exists, the corpse undergoes an ontological transformation as it too is "Westernized." No longer the focus of Buddhist meditators *or* Theist necromancers, the corpse becomes a number in a village ledger, in a police report, and in a coroner's files. The simultaneous propagation of modern medical presuppositions about the state of the dead—deanimated beyond the Buddhist in the denial even of future lives—literally destroys both the need for traditional deanimation and the possibility for traditional reanimation in one fell swoop.

More pervasively, Mrs. Bandaranaike's personal example refigured the nature of the Sinhala grave in the NCP. She entombed her assassinated husband in a magnificent monument at the family estate north of Colombo, and initiated an unprecedented paradigm for funeral practices among the rural Sinhalese.

Although Buddhist elites in Colombo had been imitating/appropriating the Christian practice of grave-marking for at least several decades prior to the 1959 assassination of SWRD Bandaranaike, burying their dead in a "Buddhist section" of the extensive (and previously exclusive—hence the nationalist interest) Kanatta Cemetery at Borella junction,[14] it was only after the creation of the Bandaranaike monument that villagers in the area I studied began emulating, if not successfully copying, the originally Western practice. By the 1970s a few of the wealthiest villagers had erected graves marked with *sohon*s—"tombstones/grave markers"—in memory of deceased loved ones. In 1985 the wealthiest local merchant, proprietor of a number of prosperous shops in the nearest mid-size town, died; he was entombed in a spectacular granite mausoleum reminiscent of Bandaranaike's monument. Since that time, especially due to the influx of immigrants from the low country, where Buddhist grave-marking is more common, the region where I did my research has become studded with permanent necropolises boasting graves every bit as ostentatious—polychrome, covered with gaudy figurines and mock-*stūpa*s and laminated photographs—as those found at the Kanatta Cemetery in Borella, Colombo. The most conspicuous mark the graves of dead soldiers, whose parents receive as death compensation a large sum of cash which they often are unwilling to use for themselves.

The practice of grave-marking is admittedly slow at catching on, though the reason appears to be economic more than nostalgic. In the village *sohompiṭiya* there are still no permanent graves, unlike the *sohompiṭiya*s in the nearby town and on by-roads from it that are quickly filling up and hence becoming unusable. But three or four households in the village have been able to afford permanent *sohon*s erected at the homesteads of deceased parents. Still, old traditions die hard, and in this region the permanent grave, however modern and Western, continues to be evaluated in part on the basis of older presuppositions about the state of the dead. Put simply, the permanent grave remains a source of pollution and danger; the deanimation of Western science does not deanimate the dead enough to eliminate the fear that they will continue to exert agency beyond the grave. The village homesteads boasting permanent graves, however prestigious, have simultaneously become depopulated; who would build a house in a cemetery? Made of limestone, the markers themselves are quickly experiencing the ravages of times, and the once-proud plots are overgrown with thorns and bramble, making them resemble *sohompiṭiya* itself. The merchant's magnificent mausoleum is better withstanding the effects of weather and time, but it is no less considered a source of danger and pollution. A whole string of shops along the stretch of road where the mausoleum is built, including, ironically enough, some of the merchant's own, were quickly forced out of business after the construction of the mausoleum by village ladies who "of course do not want to buy anything from a *kaḍe* (shop) in the graveyard; who could eat such food?" And the marked grave—the necropolis—is enough foreign to the traditions of these villagers that no healer, so far as I can tell, would even *consider* performing his necromantic rites there; no deanimating Buddhist monks need be summoned. The marked grave is wholly other, outside the battle of deanimation and reanimation that dominated traditional Sinhala necrotechnology. The only impact of the tradition upon it is its constitution as wasteland, over which no one has possession *(ayiti näta)*.

This Western transformation of the dead into nonparticipants in the world, nonagentive memories and reconstructions, is supplemented by the civil violence that has plagued Sri Lanka since independence, and especially in the last decade. This goes beyond the dehumanization of dead soldiers on both sides effected by daily radio and television broadcasts and newspaper reports; it goes beyond the displacement of Tamil necrotechnologies effected as a result of the decades-long "ethnic cleansing" of modern Sinhala culture. The simple fact is that Sri Lanka's city streets, university campuses, and remote village haunts have been so littered with corpses that the geography of the dead is now less recognizable; whether as torturer or tortured, countless Sinhalas have cohorted with death as a commonplace. In the villages where I did my research, this has resulted less from the government's drawn-out war with the Tamil Tigers than from the government's eradication of two generations of young Sinhala males (and occasional females) identified as "terrorists" for their participation in the People's Liberation Movement (JVP). Tens of thousands of Sinhala youths were extrajudicially executed by the Sri Lankan government during 1971 and again, with even greater virulence, between 1988 and 1990. These "disappearances," to borrow the euphemistic language of Amnesty International, removed the dead from the realm of the living altogether. My village friends who were murdered by government death squads in the late 1980's did not even win the deanimated deadness of marked graves, of statistics whether in village ledgers or police reports or coroners' files. All remnants of their existence, except the memories of mothers and others who are weeping still (and, in some cases, in reports to the United Nations), disappeared in burning tires and in unmarked mass graves and torture chambers that intentionally supplied human carrion to the wild animals of rural jungles. These are dead who cannot affect the living in any but the sterilely deanimating way of historiographical necromancy, for there is no corpse for necromancers to reanimate, no grave for demons to congregate around, no remnant to perform *holman kirīma*. These dead are really dead, without recourse; consummate expressions of Sri Lanka's "Westernization."

Notes

1. That is, "Gentleman of the Vedas." Unlike Sri Lanka's southern "low country," where a *Vedamahātmaya* practices only strict *vedakama*, that is, the peculiarly Sri Lankan

version of classical Indian Ayurvedic medicine, in the North Central Province where I did my research the term is much broader: here Ayurvedic practitioners simultaneously practice the wide range of gurus' arts *(gurukama)* including the recitation of *mantra*s; enpowerment of *yantra*s; divination *(anjala eliya)*, various *śāstra*s; possession *(änimitikama, māyaṃ wīma)*; and various necromantic acts such as animal sacrifice, reanimating corpses, and harnessing demons.

2. Various synonyms are also used in contemporary Sinhala, including *susānabhūmi,* "graveyard" (*susāna* = Sanskrit, *sausāna* = Sinhala *sohon*, appears in *Jātakagāthāsannaya* and *Visuddhimargasannaya*, both thirteenth century A.D.); *minipiṭiya*, "place of corpses"; *kärakoppuwa,* reportedly from the Portuguese (in the village where I studied the term is known but I was struck that several times its use by old folks produced giggles in village children).

3. I date this inhabitation archaeologically, from the age of the oldest parts of the modern temple, which includes a late Anurādhapuran *stūpa* and an inscribed stone bowl paleographically reminiscent (though now largely indicipherable) of pre-ninth century Anurādhapuran inscriptions. The former monastic graveyard (see n. 6) contains at least 30–40 graves, which counting 30 years per generation would date inhabitation of the site back 900–1,200 years.

4. With the possible exception of their own particularly close relatives (spouses, parents, children, and siblings), no one remembers who was disposed of where in *sohompiṭiya* outside the current clearing. But see the next section on the emergence of marked graves in modern Sri Lanka; this stands in clear opposition to traditional practice. See also n. 6, on an exception to the traditional rule of the unmarked grave.

5. I do not know of any monks or laypeople going there to meditate; in fact I do not know of it anywhere in Sri Lanka (but cf. Matthieu Boisvert, "Maraṇasati: Textual Interpretation and Modern Practice," *Buddhist Studies Review* [June 1996], on the autopsy ward as the site of *asubhabhāvanā* in Colombo); the only corpse meditation that I have witnessed—it is rare in the NCP, though highly honored and admired there—focuses upon skeletons installed at forest hermitages. A remarkable example is Mihindu ārāṇya near Mihintale, where in 2001 a pious patron donated his body to meditation. He was interred in a glass case in the monastery precincts which soon broke, exposing the corpse to the elements and wild animals such that its ravaged remains perfectly serve its meditative purpose. It would appear that the Theist associations with death, and their attendant notions of pollution and danger (see the next section), outweigh the Buddhist ones in the constitution of *sohompiṭiya*'s significance for contemporary village praxis. At the same time, at least one friend who went to the cemetery with me while I was researching this chapter began waxing rather philosophical about Buddhist notions of death while sifting bone and ash through his fingers.

6. See n. 4. An important exception to the rule that graves were traditionally unmarked is, ironically, the history of the treatment of dead monks. As in many if not all Buddhist countries, Sri Lankans have provided dead monks with elaborate funerals, paralleling the Buddha's own supposedly miraculous funeral, and miniature *stūpa*s modeled on those that contain relics of the Buddha's own body. These latter constitute a sort of

marked grave, and thus stand in stark contrast to the village *sohompiṭiya,* though only the most modern (as the *sohon* of the former village high priest, who died in 1982) contain inscribed plates with name and dates. On a rock plateau behind the village temple there are at least 30–40 monastic graves of a less pretentious sort, mere piles of stones covering—it became known during 1984 when treasure hunters broke open several of them—a monk's begging bowl full of the ash and bone from his funeral pyre. These help date the village, because the oldest villagers still living in the mid-1980's could remember a former high priest being cremated then interred at the site, which brings the tradition through 30 or 40 generations up to about 1900. But these graves do not help us reconstruct monastic lineages or lives, because they are still, in their way, anonymous; the only fact to which they bear testimony is that such-and-such number of village monks ended up crematory refuse in their own almsbowls. This is of course a very Buddhistic image, manifesting the reality that all life ends in death; given that in Buddhist soteriological schemas the monk's life best images the means to progress on the Path, it is not surprising that only monastic life-death should thus be permanently memorialized at all. At this writing (2002) it has been decided to remove the former high priest's *sohon* to the ancient monastic cemetery because its current proximity to the temple entrance is considered the polluting cause of the temple's recent hard times!

7. See the next section for an example of just how complex a single moment in the long tradition of confronting foreign technologies was. For general discussions of the composite tradition see Michael Ames, "Magical Animism and Buddhism: A Structural Analysis," in *Religion in South Asia,* ed. E. B. Harper (Seattle: University of Washington Press, 1964); Richard Gombrich, *Precept and Practice: Traditional Buddhism in the Rural Highlands of Ceylon* (Oxford: Clarendon, 1971); Gananath Obeyesekere, *The Cult of the Goddess Pattinī* (Chicago: University of Chicago Press, 1984); Martin Southwold, *Buddhism in Life: The Anthropological Study of the Religion and the Practice of Sinhalese Buddhism* (Manchester: Manchester University Press, 1983); John Clifford Holt, *Buddha in the Crown: Avalokiteśvara in the Buddhist Traditions of Sri Lanka* (New York: Oxford University Press, 1991).

8. On the problem of trade in particular and the Kandyan period in general see John Clifford Holt's the *Religious World of Kīrti Śrī: Buddhism, Art, and Politics in Late Medieval Sri Lanka* (New York: Oxford University Press, 1996), esp. chapter 1.

9. It should be noted that there are also many *mantra*s in the notes I have collected that are not intelligible even in Tamil, full of nonsense words and smatterings of various languages including Malayalam, Arabic and English. The *mantra*s I focus on in this chapter are in Tamil (often also including some Sanskrit).

10. The agents of *holman* are demons (*yaka,* Sanskrit, *yakṣa*), often commanded by necromancers/healers. Sometimes the dead appear directly, sitting on the side of the road beside the *sohompiṭiya* (villagers maintain oral traditions about whose mother or cousin died either of the fright or of direct blows to the head from the dead, and why). Villagers also maintain a wonderful repertoire of stories about people mistaken for zombies who turn out to be beggars or madwomen from distant villagers unaware or unconcerned that they have camped out in *sohompiṭiya*! At other times, *holman* consists of no

more than voices coming from nowhere, lights that appear in the dark of the night jungle, apparitions of leopards jumping across the road then jumping back as elephants and back again as leopards, and so forth; some of these "sightings" of the dead are taken as genuine, others laughed off as the effect of intoxicants.

11. In discussions of this phenomenon with villagers, and indeed throughout Sri Lanka's ancient heartland, I was often told of the "Dimbulāgala Loku Hamuduruwo," the high priest of an ancient temple in contested "Tamil Tiger" territory some sixty kilometers east of Polonnaruwa. This monk was widely known to be a practitioner of both *gurukama* and *vedakama,* and it was believed that his powerful protection *mantras* warded off terrorist attacks. However, this monk was murdered by Tamil Tigers in 1995, causing riots throughout the country.

12. Cf. Pradeep Jeganathan, "Authorizing History, Ordering Land: The Conquest of Anurādhapura," in *Unmaking the Nation: The Politics of Identity and History in Modern Sri Lanka,* eds. Pradeep Jeganathan and Qadri Ismail (Colombo: Social Scientists' Association, 1995), pp. 106–36.

13. Postindependence medical imperialism has been encouraged by a number of factors, including the speed/quick-cure reputation of Western medicine, government propaganda broadcast through the mass media and schools, subsidies, and district medical officers. It overlaps, as did its predecessor from South India, with numerous cognate cultural technologies including in this case Western scientific and medical philosophy/anatomic and etiologic understandings, the use of pesticides, immunization, English language training, the London system of examinations, pop music, and capitalism.

14. Scholars of cemetery architecture will have a field day at this site: juxtaposed against the austere, if not ornate, tombstones and crosses and statues of the Christian/British portion of this cemetery are the mod-art tombstones of Buddhist elites. For a provocative analysis of the complex sociology of this site, especially in relation to the 1983 communal riots, see Pradeep Jeganathan, "Traces of Violence, Spaces of Death: National and Local Identity in an Urban Sri Lankan Community" (paper presented at the Twenty-forth annual conference on South Asia, Madison, Wisconsin, October 1995). On the effects of ethnic violence upon conceptualizations of the corpse cf. Mala de Alwis and Pradeep Jeganathan, "Talking about the Body in Rumours of Death," *Pravada* 3: 6 (August/September 1994): 14–17.

6

The Suppression of Nuns and the Ritual Murder of Their Special Dead in Two Buddhist Monastic Texts*

Gregory Schopen

The compilers of the various Buddhist monastic codes that we have appear to have been very anxious men. They were anxious about—even obsessed with—maintaining their public reputation and that of their Order, and avoiding any hint of social scandal or lay criticism.[1] They were anxious about their body and what went into it; and they were anxious about women.[2] They appear, moreover, to have been particularly anxious about nuns, about containing, restraining, and controlling them. At every opportunity they seem to have promulgated rules toward these ends. Some scholars, seeing the resulting maze of legislation, have taken it to suggest that the monks were very much in charge, and have suggested that the Order of Nuns was never more than a marginalized minority that had little, if any influence, in the Buddhist community as a whole.[3] Obviously that is only one reading. That same body of legislation could, in fact, be read to suggest something like the very opposite. The mere existence of such rules might rather suggest that at the time our monastic codes were written the Order of Nuns was a force of considerable consequence, if not an actual powerful and potentially competitive rival in the world that the compilers of the *vinaya*s were trying to construct.

Certainly, when we move outside of texts and look—insofar as we can—at actual monastic communities in India, nuns and groups of nuns do not appear to have been a marginalized minority without influence. During the period from at or before the beginning of the common era up until the fourth or fifth century—the period during which I would place the final redaction, if not the composition, of all the monastic codes as we have them[4]—donative inscriptions from a

* This chapter was originally published in the *Journal of Indian Philosophy* in the December 1996 issue (Vol. 24, No. 6, pages 563–92) and is reprinted here with permission from Kluwer Academic Publishers.

significant number of Buddhist sites show clearly that approximately the same number of nuns as monks—and sometimes more—acted as donors.[5] This donative activity would seem to suggest, if nothing else, that nuns during this period had equal and sometimes superior access to private wealth.[6] This parity, moreover, is taken for granted by the monastic codes themselves: the Pāli, Mūlasarvāstivādin, and the Mahāsaṅghika-lokottaravādin *Vinaya*s all, for example, have rules to govern situations in which nuns—exactly like monks and lay brothers and sisters—donate monasteries, land for monasteries, permanent alms, meals, *stūpa*s (funerary monuments), and so on, to the monastic community, and they all assume that nuns had the financial means to do so.[7]

The fact alone that sizable numbers of individual nuns—and some groups—could and did act independently as donors, and had the means to do so, added to the fact that some of these nuns had their own disciples and significant ecclesiastical titles, might well have raised the possibility in the minds of anxious men that these nuns might also act independently in other ways as well, that, for example, their private wealth and energies might well be channeled toward more independent religious projects and away from sites or *stūpa*s that appear to have been under the control of monks, and that were in part an important source of revenue for them.[8]

Alas, some of this must remain for now at least another example of the sort of "exciting tale" I have been said to author elsewhere.[9] I sketch these possibilities only as a prelude to an attempt to make some sense of two otherwise even stranger tales, in two different *Vinaya*s, of violence and aggression directed first by monks toward nuns and their special dead; then by nuns toward monks and each other—all of it passing without sanction or censure. It may be, in fact, that these two tales are in part about the ritual murder by monks of the special dead claimed by groups of nuns. We shall see.

The first of our tales—and the hardest still to interpret—has been available in translation for a long time. It forms the frame story for the Fifty-second *Pācittiya* rule in the Pāli *Bhikkhunīvibhaṅga* and was translated in 1942 by I. B. Horner.[10] I give here another translation not so much because I can improve on hers—her translation of the Pāli *Vinaya* as a whole remains, in spite of enormous problems, a remarkable achievement—but simply to highlight and nuance certain elements of vocabulary that are used:

> On that occasion the Buddha, the Blessed One, was living in Vesāli, in the Great Grove, in the Hall of the Peaked Dwelling.
>
> At that time as well the Venerable Kappitaka, the preceptor *(upajjhāya)* of Upāli, was living in the cemetery. And at that time too a comparatively great nun among the nuns of the group of six had died.[11] When the nuns of the group of six had taken that nun out, had cremated

her near the Venerable Kappitaka's *vihāra* (monastery), and had made a *stūpa,* they went there and lamented at that *stūpa.*

The Venerable Kappitaka, then, was annoyed by the noise. Having demolished that *stūpa* he scattered it around *(taṃ thūpaṃ bhinditvā pakiresi).*

The group of six nuns talked among themselves saying "the *stūpa* of our noble one was demolished by this Kappitaka *(iminā kappitakena amhākam āyyāya thūpo bhinno).* Come, we are going to kill him!"

Another nun reported this matter to the Venerable Upāli. The Venerable Upāli reported this matter to the Venerable Kappitaka. The Venerable Kappitaka, then, having left the *vihāra,* remained in hiding.

The group of six nuns went, then, to the Venerable Kappitaka's *vihāra.* When they got there and had covered the Venerable Kappitaka's *vihāra* with rocks and clods of earth, they departed saying "Kappitaka is dead."

Then, however, when that night had passed, and when the Venerable Kappitaka had dressed in the morning and taken his bowl and robe, he entered Vesāli for alms. The nuns of the group of six saw the Venerable Kappitaka going around for alms, and having seen him spoke thus: "This Kappitaka is alive. Who now has told of our plan?"

The group of six nuns then heard that it was certainly the Noble One Upāli who had told of their plan. They verbally abused and reviled the Venerable Upāli saying "How is it, indeed, that this barber, this low born dirt wiper will tell of our plans?"

Those nuns who were decorous *(appiccha)* were critical saying "How is it, indeed, that nuns of the group of six will verbally abuse the Noble One Upāli?" . . .

The Blessed One said: "Is it true in fact, Monks, that nuns of the group of six verbally abuse Upāli?"

"It is true, Blessed One."

The Buddha, the Blessed One, upbraided them saying "How is it, indeed, Monks, that the group of six will be verbally abusive. This will not, Monks, inspire devotion in those who have none . . . therefore, monks, nuns should proclaim this rule of training: whichever nuns were to verbally abuse or revile a monk—this is an offence involving expiation."

The vocabulary here seems to be straightforward, but it almost immediately reveals our awkward ignorance about the realia of Buddhist monasticism. The text tells us that Kappitaka lived in *a* or *the susāna*—the Sanskrit term is *śmaśāna*. This is usually—really as a matter of convention—translated as "cemetery," but sometimes as "burning ground," although we know next to nothing about the precise nature of such a place or the range of activities or kinds of depositions that took place there. Our text, and others, suggest that corpses were cremated there; while other monastic texts seem to indicate that whole, uncremated bodies were left there—as well as food for, and the possessions of, the deceased—but they were not buried.[12] Then there is the question of the definite or indefinite article: is our text referring to *a* or *the* cemetery? The archaeological record makes it certain that Buddhist monastic communities had what would seem to qualify as cemeteries—Bhojpur would be an early example; Kānheri a large and late one.[13] There is too the term *vihāra:* Kappitaka's *vihāra* is in the cemetery. *Vihāra* is—again conventionally—translated as "monastery," but even a quick reading of Buddhist monastic literature will show that the word is used to designate a very large and wide range of types of dwelling places. The compiler of our tale could almost certainly not have had in mind the sort of thing still visible at places like Nālandā since he suggests that a group of nuns could seal it over with rocks and dirt all in a day's work. Moreover, although it is virtually certain that a significant number of Buddhist monastic complexes where intentionally sited near, in, or on top of old, protohistorical graveyards,[14] there is little evidence to suggest that they were established in still functioning *susānas* or *śmaśānas*; and although literary sources very rarely suggest that a *vihāra* was at least close enough to a cemetery to be off-putting,[15] they far more commonly indicate that cremations, at least, took place well away from the monastic residence: like our text, descriptions of monastic funerals in both Pāli and Sanskrit commonly use a verb like *nīharitvā*, *abhinirhṛtya,* or *nītvā*— all of which mean "to take away" or "remove"—in their accounts of the initial parts of the procedure.[16] Finally, in terms of realia, it should be noted that, like Kappitaka's *vihāra,* the exact nature of the *stūpa* erected for the deceased nun is not clear. In her translation of the text Horner renders the term *thūpa* simply as "tomb," and although elsewhere she uses the term *stūpa* in her brief discussion of the text, about all that can be said with certainty is that our author or compiler understood it to be something that could be destroyed by a single person in a very short period of time.

If there is considerable uncertainty about "things" in our text, the same can be said about persons. If, for example, the monk Kappitaka were anymore obscure he would be virtually unknown. Outside of our text, a monk named Kappitaka appears to be referred to in only one other place in the entire Pāli Canon. The *Petavatthu* refers to an elder by that name, but the latter has little in common with our Kappitaka except for the name and there is no reason—in spite of the commentarial tradition—to assume that the two are necessarily the same.[17] As for the deceased nun, she is so obscure as to not have a name, unless *mahatarā*—a strange reading—might be a corrupt version thereof. *Mahatarā,* which I have translated as "comparatively great," Horner renders by "an older nun," and adds in a note; "perhaps a leading nun." But in his very spare critical apparatus Oldenberg clearly doubts even the reading and suggests "read, *aññatarā?*" which of course would produce the even less specific "a certain nun" or "some nun."

The imprecision of our Pāli text in regard to place and person occurs as well in regard to the action of Kappitaka: we do not know precisely what he did, why he did it, and—most importantly—what it meant. At first sight the phrase *taṃ thūpaṃ bhinditvā pakiresi* appears, again, to be straightforward and I have conservatively translated it "having demolished that *stūpa* he scattered it around." But, although the verb *bhindati* in Pāli can mean "destroy" or "demolish," its basic sense seems to be "to break, break apart or split," and the same verb in Sanskrit ranges from "to split or cleave" to "transgress, violate, open and disturb." Moreover, there is no stated object for the verb *pakiresi,* "scattered." I have supplied "it," and Horner translates: "The Venerable Kappitaka . . . having destroyed that tomb, scattered (the materials)." In light of these considerations it is possible to arrive at what, from at least our point of view, would be an altogether more sinister translation: "Having broken open (or violated) that *stūpa* he scattered (its contents) around."

The question why he did it also remains. If the text had said that the nuns' activities disturbed or negatively affected Kappitaka's profound meditations, then we might see here an epic struggle between two competing styles of religiosity, the contemplative and the devotional. But of course it says no such thing. The text in fact passes no judgment on what the nuns had done in building a *stūpa* for their deceased fellow nun—they had, after all, only done what the Buddha twice elsewhere in the Pāli Canon instructed monks to do.[18] Nor does the text indicate any disapproval on the part of even Kappitaka in regard to the activities the nuns engaged in at the *stūpa:* it is not mourning per se that he reacts to, but its volume. Kappitaka's reaction, moreover, is not one of moral outrage or indignation. He was said to be simply "annoyed" or "bothered"—*ubbāḷha*. The same verb is used elsewhere in the Pāli *Vinaya:* monks are said to be "bothered" or "annoyed" by animals and "creeping things" and by demons *(pisāca)*; or even mosquitoes; the Buddha himself is said to be "annoyed" by the unruly monks of Kosambī—but he does not then go out and smash them, nor do any of the monks act similarly.[19] Both Kappitaka's reaction and his actions may seem to be out of context, if not altogether out of control. The compilers of our text, however, give us no indication that they thought so.

In the same way that our text passes no judgment on the initial activities of the nuns in regard to the *stūpa,* it also passes no judgment on Kappitaka's destruction of it, leaving us to surmise that it too was sanctioned. In fact, in the entire tale the compilers of this document find fault only in the nuns' verbal abuse of Upāli after he has betrayed their plans—verbal abuse of a monk appears, therefore, to have been considered far more serious than attempted murder and what might look to us like desecration of a grave. The only outrage at the latter in particular that I know of is in Horner. She clearly did not approve. She—in spite of the texts' silence—says, "Kappitaka's indecent and selfish behavior is symptomatic of the extremely low state to which monkdom could fall at that time"—without, unfortunately, ever making it clear when that was. She also refers to "the horror felt by these [nuns of the group of six] at the dishonor done to their dead."[20] But since the text itself again says nothing of the sort this must simply be the projection onto another time and another place of modern Western sensibilities. The text itself says nothing about how the nuns felt. It gives no indication that they were horrified or angry or outraged. They appear to be simply resolute: "that monk did this and we must kill him." If anything, this looks like an old-fashioned blood feud or—being biblical, which at least would put us closer to the desired time frame—an eye for an eye. Putting such a construction on the text, however, would seem to require that the first murder was of a dead person.

Clearly, the more carefully one looks at this text the more curious it becomes, and when we look elsewhere in the Pāli Canon for aid in understanding it, or in determining what the intentional destruction of a *stūpa* might have meant, we get only equally obscure hints. There are—as far as I know—only two other texts in the Pāli Canon that seem to talk about the destruction of a *stūpa,* though one of them occurs several times. The latter occurs at least twice in the *Dīgha-nikāya* and once in the *Majjhima,* and in all three places the statement that is of interest is repeated two or three times.[21] This statement is the concluding part of the description of the sorry state of the community of "the Nigaṇṭhas, the followers of Nātaputta"—a religious group that competed with the Buddhists—following Nātaputta's death. This community, the text says was divided and at each other's throats:

> Even the lay disciples of the white robe, who followed Nātaputta, showed themselves shocked, repelled and indignant at the Nigaṇṭhas, so badly was their doctrine and discipline set forth and imparted, so ineffectual was it for guidance, so little conducive to peace, imparted as it had been by one who was not supremely enlightened, and now wrecked as it was of his support and without a protector.

"Wrecked as it was of his support and without a protector" is the Rhys Davids's translation of *bhinna-thūpe appaṭisaraṇe,* to which they add the note: "lit. having its *stūpa* broken—a metaphor, says the Com[mentar]y, for foundation (platform, *patiṭṭhā*)"[22] Various other renderings have been given of the phrase that vacillate between the metaphoric and literal meaning of the terms: "with its support gone, without an arbiter" (Walshe); "deren Kuppel geborsten, die keine Zuflucht gewährt" (Neumann)"; "the foundations wrecked, without an arbiter" (Horner); "its shrine broken, left without a refuge" (Ñāṇamoli and Bodhi); and so forth.[23] Here then, however nuanced, the expression *bhinna-thūpa,* "a broken or demolished *stūpa*," seems to have no reference to the desecration of a grave, or anything like that. It seems rather to refer to the destruction of the central focus and—significantly—the support, refuge, or shelter of a religious community or group. Bhikkhu Ñāṇamoli and Bhikkhu Bodhi in a note added to their translation already cited give a statement that they attribute to the Commentary: "the 'shrine' and 'refuge' are the Nigaṇṭha Nātaputta, who is now dead." But this ignores the *bhinna,* "broken or wrecked." When the qualifier is allowed in, it seems almost unavoidable to suggest that if the *stūpa* is Nigaṇṭha Nātaputta, then the broken or wrecked *stūpa*—not the *stūpa* itself—signifies that he is truly dead. The necessary corollary of this is, of course, that as long as the *stūpa* is not demolished Nātaputta remains alive and—importantly—his community has a continuing shelter and refuge.[24]

Seen in this light—which is admittedly dim—Kappitaka's actions too take on a different significance: he did not desecrate a tomb; he killed a "person" who was a religious focus of the group of nuns; he destroyed their refuge and support. This is an act that it seems would have been understood to involve or precipitate the kind of chaos and disarray that befell the Nigaṇṭhas when Nātaputta's *stūpa* was destroyed. Kappitaka cut at the root of the nuns' community. Note that a form of the same verb that produced the qualifier applied to Nātaputta's *stūpa (bhinna-)* is used to express Kappitaka's action *(bhinditvā)*—he did to the nun's *stūpa* exactly what was said to have happened to Nātaputta's.

The second text that seems to refer to the destruction of a *stūpa* is in its Pāli version, both obscure in sense and uncertain in reading. The text in question makes up the Thirty-fifth Sekhiya Rule in the Pāli *Pātimokkha* and, on the surface at least, seems to deal with monks playing with their food. The text in the Pāli Text Society edition reads: *na thūpato omadditvā piṇḍapātam bhuñjissāmīti sikkhā karaṇīyā.*[25] Straining to make some kind of natural sense of this, and depending almost entirely on the interpretation of the commentary, Rhys Davids and H. Oldenberg translate this as: "'Without pressing down from the top will I eat the alms placed in my bowl.' This is a discipline which ought to be observed." And Horner: "'Not having chosen from the top will I eat almsfood,' is a training to be observed."[26]

It is probably fair to say that neither the commentator nor our modern translators were very sure about what this meant. Nor is it altogether clear that the compilers of the *Vibhaṅga* did—they essentially just restate the rule. There is, moreover, in regard to *thūpato,* taken to mean "from the top," a whole series of variants: *dhūpakoto, thupato, thutho, thūpikato,* and *thūpakato*—and this list is certainly not complete.[27] There is a distinct possibility that both the correct reading and the meaning of the rule were lost by the time the Pāli manuscripts we have were written.

Interpreted as it generally has been this rule would seem to have little to offer to our discussion. But at least one other interpretation has been suggested, one that several variants in the Pāli manuscript tradition and at least one set of thoroughly unambiguous parallels also would seem to support. André Bareau, for example, has seen in this rule an interdiction against making a *stūpa* with one's food then demolishing and eating it ("les Theravādin . . . interdisent de faire un *stūpa* avec la nourriture puis de le démolir et de le manger").[28] He has also said that the Theravādins shared this rule with the Mūlasarvāstivādins. But in Mūlasarvāstivādin sources there are much less serious doubts about the readings for this rule and virtually none about how it was generally understood.

The one verifiable Gilgit manuscript reading for this rule in the Mūlasarvāstivādin *Prātimokṣasūtra* is as follows:

> *na stūpākṛtim avamṛdya piṇḍapātam paribhokṣyāma iti śikṣā karaṇīyā.*[29]
>
> "'We will not eat alms food after having crushed that which has the form of a *stūpa*'—this is a rule of training that must be followed."

The Tibetan renderings of this differ somewhat—as they frequently do—depending on where they are found. In the Derge edition of both the *Prātimokṣa-sūtra* and the *Bhikṣuṇīprātimokṣa-sūtra* we find the following: *mchod rten 'dra bar bcos te zas mi bza' bar. . . .,*[30] "We must not eat food forming it like a *stūpa. . . .*" But in the *Vinayavibhaṅga* the same rule appears as *mchod rten'dra ba bcom ste zas mi bza' bar. . . .,*[31] "We must not eat food destroying that which has the form (or is like) a *stūpa. . . .*" And in the *Bhikṣuṇī-vinayavibhaṅga: mchod rten 'dra bar sbrus te zas za bar mi bya bar. . . .,*[32] "We must not eat food kneading it like (or into the form of) a *stūpa. . . .*" It can be seen here that if *bcos te* (forming) is not simply a graphic error for *bcom ste* (destroying)—and there is a good chance that it is—then the Tibetan translators wavered in regard to how best to translate *avamṛdya.* Since the latter can mean not only "crush" or "destroy" but also "rub," the same verb can by extension even account for *sbrus te,* "knead." When Guṇaprabha restated our rule in *sūtra* form in his *Vinayasūtra* he did so as *na stūpākṛtyavamardam,* "not (eating after) crushing (food) having the form of a *stūpa*"; this in turn was translated into Tibetan as *mchod rten 'dra bar byas te mi gzhom mo,* "not (eating after) destroying (food) that was made into the form of a *stūpa,*" and glossed by Dharmamitra in his commentary *zan la mchod rten gyi dbyibs 'dra bar byas te gzhom zhing bza' bar mi bya'o,* "making food into the likeness of the form of a *stūpa* he must not destroy and eat it."[33]

A number of niggling details will have to be worked out here, but the important point for us is that Mūlasarvāstivādin texts in both Sanskrit and Tibetan make it all but absolutely certain that this tradition—over a long period of time, Guṇaprabha may have written as late as the seventh century; Dharmamitra still later—understood our rule to interdict forming food into the shape of a *stūpa,* then crushing or demolishing and eating it. This virtual certainty may well support Bareau's interpretation of the Pāli text—we will have to return to this—but by itself it does not necessarily allow us to establish a link between it, Kappitaka's action, and the wrecked *stūpa* of Nātaputta. The Mūlasarvāstivādin *Vinayavibhaṅgas,* however, I think, will.

The possibility has already been suggested that the compilers of the Pāli *Suttavibhaṅga* that we have did not understand our rule, and it has been noted that the explanatory or frame story found there does little more than restate the rule itself. Bareau, however, has noted that this is not the case in the Mūlasarvāstivādin *Vibhaṅga,* but I cannot agree with him when he characterizes the elements of the Mūlasarvāstivādin frame story as "in fact rather poor and of little interest."[34] There are in fact two Mūlasarvāstivādin frame stories—one in the *Vinayavibhaṅga* and one in the *Bhikṣuṇī-vinayavibhaṅga*—and although in many ways similar they are both of interest. They establish a clear and coherent—if somewhat unexpected—understanding of the rule, and they both associate the destruction of a *stūpa*—however ritualistic or symbolic—with aggression by one religious group against another:

> *Vinayavibhaṅga* (Derge 'dul ba Nya 257b.7–258a.4)[35]
>
> A certain householder living in Śrāvastī was very devoted to the naked ascetics *(gcer bu pa = nirgrantha).* When at a later time he had become devoted to the Blessed One, and had invited the community of monks to a meal in his other house *(khyim gzhan du),* he distributed flour *(phye dag)* there and the group of six kneaded it *(sbrus te = avamṛdya)*[36] and arranged it *(rnam par bzhag go = vyavasthāpita)* like a *stūpa.* He distributed split pieces of radish and they were also stuck into that flour arranged like the central pole of a *stūpa.* He distributed cakes and they too were arranged like umbrellas on top of that radish. Then the monks of the group of six said: "Nanda, Upananda![37] This is the *stūpa* of Pūraṇa, Pūraṇa gone to hell." Then destroying *(bcom ste)* and eating it they said: "Nanda, Upananda! The *stūpa* of Pūraṇa, Pūraṇa gone to hell, is broken *(rdib bo = bhinna)!*"
>
> When the householder heard that he said: "Noble Ones, although I am rid of that form of evil view you persist in not being rid of hostility *(zhe sdang = dveṣa)*"

> The monks of the group of six sat there saying nothing.
>
> The monks reported this matter to the Blessed One and the Blessed One said: "Henceforth, my disciples should recite thus this rule of training in the Discipline: 'we must not eat food destroying that which has the form of (or is like) a *stūpa*. So we should train!'"

Note here first of all that unlike what we see in the Pāli *Vinaya* this frame story makes perfect—if, again, somewhat unexpected—sense of our rule: for the Mūlasarvāstivādin *vinaya* tradition it is not simply a rule about food; it is a rule about ritual aggression through the use of food. This frame story gives some interesting and precise details in regard to what making the form or likeness of a *stūpa* from ones food entailed;[38] it indicates that crushing and eating such a *stūpa* was perceived as an act motivated by hostility, hatred, or aggression, and that its avowed purpose was to do to a named person's *stūpa* what was said to have happened to the *stūpa* of Nātaputta and what Kappitaka is said to have done to the *stūpa* of the dead nun. As Nātaputta's *stūpa* is said to have been broken *(bhinna)*, and Kappitaka is said to have demolished *(bhinditvā)* that of the dead nun, so when the group of six have destroyed and eaten the *stūpa* formed from food they declare that "the *stūpa* of Pūraṇa . . . is broken" *(rdib ba = bhinna)*—all three use forms of the same verb.

Second, it might be noted that the *Vibhaṅga* text employs in one passage the whole range of verbs or meanings that occurs in the various Tibetan translations of the actual rule: "knead," "form," and "destroy." In so doing it seems to make explicit what is implied in the rule: that forming food into the shape of a *stūpa,* and destroying it and eating it are *all* forbidden. It is, moreover, difficult to avoid the conclusion that the procedure described was anything other than what we might call an act of ritual or sympathetic magic or causation. Notice that in the text once the *stūpa* is formed, and before it is demolished, the monks are made to verbally declare, "This is the *stūpa* of Pūraṇa." This formal verbal declaration was presumably—given the power of verbal declarations of several sorts in India—thought to make it so. It is the *stūpa* of Pūraṇa, not a *stūpa* made of food, which is likewise declared to have been broken at the end of the procedure. Finally, the fact that the procedure is aimed at the *stūpa* of Pūraṇa is also of interest since this same *stūpa* is referred to as well elsewhere in the *Mūlasarvāstivāda-vinaya.* In a text that is found in two slightly different versions in both the *Saṅghabheda-vastu* and in the *Kṣudraka-vastu,* for example, we read that on one of their periodic visits to hell Śāriputra and Maudgalyāyana see Pūraṇa there undergoing some fairly uncomfortable tortures. Pūraṇa says to them:

> O Noble Śāriputra and Maudgalyāyana, when you return to the world you must tell my fellow practitioners (Tib. *tshangs pa mtshungs par spyod pa rnams,* but Skt. *śrāvakā*) that I said this: "whenever you

pay reverence to my *stūpa* then my suffering becomes intolerably severe—hereafter you must not do it!" *(khyed kyis ji lta ji ltar nga'i mchod rten la brjed pa byas pa de lta de ltar nga la sdul bsngal ches mi bzad par gyur gyis / phyin chad ma byed par thong zhig; . . . yathā yathā ca śrāvakā stūpakārān kurvanti tathā tathā tīvravedanaṃ vedayāmi . . . mā tasya stūpakāraṃ kariṣyatheti).*[39]

Found in a Buddhist text this passage would seem to be an instance of preaching to the converted. The fact that it is repeated, and that the *Vibhaṅga* and—as we will shortly see—the *Bhikṣuṇī-vinayavibhaṅga* both take aim at this same *stūpa* would seem to suggest that, for reasons that I cannot explain, the compilers of the *Mūlasarvāstivāda-vinaya* saw or cast Pūraṇa and the *stūpa* of Pūraṇa in the roles of major competitor, rival, or threat.[40] In addition this passage would seem to establish in an even more explicit way the "principle" that what is done to the *stūpa* of someone who is dead directly affects the dead person him or herself. This in turn implies in yet another way that to destroy someone's *stūpa* is to definitively destroy his or her person. The *Bhikṣuṇī-vinayavibhaṅga* takes this out of the realm of implication:

Bhikṣuṇī-vinayavibhaṅga (Derge 'dul ba Ta 321b.7-322a.4)

The nuns of the group of twelve were then making their way through the countryside and came to the house of a farmer. When they had shaken out their robes there, and washed their feet and hands, they got ready to eat. Naked ascetics *(gcer bu pa)* had also assembled then in the other house *(khyim cig shos su)* and they too then got ready to eat.

The group of twelve then, with derisive intentions, having made in their food a *stūpa* which they named Pūraṇa *(kha zas la rdzogs byed ces bya ba'i mchod rten byas nas)*, and sticking a radish into it as the central pole, said to the naked ascetics: "This is the *stūpa* of your teacher" (*'di ni khyed kyi ston pa'i mchod rten yin no zhes smras nas).* Then breaking chunks from that *stūpa* and eating them they said in unison: "The *stūpa* of Pūraṇa is demolished" *(zhig go* = (?) *bhinna).*

The naked ascetics were then aggrieved, and having become dejected they said weeping: "Today our teacher is truly dead" *(de ring bdag cag gi ston pa dus las 'das pa lta zhes zer ro).*

The Blessed One said: "One must train such that...we must not eat food kneading it like (or into the form of) a *stūpa*!"

The frame story here from the *Bhikṣuṇī-vinayavibhaṅga* has obvious similarities with that cited from the *Vibhaṅga,* although they are by no means identical. There is one small piece of evidence that in this case the latter may have been derived from the former. In the text of the *Vibhaṅga* it is said that the monks were invited to a meal in the householders' "other house," but in this text there is only one. It is only in the *Bhikṣuṇī-vinayavibhaṅga* that there is reference to two houses, and only there that the reference to the "other" makes any sense. It looks as though the compilers of the *Vibhaṅga,* in adapting the *Bhikṣuṇī-vinayavibhaṅga* story, may have mechanically taken over the reference to the "other" of two houses without noticing that it did not fit in its new context.[41]

The text in the *Bhikṣuṇī-vinayavibhaṅga,* however, seems to make it even more clear than in the *Vibhaṅga* that what is being described is a ritual procedure: the *stūpa* is formed, then named, then declared to be what it had been named. When it has been torn apart and eaten, the nuns then publicly and "in unison" declare that what had been created is now demolished; that is to say that the same thing happened to it as was said to have happened to the *stūpa* of Nātaputta, and that Kappitaka is described as having done to the deceased nun's *stūpa.* The verb in this case was very probably the same. But the *Bhikṣuṇī-vinayavibhaṅga* text—as we have already intimated—also goes beyond this. It makes perfectly explicit what the destruction of a *stūpa* entailed, what it was understood to *mean.* When the *stūpa* of Pūraṇa is declared demolished the naked ascetics are made to say: "Today our teacher is truly dead." To destroy one, is to kill the other, and that—it would seem—is the point of the whole procedure. To judge by the words put into the mouths of the naked ascetics, moreover, it would appear that the compilers of this *vinaya* thought that their "readers" would think that such a procedure actually worked. Naked ascetics are also not the only ones to express such sentiments in the *Mūlasarvāstivāda-vinaya.*

Having come this far we are almost back to the frame story for the Fifty-second *Pācittiya* rule in the Pāli *Bhikkhunīvibhaṅga* that we started with. A parallel for it might simply summarize what we have seen along the way. When, however, we look for a parallel for this rule in the Mūlasarvāstivādin *Bhikṣuṇī-vinayavibhaṅga* it is not there. The Fifty-second *Pācittiya* in the Pāli tradition dealt—as we have seen—with the verbal abuse of monks by nuns. It seems at some stage to have come to form a pair with its Fifty-first *Pācittiya* that requires nuns to ask permission of the monks before entering a monk's residence, an *ārama* or *vihāra.* According to Waldschmidt's tables the same two rules in the same relative order as in the Pāli also occur in the *Bhikṣuṇī-prātimokṣa*s of the Dharmaguptas and Sarvāstivādins, but neither occur in that of the Mūlasarvāstivādins.[42] There is, however, in the Mūlasarvāstivādin *Kṣudrakavastu*—a very rich and little studied collection of odds and ends that sometimes have a prominent place in other *vinayas*—an account that is similar to, though not the same as, the frame story about Kappitaka attached to the Fifty-second *Pācittiya* in the Pāli *Bhikkhunīvibhaṅga* and, curiously, it delivers a ruling that is parallel to that found in the Pāli's Fifty-first *Pācittiya.* It does, indeed, in many respects summarize or recapitulate most of what we have seen:

Kṣudrakavastu (Derge 'dul ba Da 172b.2-174b.5)

The Buddha, the Blessed One, was staying in Śrāvastī, in the park of the Jetavana.

When the Venerable Phalguna had died, then the nuns of the group of twelve, after collecting his bones *(rus)*, built a *stūpa* with great veneration at a spacious spot. They also attached umbrellas and banners and flags to it, and adorned it with perfume and flowers, and assigned to it two nuns who spoke sweetly. Every day they provided earth and water and incense and flowers there. Then they gave to those monks who came there from other countries the washing of hands and had them pay reverence to the *stūpa* with flowers and incense and the singing of verses.

Once the Venerable *Udakapāna was moving through the countryside with a retinue of five hundred and arrived at Śrāvastī. Now, since *arhat*s do not enter into knowledge and vision without focusing their mind *(dgong pa)*, when he saw that *stūpa* from a distance he thought to himself: "Since this is a new *stūpa* of the hair and nails of the Blessed One I should go and pay reverence!"[43]

They went there and the two attendant nuns gave them earth and water for washing their hands and feet. Then the monks paid reverence to the *stūpa* by presenting flowers and incense and the singing of verses. Having paid reverence there with the retinue of five hundred Udakapāna left.

Not very far from that *stūpa* a nun, the Venerable Utpalavarṇā, was sitting at the root of a tree for the purpose of spending the day. Having watched them she said: "Venerable Udakapāna, you should focus your mind when you pay reverence to someone's *stūpa!" (khyed kyis su'i mchod rten la phyag bgyis pa dgongs shig).*

The Venerable Udakapāna thought to himself: "Why would the Venerable Utpalavarṇā say 'Venerable Udakapāna, you should focus your mind when you pay reverence to someone's *stūpa!*'?" Having thought that he said: "There is something here I should concentrate on." When that thing entered into his mind, and he saw that the *stūpa* was a *stūpa* of the bones of the Monk Phalguna, he was infected with a passion that was totally engulfed by hostility and went back and said to the Venerable Utpalavarṇā: "When an abscess has appeared in the teaching you have sat there and ignored it!" *(bstan pa la chu bur byung na khyod 'di na 'dug bzhin du yal bar bor ro zhes bya ba).*

> She sat there saying nothing.
>
> The Venerable Udakapāna then said this to his pupils and disciples: "Venerables, those who are fond of the Teacher and would spare him *(ston pa la sdug pa dang phangs par byed pa gang yin pa de dag gis. . . .)* must on that account tear out and pull down every single brick from this heap of bones and bone chunks!" *(rus pa dang rus gong gi phung po).*
>
> Since that was a large group they, tearing out every single brick from that heap of bones and bone chunks and throwing them away, demolished that *stūpa* in the snap of a finger. The two attendant nuns were crying and ran hurriedly to the retreat house and told the nuns. When the nuns of the group of twelve, and others who were not free of commitment to and feelings of affection for Phalguna, heard that they sat there crying and said: "Our brother is as of today truly dead!" *(bdag cag gi ming po deng gdod shi ba lta zhes. . . .).* And the Nun Sthūlanandā said: "Sister, who has revealed this?"
>
> The other nuns said: "It occurs to us immediately, although we do not actually know, that the Noble Utpalavarṇā was sitting there and that she actually told them."
>
> Sthūlanandā said: "Seeing that she has entered the order from among barbers and is therefore naturally inferior it is clear to me from what little has been said that this is her doing. Seeing too that the Blessed One has well said 'one who defames the assembly is not to be allowed in the midst of the assembly' how could there therefore be any considerations in regard to her?[44] Come—we must go!"
>
> Being totally engulfed by anger and taking up weapons and needles and daggers of hard wood they went to kill her. . . .

The rest of the text—although of considerable interest in other regards—adds little that is germane to our specific interest here and is in any case too long to cite in its entirety. Utpalavarṇā sees the group of twelve coming and, realizing their intentions, she wraps herself in a protective mantle and enters into the meditative state of cessation *(nirodhasamāpatti).* They attack her and leave her for dead. When she rouses herself from her meditative state she sees that she is badly punctured and goes to the monks' *vihāra.* They ask what has happened to her and when told they themselves become angry and they make an ordinance *(khrims)* forbidding all nuns to enter the Jetavana. Mahāprajāpatī comes and is turned away. The Buddha, although he already knows why, asks Ānanda why Mahāprajāpatī no longer comes to see him and Ānanda tells him about the ordinance. The Buddha, although he does not forbid the making of such ordinances,[45] then promulgates a rule that nuns must ask permission to enter a *vihāra,* as a part of which he requires that the monks, when asked for permission, must in turn inquire of the nuns if they are carrying concealed weapons!—"Sisters, having some grudge, are you not carrying weapons and needles? *(sring mo dag 'khon can mtshon cha dang khab dag 'chang ba ma yin nam zhes dris shig).*"

This Mūlasarvāstivādin tale about, in part, the monk Udakapāna is both clearly like, and clearly different from, the Pāli tale about, in part, the monk Kappitaka. Their similarities and differences may both be informative. What is perhaps most generally striking about both is that in neither case is the behavior of their respective monks anything like the main focus of the text. In both it is simply a narrative element in a larger story, an introductory device that allows the compilers to tell the main story that gave rise to the rule they presumably want to deliver. In neither is any judgment passed on the monk's behavior, and in both the unedifying and definitionally, if not doctrinally, perplexing picture of an infuriated *arhat* or irascible senior monk—the preceptor of the monk both traditions centrally associated with the *Vinaya*s—is allowed to stand. We will have to return to this.

In terms of details, the first point that might be noticed is that although the compilers of both texts use the term *stūpa* or *thūpa* they clearly did not have in mind the same thing: in the Pāli text the *thūpa* appears to have been a small, relatively insubstantial construction—it could be destroyed by one man in a short time—in or near a cemetery; in the Mūlasarvāstivādin text the *stūpa* was at least more substantial—it took five hundred men to destroy it, although they made quick work of it—it was made of brick and sited "at a spacious spot." The *stūpa* in each was also the object of different kinds of activity and had different clientele: the Pāli text presents its *thūpa* as a focal point for mourning—at least no other forms of activity are mentioned—and it draws, apparently, only local nuns; the *stūpa* in the Mūlasarvāstivādin text, on the other hand, is clearly the focal point of cult activity—although this too may have included mourning—had two attendant nuns assigned to it, and drew, apparently, monks from far away ("monks who came there from other countries" are explicitly mentioned). Differences of this sort are, of course, almost chronically 'explained' by chronology, but here—as in many other cases—they might be explained as well by cultural geography. We admittedly know little about any cult of the local monastic dead in Sri Lanka, though the Pāli commentaries—as I have pointed out elsewhere—seem to suggest some resistance to it.[46] Moreover, what little we know about *stūpa*s for local monks in Sri Lanka suggests that they were insubstantial affairs. Long ago A. H. Longhurst reported in regard to what he had seen in Sri Lanka that "the *stūpa*s erected over the remains of ordinary members of the Buddhist community were very humble little structures"; Richard Gombrich, more recently, that "small *stūpa*s (closer to molehills than mountains) cover the ashes of monks in Sri Lanka to this day"[47] In communities accustomed to this sort of thing the architectural detail suggested by the story of Kappitaka would have made narrative and cultural sense—"readers" of the text in Sri Lanka could have easily envisioned what was said to have occurred. But the same account probably would not, perhaps could not, have been written on the subcontinent. There things seem to have been very different very early.

Although the situation is somewhat better than it is in regard to Sri Lanka, still we are very far from being fully informed about the cult of the local monastic dead in India proper. What is clear, however, is that from our earliest datable evidence *stūpa*s for the local monastic dead could and did take impressive and substantial monumental form. *Stūpa* no. 2 at Sanci, for example, which contained the inscribed reliquaries of several local monks, was 47 feet in diameter and 29 feet high. It was provided with a crowning umbrella that raised its height to 37 feet, was made of carefully cut and finished stone, and eventually surrounded by a sculpted railing.[48] This very substantial construction—which could have easily taken five hundred men to dismantle—is, moreover, not late: it stands at the very beginning of the series of known *stūpa*s of this sort. Bénisti has argued that the carvings on the rail of *Stūpa* no. 2 predate Bharhut and that they go back to the first half of the second Century B.C.E.[49] There is general agreement that they are very early, but since the *stūpa* itself must already have been in existence before the railing was erected, that would make it even earlier—although by how much is not clear. To judge by the inscriptions on the rail, this *stūpa*—like that of Phalguna—attracted people and gifts from other regions or "countries." Likewise, some of the inscribed *stūpa*s of the local monastic dead at Bhaja are both substantial and very early. Carved from the living rock, they are—or were when complete—at least 15 to 20 feet high, and some of these have been assigned to the late third Century B.C.E.[50] These and other examples would seem to suggest that the Pāli tale told on the continent might well not make very good cultural sense, whereas the monks of central or western India would have no difficulty in understanding the details of the story of Udakapāna. There need not necessarily be, therefore, any chronological gap between the two tales, and it may well only be that each is simply telling its story in a language of detail adapted to its local environment.[51] The important point for us, however, is that in both a monk was allowed to destroy, without censure or blame, an important focus—however that was understood—of the activities of a group of nuns.

The individual monks who did the deed in the two tales also have some things in common, though here too the specific details differ. Both were not just monks; they were monks with disciples and therefore senior monks. One is specifically said to have been an *arhat;* the other a cemetery-dweller. But above all else, they have in common the fact that they are virtually unknown elsewhere. Kappitaka may be referred to nowhere else in the Pāli Canon; Udakapāna is so obscure that I probably do not even have his name right. In Tibetan the name occurs as *chu 'thung,* but I have not been able to find an attested Sanskrit equivalent for this and *Udakapāna is simply a wild guess. Since in Tibetan the name seems to mean something like "a drink of water," it is not impossible that it might be connected with the Pāli name Udakadayaka, "Provider of Water," carried by two monks and a nun—all equally obscure—in the *Apadāna*. But this too is a wild guess.[52] This obscurity of the main actors may point in at least two directions. Given the enormous degree of standardization of both personal and place names that the "editing" process seems to have imposed on both the Pāli and Mūlasarvāstivādin *Vinaya*s—the latter in fact contains a set of rules telling monks exactly how to do this—the strikingly nonstandard nature of our characters' names may point to the relative authenticity of the account. But it is equally possible that there might have been some unease in ascribing the actions described to a Śāriputra or Maudgalyāyana, so the choice of characters we find may be connected to an attempt to avoid indelicate questions. Ironically this would also have lessened the authority of the model.

Obscurity of character, however, does not just mark the main actors—the deceased are equally unknown. In the Pāli text the *stūpa* was built for the remains of an apparently nameless nun. In the Mūlasarvāstivādin text the *stūpa* contains the bones of a monk who appears to have been named Phalguna, that is if I am right in thinking that the Tibetan *gre las skyes* is an alternative translation of the second element of the name Mūlaphalguna which occurs in the *Cīvaravastu*. The monk so named there—and only there as far as I know—*may* be the same as Moliya-Phagguna in Pāli sources. The latter is described as excessively close to the nuns and their staunch defender; and Mūlaphalguna as "fondly looked after by the nuns." Although much remains uncertain here, if the *Kṣudrakavastu* account is referring to this same monk then he was, indeed, an important figure for groups of nuns, though he, typically, receives little attention in monastic sources.[53]

Curiously, the only role occupied by individuals of any standing elsewhere in monastic literature is that of *révélateur,* and in both texts these are precisely the individuals who are the objects of the censored attacks, both verbal and actual. Upāli is, of course, in both traditions one of the most prominent of the Buddha's immediate disciples—it was he who is said to have preserved the whole of the *vinaya*. In the Pāli tradition Utpalavarṇā is almost equally eminent and is said to have been "one of the two chief women disciples of the Buddha."[54] In the Mūlasarvāstivādin *Vinaya* she has a more checkered career—she is rebuked by the Buddha for showing off her magical powers, for example—but is still well-known.[55] As a kind of final inversion, note that whereas the obscure characters in both the Pāli and Mūlasarvāstivādin tales have clear roles, the roles of the well-known characters are ambivalent—in both cases they start what the compilers seem to have seen as the real trouble. Both, incidentally, are also slurred for their low birth or inferior social status. This is, however, the only indication that I know that would suggest that Utpalavarṇā was of low-caste origin.

When we turn to the explicit motives behind Udakapāna's action it is clear that they are not. Although Udakapāna expresses himself much more verbally than Kappitaka, this is not difficult since the latter doesn't say anything. But what Udakapāna says is difficult to interpret. He is described as extremely angry, but the narrative leaves the impression that this might be because he was hoodwinked by a group of nuns. Apparently referring to the *stūpa* he says "an abscess has appeared in the teaching," and clearly referring to the *stūpa he* calls it a "heap of bones and bone-chunks." But if this strong talk is based on a disapproval of the monk Phalguna the text, as we have noted, gives no indication of this, and he presumably could not—if he knew his *vinaya*—be objecting to the erection of a *stūpa* for a deceased monk: this is elsewhere explicitly allowed with rules provided to govern it, and narratively described.[56] Perhaps the most significant thing Udakapāna says is in his exhortation to his disciples to tear the *stūpa* down. They should do it, he says, because they "are fond of the Teacher and would spare him." But spare him from what? It can only be, it seems, from a loss of veneration as a result of what was meant for him being "misdirected" toward something else: "a heap of bones and bone chunks." Notice that those concerned with the *stūpa* of Phalguna are described as having feelings of affection *(mdza' ba 'dod chags)* for him, and Udakapāna's monks are exhorted to act because they are fond of the Teacher *(ston pa la sdug pa . . . byed pa).* The conflict, it seems, is about competing loyalties, if not affections. And the real point that is narratively made is that from the monk's point of view it is a very dangerous conflict, because even an *arhat* can, if he is not careful, be led astray. The whole text turns in a sense on the fact that Udakapāna thought he was worshiping a *stūpa* of the Buddha.[57]

The *stūpa* of Phalguna—erected, maintained, and promoted by the nuns—appears, therefore, as a potentially dangerous competitor to the *stūpa* of the Buddha and the monks' response is a brutal one, one that we view differently than the nuns are reported to have. Where we would see the destruction of a monument, they—confirming much of what has been said—are presented as seeing the death of a person. When the nuns are informed of the destruction of Phalguna's *stūpa* they say almost exactly what the followers of Pūraṇa said when the nuns ritually demolished his *stūpa:* "Our brother is as of today truly dead!" He too in fact appears to have been ritually murdered.

It is not just our analysis, then, which links the rule about food and the text concerning the *stūpa* of Phalguna: they are linked by a shared key statement. The end result of the ritual manipulation of food triggers exactly the same exclamation as the end result of the actual destruction of the *stūpa.* But if one is ritual, so too must be the other, at least in meaning. They both moreover effect a definitive change in one thing by manipulating another: in the one case the destruction of kneaded food destroys a person; in the other case this is effected by the destruction of an arrangement of bricks; in both cases the person destroyed is—

from our point of view—already dead. Here I think it is important to note that both kneaded food and arranged bricks are also employed in Brahmanic rites for manipulating the "dead." The most obvious, perhaps, is the use of balls of rice to "be" the dead in the *sapiṇḍa* ritual; or the use of bricks in the fire altar to reconstitute the dismembered Puruṣa. The pattern runs deep.[58]

But our texts also intersect or link up with another Indian pattern as well, this one more specifically Buddhist. It has been argued elsewhere on the basis of both archaeological and epigraphic sources that the *stūpa* of the Buddha was—to use again the formulation of the late Prof. André Bareau—"more than the symbol of the Buddha, it is the Buddha himself"; it is the living Buddha.[59] It has also been suggested that this must apply as well to the *stūpa*s of local monks like those of Gobhūti at Bedsa or the Elder Aṃpikiṇaka at Bhaja.[60] But if this is correct, if the *stūpa is* the living person, then it would seem that as a necessary corollary such a "person" must also be subject to death. If, in other words, a *stūpa* could live, it also—by necessity—should be able to die or even, indeed, be murdered. Our texts, it seems, explicitly establish this. They confirm, if you will, from yet another angle that *stūpa*s were thought to be living by showing that it was also thought that they could be killed. And they show as well that this conception was a monastic one found in decidedly monastic sources.[61]

Then there are the compulsory caveats and "final" conclusions. It may not be too difficult to assent to the suggestion that the Pāli account of the destruction of the nameless nun's *stūpa* be read in light of the more explicit Mūlasarvāstivādin text, and to see in it that the destruction of her *stūpa* meant both the destruction of her and the suppression by a monk of a focal point for the activities of the group of nuns that sought it and her out, the destruction—if you will—of either an actual or potential organizational center. We have, after all, the repeated reference elsewhere in the Pāli Canon to fragmented religious groups who are characterized as having their *stūpa* broken or demolished, *bhinna-thūpa.* There may, however, be more resistance to reading the Pāli rule about food in light of the Mūlasarvāstivādin "parallel."

The Mūlasarvāstivādin understanding of the rule in question may indeed be "late." At least one person has in fact asserted that this Mūlasarvāstivādin reading "is clearly a later derivation which was produced by mistaking the first member of the compound *[stūpākṛti] stūpa* as 'a tope'." But this observation is based on a rather confused presentation and analysis of purely philological data and on the very questionable assumption that there was an *ur* or "original" text of such rules, rather than a number of competing versions.[62] Moreover, the data could as easily be argued the other way around. Sylvain Lévi, for example, has shown that in other cases where other *vinaya* traditions are confused or garbled, or where the sense of a term appears to have been forgotten, that sense has been accurately preserved in the Mūlasarvāstivādin tradition.[63] We could very well be dealing with a similar case, especially if the Mūlasarvāstivādin interpretation can indeed be linked to old Indian patterns. The confusion in the manuscript tradition for the Pāli rule has already been noted, as has the fact that the compilers of the Pāli *Vibhaṅga* seem no longer to have known what it meant—at least they give no explanation.[64] Over against this stands the Mūlasarvāstivādin tradition in considerable contrast. It has everywhere understood the rule in the same way—in its two *Prātimokṣa*s, in both the *Bhikṣu-* and *Bhikṣuṇī-vinayavibhaṅgas,* even in Guṇaprabha's *Vinaya-sūtra* and its four commentaries. It has, moreover, consistently given an interpretation of the rule that is clear and in conformity with both its readings and with texts like the tale of Phalguna's *stūpa* found elsewhere in its *vinaya.* Ironically, even if the Mūlasarvāstivādin interpretation would turn out to be relatively "late" it would still give us a consistent Buddhist interpretation of a difficult text that would otherwise remain all but meaningless, an interpretation, moreover, that would be much closer in time and culture to the compilers of the Pāli Canon than anything that could be produced in modern Europe or in the United States—the latter leaves us with little more than a seemingly silly rule about monks playing in their food. Moreover, in assessing the Mūlasarvāstivādin interpretation of the rule it must always be kept in mind that we have an extant manuscript containing this rule that predates anything we have for the Pāli by six centuries or more. The Gilgit manuscript of the Mūlasarvāstivādin *Prātimokṣa* contains in fact—as far as I know—the earliest attested form of this rule in an Indian language, and there are at least two comparatively early manuscripts from Central Asia ascribed to the Sarvastivadins that have very similar readings.[65]

Finally, we might conclude by trying to place the Pāli tale of the nameless nun's *stūpa* and the Mūlasarvāstivādin account of the *stūpa* of Phalguna in the context of what else has been said—or not said—about *stūpa*s elsewhere in the literature they come from. Both the Pāli Canon and the Mūlasarvāstivādin *Vinaya,* for example, explicitly mandate the erection of *stūpa*s by monks for deceased fellow monks, but in neither is there—as far as I know—a similar statement in regard to nuns. This omission is also narratively or hagiographically highlighted in at least the *Mūlasarvāstivāda-vinaya:* when the monk Śāriputra dies he gets a *stūpa;* when the monk Kāśyapa dies he too gets a *stūpa;* when the monk Ānanda dies he gets two—he also refers to the *stūpa*s of the others when, on the point of dying, he describes himself by saying: "I am alone, isolated, like the remaining tree in a forest of *stūpa*s." When, however, Mahāprajāpatī—the seniormost nun and in a sense the foundress of the Order of nuns—dies, she gets none, and the funeral proceedings, which are elaborately described, are entirely in the hands of the monks.[66]

The Pāli tale of the nameless nun's *stūpa* and the Mūlasarvāstivādin account of the *stūpa* of Phalguna are the only references I know in either *vinaya* to *stūpa*s built for or by nuns, and in both cases these *stūpa*s are destroyed by monks who receive no censure for their acts. Generally speaking the attitude toward such destruction in Buddhist literature is firm and unequivocal: "to destroy a *stūpa* is a grave offence which could be committed only by men who have no faith in the law."[67] If the interpretation of the *Prātimokṣa* rule proposed above is correct, even the purely symbolic or ritual destruction of the *stūpa* of a "heretic" is strictly forbidden to both monks and nuns. Moreover, apart from the two *stūpa*s built by nuns that we have studied here, the only other *stūpa*s whose destruction is contemplated or referred to are, in fact, those of "heretics" or members of rival religious groups. If by nothing else, then, nuns are by association, at least, classified with such groups.

It is clear from the references to the *stūpa* of Nātaputta in the Pāli Canon that the destruction of a group's *stūpa* was associated with that group's disarray and loss of an organizational center. It is clear as well from the *Mūlasarvāstivāda-vinaya* that the *stūpa* of a monk was a source of revenue and support for his fellow monks: what was given to it belonged to them.[68] The actions of the monks Kappitaka and Udakapāna would, then, have left the two groups of nuns involved with neither an important means of support nor an organizational focus. Such actions would not have been just ritual murder, but in fact something more akin to the political assassination of a group's special dead. That such actions did occur in Buddhist India may account, far better than does historical accident, for the fact that nowhere in either the archaeological or epigraphic records do we find an instance of a *stūpa* having been built for a nun. It is perhaps unlikely that once having built such structures, and having had them pulled down, groups of nuns would have continued doing so knowing that this would be again for them—as it must now be for us—the end.[69]

Abbreviations

BD = I. B. Horner, *The Book of the Discipline* (Oxford-London:1938–66), vols. 1–6

BEFEO = *Bulletin de l'école française d'extrême-orient*

BHSD = F. Edgerton, *Buddhist Hybrid Sanskrit Grammar and Dictionary* (New Haven:1953), Vol. 2

Derge = *The Tibetan Tripitaka. Taipei Edition* (Taipei:1991)—cited according to original section, volume, and folio

DPPN = G. P. Malalasekera, *Dictionary of Pāli Proper Names* (London: 1937–38), vols. 1–2

GMs iii = N. Dutt, *Gilgit Manuscripts* (Srinagar-Calcutta:1942–50), vol. 3, parts 1–4

GMsSA = R. Gnoli, *The Gilgit Manuscript of the Śayanāsanavastu and the Adhikaraṇavastu* (Serie Orientale Roma, 50) (Rome:1978)

GMsSB = R. Gnoli, *The Gilgit Manuscript of the Saṅghabhedavastu* (Serie Orientale Roma, 49.1 and 2) (Rome:1977–78), parts 1–2
JA = *Journal asiatique*
JIABS = *Journal of the International Association of Buddhist Studies*
JIP = *Journal of Indian Philosophy*
JPTS = *Journal of the Pāli Text Society*
MSV = *Mūlasarvāstivāda-vinaya*
Pāli *Vinaya* = H. Oldenberg, *The Vinaya Piṭakaṃ* (London:1879–83), vol. 1–4
Tog = *The Tog Palace Manuscript of the Tibetan Kanjur* (Leh:1979)—cited according to original section, volume, and folio
TSD = L. Chandra, *Tibetan-Sanskrit Dictionary* (New Delhi:1959–61), parts 1–12
WZKS = *Wiener Zeitschrift für die Kunde Südasiens*

Notes

1. See G. Schopen, "On Avoiding Ghosts and Social Censure: Monastic Funerals in the *Mūlasarvāstivāda-vinaya,*" *JIP* 20 (1992): 1–39, esp. 17ff.

2. There is as yet no good study of food in the various *vinaya*s, but the potential of such can be glimpsed in what has been done in studies of food in other Indian contexts; see, for example, R. S. Khare, ed., *The Eternal Food: Gastronomic Ideas and Experiences of Hindus and Buddhists* (Albany:1992); P. Olivelle, "Food in India," *JIP* 23 (1995): 367-80 and the sources cited in this review of Khare. In spite of a growing list of monk bashing papers, there is still not a good study of the complex monastic attitudes towards women either.

3. This position — still influential — was very early in place; see H. Oldenberg, *Buddha: His Life, His Doctrine, His Order,* trans. W. Hoey (London:1882), p. 381. Very recently it has been said: "The findings of Paul [D. Y. Paul, *Women in Buddhism: Images of the Feminine in the Mahāyāna Tradition,* 2d ed. (Berkeley: 1985)] and K. C. Lang [Lang, "Lord Death's Snare: Gender-related Imagery in the Theragāthā and the Therīgāthā," *Journal of Feminist Studies in Religion* 2:2 (1986)] would suggest that, in the period prior to the composition of *Apadāna*, Buddhist women were decidedly marginalized"; J. S. Walters, "A Voice from the Silence: The Buddha's Mother's Story," *History of Religions* 33:4 (1994): 370. Here, as I think Walters suggests, this position is in part maintained so as to cast "The Mahāyāna" in a supposedly more favorable light.

4. See Schopen, "Deaths, Funerals, and the Division of Property in a Monastic Code," in *Buddhism in Practice,* ed. D. S. Lopez (Princeton:1995), pp. 473–502, esp. pp. 475–77.

5. Schopen, "On Monks, Nuns and 'Vulgar' Practices: The Introduction of the Image Cult into Indian Buddhism," *Artibus Asiae* 49:1/2 (1988–89): 153–68 esp. 163–65; the findings here seem now to be confirmed by P. Skilling, "A Note on the History of the

Bhikkhunī-saṅgha (II): The Order of Nuns after the Parinirvāṇa," in *Pāli & Sanskrit Studies. Mahāmakut Centenary Commemorative Volume and Felicitation Volume presented to H.H. The Supreme Patriarch on the Occasion of his 80th Birthday,* ed. P. Bodhiprasiddhinand (Bangkok: 1993), pp. 208–251, esp. pp. 211–16, 229, and n. 167. I cannot account for the assertion in A. Hirakawa, *A History of Indian Buddhism. From Śākyamuni to Early Mahāyāna,* trans. P. Groner (Honolulu:1990), p. 226, that at Sanci "the names of many more nuns than monks are recorded." He cites no source and my own count indicates the numbers were about equal: 129 monks and 125 nuns.

6. On the private means of Buddhist monastics see most recently Schopen, "Monastic Law Meets the Real World: A Monk's Continuing Right to Inherit Family Property in Classical India," *History of Religions* 35:2 (1995): 101–23.

7. See Schopen, "The Ritual Obligations and Donor Roles of Monks in the Pāli Vinaya," *JPTS* 16 (1992): 87–107.

8. Two of the three main *stūpa*s at Sanci contained the remains of deceased monks: Stūpa no. 2 was built for the deposit of the remains of several local monks, no. 3 for those of Śāriputra and Maudgalyāyana, and at least the Mūlasarvāstivādin tradition explicitly declares "that which is given to the *stūpa* of a disciple belongs indeed to his fellow-monks" (See Schopen, "Ritual Rights and Bones of Contention: More on Monastic Funerals and Relics in the *Mūlasarvāstivāda-vinaya,*" *JIP* 22 (1994): 31-80, esp. 56ff. See also the second version of the *Vinaya-uttara-grantha,* Derge 'dul ba Na 260b.5: *nan thos kyi mchod rten la bsngos par gyur pa ni shi ba'i yo byad pas na bgo bar bya'o:* "Since what is dedicated to the *stūpa* of a disciple *(śrāvaka)* is (a part of) the estate of the deceased *(mṛtapariṣkāra)* it should be distributed (among the monks)." It has been said that "the *Vinaya-uttara-grantha,* just like the Pāli *Parivāra,* is an appendix to the Vinaya" and that "this work tells us nothing new" (A. C. Banerjee, *Sarvāstivāda Literature* (Calcutta: 1957) 99; neither assertion, however, has yet been demonstrated and the latter is far from true. Here the *Uttaragrantha* has assimilated what is given to the *stūpa* of a deceased *śrāvaka* to his estate. This, of course, means in turn that the rules that apply to the latter (which are detailed, for example, at GMs iii 2, 120.3ff and digested in the *Ekottarakarmaśataka,* Derge bstan 'gyur, 'dul ba Wu 221b.3–7) now apply to the former as well.).

This same *Vinaya* also lists as one of the eight categories of "acquisitions" *(lābha)* or revenue that which is offered at "The Four Great Shrines," i.e. those at the sites of the Buddha's birth, awakening, first teaching and *parinirvāṇa*—see MSV: GMs ii 2, 113.8, and note that these four are not relic or mortuary *stūpas* and therefore, technically, not subject to the rules that govern *stūpas* of the Buddha.

9. R. Gombrich, "Making Mountains without Molehills: The Case of the Missing *Stūpa,*" *JPTS* 15 (1991): 141–43. Notice, however, that in a characteristically fine paper that revisits the question of the role of nuns in early and medieval Sri Lanka R. A. L. H. Gunawardana uses some of the same sort of language for some of the same reasons: he notes the economic independence of women in Sri Lankan inscriptions; and refers to "the independent spirit displayed by nuns," "the concern shared by some monks about this situation," and the "challenge" presented (Gunawardana, "Subtile Silk of Ferreous Firmness:

Buddhist Nuns in Ancient and Early Medieval Sri Lanka and Their Role in the Propagation of Buddhism," *The Sri Lanka Journal of the Humanities* 14 (1988, but 1990): 1–59. It is ironic that whereas in most areas of Buddhist studies interpretation, analysis, and conjecture frequently go far beyond their available evidential base, the study of the history of the Order of nuns in India has yet to fully use even the rich textual data that has accumulated over the years. In 1884 W. W. Rockhill published a translation of the Mūlasarvāstivādin *Bhikṣuṇī-prātimokṣa* (Rockhill, "Le traité d'émancipation ou Pratimoksha Sutra traduit du tibétan," *Revue de l'histoire des Religions* 9 (1884): 3–26; 167–201); in 1910 L. Wieger translated both the Dharmaguptaka *Bhikṣuṇī-prātimokṣa* and extracts of its *Vibhaṅga* (Wieger, *Bouddhisme Chinois I: Vinaya: Monachisme et discipline; Hinayana, Véhicule inférieur* (Paris:1910, reprinted in 1951); in 1920 appeared C. M. Ridding and L. de la Vallée Poussin, "A Fragment of the Sanskrit Vinaya. Bhikṣunikarmavacana," *Bulletin of the School of Oriental and African Studies* 1 (1920): 123–43; the important study of E. Waldschmidt, *Bruchstücke des Bhikṣuṇī-prātimokṣa der Sarvāstivādins. mit einer Darstellung der Überlieferung des Bhikṣuṇī-prātimokṣa in den verschiedenen Schulen* was published in Leipzig in 1926; then followed significant work on Mahāsāṅghika texts dealing with nuns; G. Roth, *Bhikṣuṇī-vinaya, including Bhikṣuṇī-prakīrṇaka and a Summary of the Bhikṣu-prakīrṇaka of the Ārya-Mahāsāṃghika-Lokottaravādin* (Patna:1970); A. Hirakawa, *Monastic Discipline for the Buddhist Nuns. An English Translation of the Chinese Text of the Mahāsāṃghika-Bhikṣuṇī-Vinaya* (Patna:1982); É. Nolot, *Règles de discipline des nonnes bouddhistes* (Paris:1991); and so forth. Little of this and similar work has made its way into more general works and we still get studies like that of R. Pitzer-Reyl's which, in spite of its title *Die Frau im frühen Buddhismus* (Berlin:1984), is based almost exclusively on Pāli or Theravādin sources.

10. Pāli *Vinaya* iv 308–09; Horner, *BD* iii 343–44.

11. "The nuns of the group of six," *chabbaggiyā,* are of course the female counterparts to "the group of six monks," the later being described in T. W. Rhys Davids and W. Stede, *The Pāli Text Society's Pāli-English Dictionary* (London:1921–25), p. 273 as "a set of (sinful) Bhikkhus taken as exemplification of trespassing the rules of the *Vinaya"* (the *Dictionary* makes no reference to the nuns' group!). The *Mūlasarvāstivāda-vinaya* has an exact counterpart to the Pāli's group of monks who are called *ṣaḍvārgika.* Edgerton, *BHSD* (New Haven:1953), p. 538, says: "In Pāli they seem to be represented as followers of the Buddha, though very imperfect ones, often transgressing rules of propriety. In BHSD, at least in Divy. they seem to be heretics from the Buddhist standpoint" —the last sentence here must be corrected. In the *Mūlasarvāstivāda-vinaya* and in the *Divyāvadāna* (much of which appears to have been borrowed from the former) there can be no doubt that the *ṣaḍvārgika* monks were Buddhists. Interestingly, the Mūlasarvāstivādin counterpart to the Pāli's group of six nuns is called, as we will see, "the group of twelve," *dvādaśavargīya,* making them, presumably, twice as bad (here too Edgerton, p. 273, needs to be corrected and supplemented, though he does recognize that they cannot be "heretics"). The members of both groups, male and female, appear as stereotypical rogues, scoundrels, tricksters, deviants, and sometimes downright nasty customers, but they are always represented as regular members of the Order, and some of their stories provide some of the finest humor in both *vinaya*s. At the same time, though, the com-

pilers of the various *vinayas* seem to have used these groups or individuals belonging to them to articulate and work out some of the most disturbing and highly charged issues that confronted them. (For a representative sampling of passages from the Pāli *Vinaya* in which the group of six occurs see the references given in *DPPN* i 926; J. Dhirasekera, *Buddhist Monastic Discipline. A Study of its Origin and Development in Relation to the Sutra and Vinaya Pitakas* (Colombo, Sri Lanka:1982) is one of the few works that gives serious consideration to the group; see pp. 46, 135, 150-51 (nuns), 164-70. For references to the group or individuals belonging to it in *MSV* See GMs iii 1, 8.4; iii 2, 98.9; 117.8; *GMsSA* 36.14, 37.19, 39.7, 40.13, 41.13, 43.4, 53.24; Derge 'dul ba Nya 257b.7; Ta 123a.5, 321b.7; Tog 'dul ba Ta 6a.6, 8b.4, 11a.2, 9lb.7, 15la.4, 304a.3, 332a.4, 337b.2, 346b.1—all references here are to the beginning of the texts in which the group or its members appear.

12. Pāli *Vinaya* iii 58.11 = Horner, *BD* i 97 = *MSV*: Tog 'dul ba Ta 332a.4ff; Pāli *Vinaya* iv 89.17 = *BD* ii 344 = *MSV*: Derge 'dul ba Ja 154b.2ff; etc. (Note that when a *MSV* text is joined to a Pāli text by equal marks this does not imply that it is an exact equivalent, but only that it is more or less parallel or broadly similar.)

13. See Schopen, "An Old Inscription from Amarāvatī and the Cult of the Local Monastic Dead in Indian Buddhist Monasteries," *JIABS* 14:2 (1991): 281-329.

14. See Schopen, "Immigrant Monks and the Proto-Historical Dead: The Buddhist Occupation of Early Burial Sites in India," in *Festschrift Dieter Schlingloff,* Hrsg. F. Wilhelm (Reinbek: 1996) 215–38.

15. See, for example, *MSV*: GMs iii 1, 223.7–224.12.

16. See *JIP* 20 (1992): 27 ns. 31–33.

17. See *DPPN* i 524 s.v. Kappitaka Thera.

18. References at *JIABS* 14:2 (1991): 281 n.1.

19. Pāli *Vinaya* i 148–49 = Horner, *BD* iv 196; Pali *Vinaya* ii 119 = Horner, *BD* v 163 (here translated by "*pestered*"); Pali *Vinaya* i 353 = Horner, *BD* iv 505.

20. I. B. Horner, *Women under Primitive Buddhism. Laywomen and Almswomen* (London:1930), p. 158.

21. T. W. Rhys Davids and J. E. Carpenter, ed. *The Dīgha Nikāya* (London:1911), 3:117–18; 209–10; R. Chalmers, *The Majjhima-nikāya* (London:1898), 2: 244.

22. T. W. Rhys Davids and C. A. F. Rhys Davids, *Dialogues of the Buddha* (Oxford:1921), part 3, pp. 111–12 n.1, also 203–4.

23. M. Walshe, *Thus Have I Heard: The Long Discourses of the Buddha* (London:1987), pp. 427, 480; K. E. Neumann, *Die Reden Gotamo Buddhos. Aus der Mittleren Sammlung Majjhimanikāyo des Pāli-Kanons* (München:1922) 3:52–53; I. B. Horner, *The Middle Length Sayings* (London:1959), 3:30–31; Bhikkhu Ñāṇamoli & Bhikkhu Bodhi, *The Middle Length Discourses of the Buddha* (Boston:1995), pp. 853, 854.

24. There are of course a number of problems with the Pāli passages about the *stūpa* of "the Nigaṇṭha Nātaputta," not the least of which is whether this refers to the Jains. A. L. Basham, *History and Doctrines of the Ājīvakas* (London:1951), p. 75, suggests it does not, but refers rather to the death and community of Gosala, a founding figure of the Ājīvakas, another group competing with the Buddhists (cf. K. R. Norman, "Observations on the Dates of the Jina and the Buddha," *The Dating of the Historical Buddha/Die Datierung des historischen Buddha* (Gottingen:1991), pp. 300–12; esp. p. 301). If it does refer to the Jains, then there is the problem of the *stūpa* in Jainism. See P. Dundas, *The Jains* (London-New York:1992), pp. 188, 97–98; K. W. Folkert, "Jain Religious Life at Ancient Mathurā: The Heritage of Late Victorian Interpretation," in *Mathurā: The Cultural Heritage*, ed. D. M. Srinivasan (New Delhi: 1988), pp. 102–12. This will involve the further questions of the relative age and exact nature of Jain *nisidhis*. See A. N. Upadhye, "A Note on *Nisidhi* (Nisīdiya of Khāravela Inscription)," *Annals of the Bhandarkar Oriental Research Institute* 14 (1932–33): 264–66. None of this will, however, affect the basic interpretation of the passages: regardless of which religious group is being referred to, the fact remains that the compilers of the Pāli texts used the expression *bhinna-thūpa* to characterize the destruction of the central focus of a competing religious group and that group's fragmentation. There is in fact a great deal of confusion about other religious groups in "early" Buddhist literature; see, for example, C. Vogel, *The Teachings of the Six Heretics* (Abhandlungen für die Kunde des Morgenlandes, 39:4) (Wiesbaden:1970); D. Schlingloff, "Jainas and Other 'Heretics' in Buddhist Art," in *Jainism and Prakrit in Ancient and Medieval India. Essays for Prof. Jagdish Chandra Jain,* ed., N. N. Bhattacharyya (New Delhi:1994), pp. 71–82. Note, finally, that the one Sanskrit parallel to the Pāli passages that I have noticed has—as it has been reconstructed—a different reading; see V. Stache-Rosen, *Dogmatische Begriffsreihen im älteren Buddhismus II. Das Saṅgītisūtra und sein Kommentar Saṅgītiparyāya* (Berlin:1968), Teil pp. 1, 45.

25. Pāli *Vinaya* iv 192.15—see also Sekhiya 30, . . . *chabbaggiyā bhikkhū thūpikataṃ piṇḍapātaṃ paṭigaṇhanti,* which is also problematic, but ignored here in spite of its similarity.

26. T. W. Rhys Davids and H. Oldenberg, *Vinaya Texts* (The Sacred Books of the East, vol. 13) (Oxford:1885), part 1, p. 63, n. 2; Horner, *BD* iii, 130.

27. The first three variants are cited from Pāli *Vinaya* iv 374 (the only edition that is available to me), the last two from H. Matsumura, "A Lexical Note on the Vinaya Literature: *Stūpa* in the Śaikṣa Rules," *WZKS* 33 (1989): 57 (I cite this paper here and below with some hesitation since it seems that one cannot be sure whose work appears under this author's name—see Professor Bechert's postscript to K. Wille, *Die handschriftliche Überlieferung des Vinayavastu der Mūlasarvāstivādin* (Verzeichnis der orientalischen Handschriften in Deutschland. Supplementband 30) (Stuttgart:1990), pp. 173–74; this "author" has made the same sort of unacknowledged "use" of material from my Canberra dissertation: "his" paper entitled "The *Stūpa* Worship in Ancient Gilgit," *Journal of Central Asia* 8:2 (1985): 133–47, for example, is almost entirely based on texts I refer to or cite and translate in that dissertation; cf. Schopen, "The Bhaiṣajyaguru-sūtra and the Buddhism of Gilgit" (Ph.D. diss., Australian National University, 1978), pp. 148–50, 298ff., 315. The inane comments, however, are entirely his own.

28. A. Bareau, "La construction et le culte des stūpa d'après les vinayapiṭaka," *BEFEO* 50 (1960): 271.

29. A. C. Banerjee, *Two Buddhist Vinaya Texts in Sanskrit: Prātimokṣa Sūtra and Bhikṣukarmavākya* (Calcutta:1977), p. 51.10, but in light of Matsumura, *WZKS* 33 (1989): 49.

30. *So sor thar pa'i mdo*, Derge 'dul ba Ca 18b.7; *Dge slong ma'i so sor thar pa'i mdo*, Derge 'dul ba Ta 23a.5.

31. *'Dul ba rnam par 'byed pa,* Derge 'dul ba Nya 258a.4.

32. *Dge slong ma'i 'dul ba rnam par 'byed pa*, Derge 'dul ba Ta 322a.44.

33. R. Sankrityayana, ed., *Vinayasūtra of Bhadanta Gunaprabha* (Singhi Jain Śāstra Śiksāpītha. Singhi Jain Series—74) (Bombay:1981), p. 63.4; *'Dul ba'i mdo*, Derge bstan 'gyur, 'dul ba Wu 49b.2; *'Dul ba'i mdo'i rgya cher 'grel pa*, Derge bstan 'gyur, 'dul ba Yu 16b.7.

34. Bareau, *BEFEO* 50 (1960): 272.

35. There is—to use an expression he himself applies to the translation of another—a "queer translation" of this passage in Matsumura, *WZKS* 33 (1989): 49–50, where he has completely misunderstood the structure of the first part of the text.

36. So *TSD* 1755, citing *Mahāvyutpatti.*

37. Nanda and Upananda are the names of the first two monks of the group of six in *MSV*. But they are often—as here—compounded and used as a vocative at the head of an exclamation by the group of six. E. B. Cowell and R. A. Neil, *The Divyāvadāna. A Collection of Early Buddhist Legends* (Cambridge:1886), p. 682, recognize something of this ejaculatory function when they say: "Nandopananda, in exclamation (Gemini!)."

38. Compare the instructions for making "miniature" *stūpas* of the Buddha out of a lump of clay in Y. Bentor, "The Redactions of the *Adbhutadharmaparyāya* from Gilgit," *JIABS* 11.2 (1988): 21-52; esp. 40, 41ff. Although going in two different directions, and having quite different ends, the two practices appear to be based on the same sort of thinking: by making a model or miniature of the thing—whether in clay or food—one makes the thing itself.

39. *MSV*: Tog 'dul ba Ta 354b.6; GMs iii 4, 239.14 = GMsSB ii 264.14.

40. The traditions about Pūraṇa are as confused as are the traditions about other 'heretical' teachers—see *BHSD* 351 for references, and the sources cited above n. 24, end.

41. Although this is obviously only one case, it is perhaps sufficient to suggest that the relationship between the *Bhikṣu-* and *Bhikṣuṇī-vinayavibhaṅgas* in the Mūlasarvāstivādin tradition differs—at least in part—from that posited, but not yet proven, for the Pāli *Bhikkhu-* and *Bhikkhunī-vibhaṅgas;* cf O. von Hinüber, "Sprachliche Beobachtungen zum Aufbau des Pāli-Kanons," *Studien zur Indologie und Iranistik* 2 (1976): 27–40, esp. 34 [=O. von Hinüber, *Selected Papers on Pāli Studies* (Oxford:1994), 69]. But note also

that there is a Tibetan tradition, starting, it seems, with Bu-ston, that the *Bhikṣuṇī-vinaya-vibhaṅga* is not a Mūlasarvāstivādin text "(but has been taken over) from the Āgama of another sect by mistake"; C. Vogel, "Bu-ston on the Schism of the Buddhist Church and on the Doctrinal Tendencies of Buddhist Scriptures," *Zur Schulzugehörigkeit von Werken der Hīnayāna-Litertur,* Hrsg. H. Bechert (Gottingen: 1985) Erster Teil, 104–10. At this stage of our knowledge it is possible to neither confirm or deny this, however.

42. Waldschmidt, *Bruchstücke des Bhikṣuṇī-Prātimokṣa der Sarvāstivādins,* 61 (3.I.A); the references in both C. Kabilsingh, *A Comparative Study of Bhikkhunī Pāṭimokkha* (Varanasi:1984), p. 124; and Hirakawa, *Monastic Discipline for the Buddhist Nuns,* 285 n.104, seem to have gone awry.

43. *Arhat*s getting themselves into awkward situations by not focussing their mind *(asamanvāhṛtya)* before they act is something of a narrative motif in *MSV.* See GMs iii 1, 79.3ff and literature associated with it; cf. BHSD, s.v. *asamanvāhṛtya*; for a discussion of the problem in scholastic literature see P. S. Jaini, "On the Ignorance of the Arhat," in *Paths to Liberation: The Mārga and Its Transformation in Buddhist Thought,* eds. R. E. Buswell, Jr. and R. M. Gimello (Honolulu:1992), pp. 135–45. References to *stūpa*s of the hair and nails of the Buddha *(keśanakhastūpa)* are also frequent in *MSV:* GMs iii 2, 143.12; 3, 98.4; Derge 'dul ba Ta 7b.2, 137a.5, 138a.4, 157a.7, 185b.1, 293a.4, .6, etc.

44. One of the characteristics of the group of six monks and the group of twelve nuns in the *MSV* is that they—far more than other "good" monks and nuns—quote "scripture" (i.e., passages from the *vinaya*) to justify their actions or make a point (for some examples see *MSV:* Tog 'dul ba Ta 154a.2, 346b.7; GMs iii 2, 101.7; GMsSA 43.27). The obvious incongruity of this could hardly be unintentional and was almost certainly a source of some amusement for both the compilers and their readers.

45. For other texts in the *MSV* that deal with local monasteries making their own "ordinances" and some of the problems this could create see Tog 'dul ba Ta 107a.4–108a.6: 318a.1-319a.6 (that the Sanskrit being translated by *khrims su bya ba* or *khrims su bca' ba,* "to make an ordinance," was *kriyākāraṃ kṛ-* is made relatively certain by Guṇaprabha's restatement of Ta 107a.4–108a.6 at Sankrityayana, *Vinayasutra* 9.22, but with a better reading at P. V. Bapat and V. V. Gokhale, *Vinaya-Sutra and Auto-Commentary on the Same* (Patna:1982), p. 42.13). Evidence for the compilation of local monastic ordinances comes from several places. The earliest such compilation that I know was found among the third-centruy C.E. Kharoṣṭhī documents that Sir Aurel Stein recovered from Niya, Sāca, and Lou-lan (See A. M. Boyer, E. J. Rapson, and E. Senart, *Kharoṣṭhī Inscriptions. Discovered by Sir Aurel Stein in Chinese Turkestan* (Oxford:1927), part 2, p. 176 (no. 489); T. Burrow, *A Translation of the Kharoṣṭhī Documents from Chinese Turkestan* (London:1940), p. 95 (no. 489)—the document is headed *bhikhusaṃgasa kriyakara,* "regulations for the community of monks," and since only the beginning has been preserved it is impossible to know how long it was. It is likely, though now hard to tell, that a sadly fragmentary inscription from Amarāvatī that has been assigned to the fifth or sixth centuries, also contained local monastic ordinances (see R. Sewell, *Report on the Amaravati Tope and Excavations on Its Site in 1877* [London:1880], pp. 63–66). For Sri Lanka see the references to inscriptions given by N. Ratnapala, *The Katikāvatas.*

Laws of the Buddhist Order of Ceylon from the 12th Century to the 18th Century (München:1971); p. 7 ns. 13–18 (following earlier Sri Lankan usage Ratnapala calls these "Vihāra katikāvatas" as opposed to "Sāsana katikāvatas"); for Tibet see T. Ellingson, "Tibetan Monastic Constitutions: The Bca'-yig," in *Reflections on Tibetan Culture. Essays in Memory of Turrell V. Wylie,* eds., L. Epstein and R. F. Sherburne (Lewiston:1990), pp. 205–29ff.

46. See Schopen, "The Stūpa Cult and the Extant Pāli Vinaya," *JPTS* 13 (1989): 91 n. 9, end.

47. A. H. Longhurst, *The Story of the Stūpa* (Colombo:1936), p. 14; Gombrich, *JPTS* 15 (1991): 142.

48. J. Marshall, A. Foucher and N. G. Majumdar, *The Monuments of Sāñchī* (Delhi:1940), vol. 1, p. 79; vol. 3; pls. 71ff.

49. M. Bénisti, "Observations concernant le stūpa n°2 de sāñcī," *Bulletin d'études indiennes* 4 (1986): 165–70, esp. 165.

50. There is a fine old photograph of some of these *stūpa*s in H. Bechert and R. Gombrich, *The World of Buddhism: Buddhist Monks and Nuns in Society and Culture* (London:1984), p. 64 (6); for the inscriptions and dates see Schopen, *JIABS* 14:2 (1991): 293–94.

51. For what might be another case of the adaptation of a canonical *vinaya* text to local architectural traditions, see Schopen, "The Monastic Ownership of Servants or Slaves: Local and Legal Factors in the Redactional History of Two Vinayas," *JIABS* 17:2 (1994): 145–73.

52. *DPPN* i 368.

53. For Moliya-Phagguna see *DPPN* ii 674 and in particular *Majjhima* i 122 ff; for Mūlaphalguna *BHSD* 437 (Edgerton says of him: "evidently same as Pali Moliya-Phagguna; like him a friend of the nuns:); in the *Cīvaravastu* (GMs iii 2, 143.15), where the "group of twelve" is explicitly mentioned in association with him, the name is translated by *khrums stod.*

54. *DPPN* i 418–21.

55. *BHSD* 125; also the passages cited and summarized in J. L. Panglung, *Die Erzählstoffe des Mūlasarvāstivāda-Vinaya. Analysiert auf Grund der tibetischen Übersetzung* (Tokyo:1981), pp. 123, 140, 159–60, 193; Ét. Lamotte, *Le traité de la grand vertu de sagesse* (Louvain:1949) T. II, 634–36, 844–46; in the *MSV Bhikṣuṇī vinayavibhaṅga* she is declared to be the foremost of those possessed of miraculous power (Derge 'dul ba Ta 295a.5); she may be, finally, the only nun clearly identifiable, or even visible, in early Buddhist art (see the good photograph of a "panel" from Swat illustrating "The Buddha's Descent at Sankissa," in V. Dehejia, "Aniconism and the Multivalence of Emblems," *Ars Orientalis* 21 (1991): 563, fig. 9.

56. Schopen, *JIP* 22 (1994): 31–80.

57. Though it is not formally parallel, the text at *MSV:* GMs iii 2, 49.1-51.6 in which the Buddha prescribes a distinct and identifiable form of robe to distinguish Buddhist monks from members of other religious groups seems to be addressing at least a part of the same issue that our text may be. That text says that it was the usual practice of Bimbisāra to dismount from his elephant whenever he saw a monk or nun and to venerate their feet. Once he did this in view of others to an Ājīvaka that he mistook for a Buddhist monk, much to the consternation *(sandigdhamanas)* of devout Buddhists. When this is reported to the Buddha he points out that the problem here is that the Ājīvaka "appropriated as his own the veneration intended for one who had seen the truths" *(dṛṣṭasatyasyāntikād vandanā svīkṛteti).* However, in neither case do the texts indicate that there was a conscious deception: the Ājīvaka did not claim to be a Buddhist, nor did the nuns of the group of twelve present their *stūpa* as a *stūpa* of the Buddha. But in both cases similarity provided an opportunity for confusion and the 'misdirection' of veneration.

58. For the *sapiṇḍa* especially see D. M. Knipe, "Sapiṇḍīkaraṇa: The Hindu Rite of Entry into Heaven," in *Religious Encounters with Death: Insights from the History and Anthropology of Religions,* eds., F. E. Reynolds and E. H. Waugh (University Park and London:1977), 111–24. It is worth noting that the compilers of *MSV* were well aware of Brahmanic funeral practices; see Tog 'dul ba Ta 377a.2ff that refers to two sons performing *śrāddha (shid btang ba)* for their deceased father, and GMsSB ii 34.14ff that refers to the giving of five *piṇḍa*s at the site of the cremation of a dead relative *(pañca piṇḍān datvā*—this text is also of interest because it contains what may be a very early [comparatively] reference to depositing the postcremational bones in the Ganges: *asthīnāṃ bhasmanāṃ ca karparakaṃ pūrayitvā gaṇgāyāṃ prakṣipya. . . .).*

59. Bareau, *BEFEO* 50 (1960): 269. For the archaeological and epigraphical evidence see Schopen, "Burial 'ad sanctos' and the Physical Presence of the Buddha in Early Indian Buddhism: A Study in the Archeology of Religions," *Religion* 17 (1987): 193–225.

60. See Schopen, *JIABS* 14:2 (1991): 281–329, esp. 299–301.

61. There is also evidence that Indian Buddhist images, like *stūpa*s could both live and, significantly, die; see Schopen, "The Buddha as an Owner of Property and Permanent Resident in Medieval Indian Monasteries," *JIP* 18 (1990): 181–217, esp. 203; "dead" *sūtra*s and other texts were also handled like "dead" Buddhas; see, for example, A. F. R. Hoernle, *Manuscript Remains of Buddhist Literature found in Eastern Turkestan* (Oxford:1916), p. 1ff.

62. Matsumura, *WZKS* 33 (1989): 59. The idea or assumption of an *ur* text has probably nowhere been more influential than in studies of the *prātimokṣas* where virtually all the energies have been directed toward finding a hypothetical "original" of the various rules. This has frequently been done by forcing disparate versions together and rejecting those that cannot be so forced as "late" or "corrupt." The whole procedure is in need of reappraisal and may be particularly unsuitable for the *Sekhiya/Saikṣa* rules. The latter are frequently described as the most "disparate" or "divergent," but this is only a negative and misleading way of saying that it is in these rules that the individual Orders express and define themselves most individually. This, I should think, would make them not less, but more valuable. Matsumura's argument—insofar as he has one—is very

much of the *ur* variety. He tries to force a good deal of material together that probably should not be and in doing so ignores or questions what would otherwise appear to be clear.

63. See, for example, Sylvain Lévi, "Observations sur une langue precanonique du bouddhisme," *JA* (1912): 495–514, esp. 510.

64. Cf. some of the cases in D. Schlingloff, "Zur Interpretation des Prātimokṣa-sūtra," *Zeitschrift der Deutschen Morgenländischen Gesellschaft* 113:3 (1964): 536–51.

65. Matsumura, *WZKS* 33 (1989) 72-73 cites both. The more sure of the two reads: *na stūpākāraṃ piṇḍapātaṃ paribhokṣyāma iti.* He says that "the meaning of the whole sentence is not very intelligible," but it seems to me to be perfectly straightforward: "we will not eat alms food having the shape of a *stūpa.*" He also says that the Chinese translation of the Kāśyapīya *Prātimokṣa* gives the rule as "not to eat making a shape of [a] tope." The Mūlasarvāstivādin understanding of the rule is, therefore, not an isolated one. (Incidentally, the Chinese translations "like a well" that he cites might be accounted for by a confusion somewhere in the transmission that transformed *stūpākāra* into *kūpākāra.*).

66. For the death of Śāriputra see *MSV:* Tog 'dul ba Ta 354a.5-368a.5 (Schopen, *JIP* 22 (1994): 45–56; Schopen, in *Buddhism in Practice,* pp. 491–94); for Kāśyapa, Tog 'dul ba Tha 463b.4–465b.7 (J. Przyluski, "Le nord-ouest de l'inde dans le vinaya des mūlasarvāstivādin et les textes apparentés," *JA* (1914): 522–28, from the Chinese); for Ānanda, Tog 'dul ba Tha 467b.2-470b.7 (Przyluski, *JA* (1914): 529–35); for Mahāprajāpatī, Tog 'dul ba Ta 167a.6-172b.3—Walters, *History of Religions,* 33.4 (1994), pp. 358ff. makes an interesting argument to the effect that at least in the *Apadāna* Mahāprajāpatī is being presented as "the female counterpart of Buddha" or "the Buddha's counterpart." If that is the case then it is particularly interesting that the equation is not complete in at least one significant way: neither in the *Apadāna* nor elsewhere in canonical literature, in so far as I know, is there any reference to a *stūpa* for Mahāprajāpatī. (The text Walters is referring to is now available in translation: J. S. Walters, "Gotamī's Story," in *Buddhism in Practice,* pp. 113–38; it gives evidence of some possible contact with the *MSV* text, especially in regard to the "sneezing" incident that in both occasions Mahāprajāpatī's decision to enter *parinirvāṇa*—Walters fudges his translation here by rendering *vandiya* and *vandasi* as "bless" and misses the fact that this is a rebuke of Mahāprajāpatī similar to the one addressed to the trees that drop their flowers on the Buddha in the Pāli version of the *Mahāparinirvāṇa-sūtra* (V.3). The absence of any reference to *stūpa*s for women "saints" is also noticeable in, and creates some problems for, the interesting study of R. A. Ray, *Buddhist Saints in India. A Study in Buddhist Values and Orientations* (New York-Oxford:1994).

67. Bareau, *BEFEO* 50 (1960): 253. Also, among many other possibilities, see L. de la Vallée Poussin, "À propos du Cittaviśuddhiprakaraṇa d'Āryadeva," *Bulletin of the School of Oriental Studies* 6:2 (1931): 412 where he says in regard to the destruction of a *stūpa:* "On sait que ce sacrilège est un des cinq *upānantaryas,* un des cinq péchés quasi mortels: c'est détruire le corps même du Bouddha."

68. Schopen, *JIP* 22 (1994): 68.

69. I hasten to add, though, that much remains to be seen. The accounts treated here are drawn from only two *vinayas,* the Pāli (often said to be the earliest) and the Mūlasarvāstivādin (equally often said to be the latest). But the chances of there being similar or related accounts in other *vinayas* is very good. In fact, J. Silk refers to what seems to be just such an account in the Dharmaguptaka Vinaya (T.1428 (XXII) 766c 3–10—Silk, "Further Remarks on *yogācāra bhikṣu,*" in *Dharmadūta. Mélanges offerts au Vénérable Thích Huyên-Vi*, ed. Bh. T. Dhammaratana and Bh. Pāsādika (Paris: 1997) 244.

7

A Funeral to Part with the Living: A Tamil Countersorcery Ritual[1]

Isabelle Nabokov

In the Tamil village where I conducted ethnographic fieldwork in 1990–91, as soon as a death occurred the women of the household huddled on the ground near the feet of the corpse and began their ritual lamentations. Almost immediately, the local troupe of untouchable (Paṟaiyar) musicians arrived from their compound to beat the funeral drums. This communicated to all within a radius of six kilometers that, as one man once told me, "we must prepare to lose a relationship." What followed then was indeed the ritualized removal of the dead from society, a polluting task that fell on the untouchables and other low-caste mortuary specialists of the village, such as the barber and the washerman.

In this chapter I present the ritual that is performed in response to the inauspicious signal of these drums. But I will be concerned with no ordinary funeral; the "removal" described here is enacted by folk healers to counter sorcery spells. Although the drums are not literally played, they still resound in a metaphoric sense, for one of the Tamil glosses for sorcery is the word *cahaṭai,* which designates the largest of the funeral drums played by untouchables at death.[2] Like that mortuary instrument, sorcery in Tamilnadu also alerts everyone about a sort of death, about the unleashing of mystical, evil forces that deliberately aim to harm or even eliminate another person. And even if victims are not physically killed, they are nonetheless intended by their injurers to be socially dead. Much like at a "real" death, therefore, this kind of symbolic annihilation requires the performance of a funeral.

Anthropologists have long observed that funeral rituals, and particularly Hindu funerals, are encoded with symbolism of regeneration.[3] All have noted the two phases to the mortuary rituals: disaggregation (represented by the temporary disposal of the corpse) followed by reinstallation (represented by subsequent rites), when the deceased and the living overcome the finality of death.[4] So it seems fitting that the Tamil counter-sorcery rite would co-opt funeral symbolism to neutralize deadly spells. But my documentation of some thirty-six countersorcery rituals in the South Arcot district suggests that, paradoxically, in this context the resumption of life is facilitated not through the enactment of the second or regenerative phase of the Tamil mortuary cycle. Instead it is actually effected through the first set of procedures, as indicated by the fact that this ritual is termed removal (*kaḻippu*). In what follows we will see how this "removal" works to cure the living.

Tamil Sorcery

I must begin by explaining how this topic of South Indian sorcery has gone virtually undocumented in the region's ethnography.[5] The scant scholarship may not be surprising for the reason that, as the Reverend Carl Gustave Diehl already noted in 1956, such practices in Tamilnadu evoke widespread feelings of "disgust and hatred."[6] And so, much as John Beattie observed among the Bunyoros, "the less it is spoken of the better," which may also explain why, in Tamilnadu, drums do what voices should not.[7]

Indeed, in fourteen months of fieldwork I never heard anyone admitting that he or she had paid a sorcerer to harm anyone else, never witnessed the execution of a sorcery spell, nor met a sorcerer (*mantiravāti,* "one who says mantras"). Yet, despite the fact that any "sorcerer" was always somebody else, that spells appeared to be wholly imaginary, and that feelings of disbelief, fear, and abhorrence surrounded the entire subject, I learned that sorcery verdicts constituted approximately a third of the divining seances that male practitioners, known in Tamil as *cāmi*s, held on a regular basis. I also observed that these *cāmi*s performed countersorcery rituals on an impressive scale, and I tried to learn why.

The term *cāmi* is a contraction of the Sanskrit word *swami* that literally means "God." By extension the term can be used to refer to, and address, most categories of religious men one might encounter in Tamilnadu: the priests (*pūcāri*s) who preside over the daily worship or *pūcā* of temple deities, the holy men (*samnyasis*) who renounce society, the so-called "god-dancers" (*cāmiyāṭis*) who embody and dance *(āṭu)* a deity at major temple festivals. What distinguishes the specialists who are empowered to diagnose and cure sorcery from both orthodox priests of major Hindu temples and the ceremonial "god-dancers" is that they have not been handed down their religious role by institutional means, such as inheritance through the male line.[8] And unlike the renouncers, these practitioners rarely choose to embrace a spiritual path. Rather, the six *cāmi*s I worked with in the South Arcot district told me that they had been forcibly initiated by various South Indian goddesses, all of whom are known under the generic term Amma or "mother," through a life-changing dream *(kaṉavu)* or through what was usually called *taricanam (darśan)*, or vision, in times of deep personal crises or severe illness. This is how, for instance, Suresh, a fifty-year-old member of the *Tēnpaḷḷi* caste, was instructed in his new calling, back in 1973:

> I was plowing my field when something cut my foot. It began to swell up. Like a trident it pierced my foot, but I did not see the trident. This was the first time that Ammā came. She came as a trident and pierced my leg. For a month I was sick and unable to eat properly. I did not know what was happening to me until Ammā came in my dream and told me, "I am with you. Don't worry, you need not to seek any treatment. I will protect you. Through you I will decode the signs *(kuṟi collutal)*. You must do good things for people."

After he experienced this dream Suresh recovered from his infection, and from then on he began to receive regular visitations from the goddess. As Suresh explained to me, she "came on me," by which he meant that the Goddess possessed him. Within a few weeks he learned to control the timing of his trances by beating a drum and singing her praises and to "interpret the signs" that are beyond human knowledge. Word of his new powers spread throughout the neighboring villages, and the needy and curious came to test the accuracy of his predictions and the efficacy of his therapeutic treatments. As his spiritual reputation grew, he built a small sanctuary roofed with palm leaves for his goddess who was named Kaṉṉiyammā (Virgin Lady). In this simple shrine located next to the field where Ammā cut his foot, he had presided for more than fifteen years over the worship of this goddess, entering states of trance whenever clients arrived for consultation.[9]

It was at such homemade sanctuaries that I observed other *cāmi*s, like Suresh, also informing their petitioners on a regular basis that they suffered from what is known in Tamil as *ēval*. This word glosses as "command" and implied that someone was under the control of a sorcery spell. Over time I came to learn that this extraordinary act of aggression always required three participants.

First, it involved a sorcerer whose name was never disclosed but whose practices were common knowledge to specialists like Suresh whose counter-sorcery rites were premised upon them. To cast his "command," this sorcerer was believed to have shaped little effigies in the form of his targeted victims. To activate these figures with a human lifeforce *(uyir)*, he dotted their bodies, especially the eyes, with a black substance *(mai)* said to be concocted from the boiled and charred skulls of firstborn sons.[10] Observing the proper ritual precautions of austerity, avoidance of pollution and other procedures, the sorcerer next directed his "commands" to these effigies in order to damage his victim's ability to move, speak, and reproduce.[11] These spells were specific: there was *tampaṉam*, the spell that "paralyzed": *vāy kaṭṭu,* the spell that "tied the mouth";

pētaham, the command that brought marital divorce, or *māraṇam,* which could actually kill.[12]

The second agency involved in sorcery were specific supernatural beings. More than activating impersonal forces, in the mind of the *cāmi*s, the real expertise of the sorcerer lay in his ability to recruit demons, known in Tamil as *pēy*s. This term derives from the Sanskrit *preta,* meaning "departed," and usually characterizes the spirits of people who are barred from transiting into the hereafter because they have met an untimely *(ahālamaraṇam)* death.[13] Rather than being ordinary victims of this inauspicious *(turmaraṇam)* fate, most of these sorcery demons were what Gananath Obeyesekere calls, in reference to the Sinhalese *yakas*-demons, "named beings in the pantheon, with fairly clear-cut identities and myths of origin."[14] All were said to enforce the sorcerer's spells by casting negative glances or the evil eye (*kaṇ dristi*) which infused recipients with fear *(payam)*, an emotional reaction that in South Asia can strip the self from protection against malevolent or "commanding" forces.[15]

Finally, sorcery in Tamilnadu incriminated a third participant, the alleged person or persons who deliberately ordered and paid for the sorcerer's spell. In the public ritual of divination, these personal enemies were never identified by the *cāmi*s and their victims were the only ones who could answer the crucial question: "Who did it?"

To my consultants, however, sorcery spells were not the result of unprovoked malice. They suspected persons whom they had in some way wronged or given some good cause for resentment. One *cāmi* put it succinctly when he told me: "The person who orders the sorcery is like a plaintiff *(vāti)*; he holds a grudge *(kuṟai)*. The person who suffers the sorcery is like a defendant *(pirativāti)*; he has caused the grievance of his injurer." When I asked why these "plaintiffs" and "defendants" did not seek legal redress, he replied, "They are not conflicts that the Panchayat [the local adjudicative counsel] can solve." For at stake here were dramas and conflicts between blood kin, in-laws, lovers, and cowives that often revolved around contradictions between moral norms of kinship behavior and individualistic conduct, rather than legal codes. Alleged victims had behaved selfishly, reneging, for example, on a financial obligation with relatives, or a marriage transaction. Since money, property, and business were often the cause of the dispute, it was not surprising that males—and particularly well-off, urban men—were the prominent "plaintiffs" and "defendants" in this discourse.[16]

To the extent that alleged victims and injurers were entangled in some hostile relationship that could not be redressed by customary legal channels, my research seems to confirm the argument made by Africanists in the 1950s and 1960s, that sorcery (or witchcraft) allegations serve to fill gaps of the legal order.[17] But all indications also suggest that Tamil sorcery is more than a kind of self-help adjudication by those who have no other avenue for redress. For these "plaintiffs" the idea of justice is to disempower and suppress those who failed to behave according to their expectations. We should not forget that the key characteristic of sorcery victimization is powerlessness over the self and that spells can kill. If they are to stop this degenerative process and regain their capacity for independent action in the world victims must take remedial action by mounting a counterattack in a private, secret ritual.[18]

The Kaḻippu Ritual

All of the thirty-six countersorcery rites that I observed, performed by at least five different exorcists, were invariably carried out on new or full moon nights by the same specialists *(cāmis)* who had delivered the diagnoses of sorcery in the first place. In their minds the rituals that I am about to describe were considered counterattacks on an opposing sorcerer. To neutralize his spells they had to strike back in precisely the same manner that he had operated.[19]

The procedure to counteract an evil "command" is glossed in Tamil as *kaḻippu*, which means "removal," "casting out," or "rejection."[20] This word also commonly describes rites regularly performed in households to ward off "evil eyes." In that domestic context circular motions draw the malevolence into absorbing and purifying substances that either leave no residue, such as a camphor lump that is lit outside the home, or that can be discarded, like cooked rice.[21] As we will soon see, the same logic underlies the countersorcery rite and this makes sense, for sorcery victims have been likewise incapacitated by visual means, only ensnared in the gaze of sorcery demons rather than by envious neighbors.

However, their visual assaults do require a more elaborate intervention due to the fact that human "eye-focused" malevolences are often considered involuntary without a conscious capacity to harm, a sort of "witching" power, if you will, whereas the demons are focused on doing ill. Moreover, the effects of the human-cast "evil eye" are relatively benign and may be neutralized without the help of specialists while demonic gazes can kill and their "removal" entails a complex rite and irrevocable separation from the alleged injurer.

To begin the *kaḻippu* ritual, at exactly midnight, the same hour when the original spell was cast, the *cāmis* duplicated the small effigies *(pāvai)* that the sorcerer was believed to have shaped. As each "command" was a personalized attack, requiring customized counterprocedures, the seven-inch effigies were fashioned out of the identical ingredients—rice or wheat dough, dung, clay, or ashes from funeral grounds. Each was also encoded with the distinctive iconographic features believed to be applied by the original sorcerer. But most had protruding tongues rouged with red vermillion powder, bulging eyes, and oversize sexual organs.

Through these little visualizations of the invisible powers that "commanded" and "blinded" them, victims could begin to separate themselves from them. Symbolism for this separation was also encoded into the very crafting of the effigies, many of whom were placed on their backs in a winnowing fan known in Tamil as *muṟam* or in a pot with limbs stretched over the rim. Used daily to sort grain from chaff, these fans can be construed as markers of differentiation between "pure" and "impure." Elsewhere in India, anthropologists have noted that at rituals the winnowing fan specifically denotes what Christopher J. Fuller calls "the separation out of polluting and inauspicious elements that can then be cast away."[22] During Tamil funeral processions for caste Hindus, I also observed village washermen carry such a fan in order to signify, as one such specialist told me, that the living wanted no more to do with the polluting corpse. In the healing context of antisorcery rites, the fan underscored the desired dissociation between the afflicted and the healthy self.

The healers completed the effigies by dotting them with charcoal paste to open the eyes *(kaṇ tiṟappu)* and to bestow life *(uyir)* on them, another hint of the link between sight and vitality. After this activating process—known in Tamil as *ceyviṉai*[23] *ceytal*—the healers could now destroy the icons of affliction to which they had just given birth.

With yellow turmeric powder they drew an "enclosure," or *cakkaram,* around the patients, symbolically circumscribing the malevolent forces and preventing their escape.[24] Then they proceeded with their symbolic funeral.

First, uncooked rice was poured into a cloth stretched above the effigy, which the victim then "fed" to the doll. At normal death rites, this ritual action is performed by living kin on behalf of their dead. Prior to any formal procession to the cremation grounds, a towel stretched above the corpse is filled with what is called in Tamil *vāykkarici* (literally, "mouth rice"). Each holding a handful of this rice, consanguineal and affinal kin circumambulate the corpse and "feed" it. "At times of separation," one female consultant said of this moment, "one always gives uncooked rice."

At exorcisms, however, the cloth was dropped, enshrouding the doll, whereupon a rupee coin was often tied into one end and abruptly ripped off at the knot. This also seemed to derive from funeral symbolism. At a real death, the village barber tears the knot *(muṭittuṇṭu)* which contains the rupee coin just before cremations or burials (there are ≃ 40 rupees to a dollar). As one of them explained to me: "At birth the God Brahmā gives man a knot, the umbilical cord. On the last day of life that knot must be removed. In doing so the dead person's relationships are torn apart."

The following phase of the *kaḻippu* ritual was even more suggestive. Water was poured in a new clay pot bought by the client's family and carried on the right shoulder around the effigy, clockwise, three times. But before the first circuit, the healer punched a small hole in the pot so that water dripped out. By the end of the third round, the pot was empty. Then the clients were told to smash it on the ground.

Here, too, at Hindu funeral rites there is what is called in Tamil, the breaking of the trickling pot *(kalikuṭam uṭaittal)*.[25] At death it is the chief mourner, the son, who concludes his three circumambulations by breaking the pot. Again, a village barber, whose ceremonial role was to perforate the vessel, shed some light; "At birth we come out of a pot, our mother's womb. The breaking of this pot symbolizes the end of life." In the real funeral context, this segment preceded the internment or cremation and climaxed the ceremony. Here it seemed the same, for healers now set the cloth covering the effigy on fire while its "victims" stared intensely at the flames.

Finally, the healers invited their patients to take an active part in destroying the evil forces, to work their own way to recovery. For now they handed them metal nails that they inserted into the doll's arms and legs.

At this point the *ka<u>l</u>ippu* ritual was essentially over. The doll was officially "dead;" the spell was neutralized. Healers lit a small lamp near the crucified effigy, which likewise was reminiscent of funeral practices. For once a human death has occurred, an oil lamp burns for sixteen days until all ceremonial arrangements have been completed to assure the soul a successful journey to the afterworld.

Still to be performed, however, was the finale. In Sinhalese sorcery rituals, according to Gananath Obeyesekere, this "is generally achieved by cutting some object."[26] Here, too, the Tamil exorcists had their patients crush limes in the northeast corner of the ritual enclosure. Lighting a lump of camphor on a pumpkin, they had them smash it on the ground and chop the broken pieces with a large knife.

In Tamil ritual symbolism, limes and pumpkins are common deflectors of inauspicious influences. Crushing pumpkins customarily concludes "beginning" rites such as consecrations for new houses, while stamping on limes is associated with blessing newly purchased vehicles, such as bicycles and rickshas. Here these rites seemed to protect the recovery of victims' capacity for action and mobility, since the healer immediately ordered them to hop over the winnowing tray three times.

Close to dawn the healers collected the used or "dead" effigies and proceeded to the nearby riverbank. Because they insisted that only men join this expedition, I never saw what happened. But one *cāmi* told me that near the water he enclosed them in another circle drawn on the ground with rice flour. "This *cakkaram*," he said, "was a form of arrest. It meant to say, 'do not come back'!" Then he pulled together some brush to cremate all of them.

Interpretations of the Funeral Symbolism

We have seen how the Tamil countersorcery ritual is saturated with funeral symbolism, which is consistent with W. T. Elmore's description of one "method of exorcism" he observed in 1913 from the adjacent state of Andhra Pradesh in which an "image of dough" was placed in a pot that was then interred in the funeral grounds with the "usual burying ceremonies."[27] But it is important to note that these contemporary, Tamil "removals," at least, do not actually incorporate all of the "usual burying ceremonies." They seem to skip rites that are integral to a "real" funeral in the South Arcot District, and once we examine what is left out we begin to understand how this funeral symbolism works.

First, the *kaḻippu* sorcery rite differs from a usual funeral by the conspicuous absence of formalized mourning. As previously recounted, as soon as a death occurs the women of the household huddle in arm-linked clusters on the ground near the feet of the corpse and sway, moan, weep, beat their chests, and drawl laments, a genre called *oppāri,* meaning "comparison." By means of metaphors and hyperboles they commemorate the dead as the prototype of the ideal kin and deplore his or her absence.

Second, the *kaḻippu* ritual also suppresses other representations of the social order that are constitutive of a "real" funeral. Male lineage members *(paṅkali)* do not observe strict pollution taboos, grandchildren do not ceremonially circumambulate around the corpse while holding a torch *(neypantam)*, in-laws do not make ceremonial prestations *(varicai)*, and the victim himself, rather than the son or a close lineage member, performs "the breaking of the trickling pot." It is as if the individual whose "funeral" is underway had been a complete stranger, with no social identity, no kinship role, indeed no kin at all.

What is additionally striking, almost shocking, about the "funeral" is that it pays no attention to the fate of the soul. This is in sharp contrast with the prototypical Hindu funeral—after the disposal of the polluting corpse, there is a second, crucial ceremony, known in Tamil as *karumāti*, which dispatches the departed *(preta)* to the hereafter as an honored ancestor *(pir)*.[28] All preoccupation with reincorporating the deceased into the extended kinship web of ancestors, which for scholars such as David M. Knipe constitutes the hallmark of Hinduism, is entirely missing.[29] The funeral that begins with no emotional "comparison," no public display from the living kinship community, simply ends with a crude cremation or, as Elmore noted, with a burial.[30]

From beginning to end the living remain unmoved and unaffected, appropriating from the symbols of an ordinary funeral only that sequence of actions that are strictly necessary for the disposal of a corpse. The healers only manipulate those mortuary symbols and rites that connote the sifting of impurity (the winnowing fan) and separation from the living collectivity ("the feeding of the corpse," "the tying of the knot," and "the breaking of the trickling pot"). Our question, then, is what exactly does this funeral "remove"? In searching for an answer we must reexamine the key symbols of this ritual and especially the effigies themselves, for we should not forget that it is the dolls that actually undergo the death rites.

These little figures are encoded with distinctive features but share a common appearance. All look avaricious (tongues out), shameless (oversize sexual organs), and scary (bulging eyes). Save for their diminutive size, their iconography is typical of the large horizontal effigies that are sculpted in certain ceremonial occasions in the South Arcot District.[31] These earthen, anthropomorphic figures often represent demonic characters that threaten the moral and physical order of the social or cosmic world and are imparted with life for the sole purpose of being destroyed or cremated. This is particularly indicated by the fact that their heads, just like that of corpses at funeral rites, generally face south, the realm of Yama, God of death.

Such symbolism suggests that the little effigies fashioned and cremated by sorcery healers also stand for the demons recruited by the sorcerer, and some exorcists clearly modeled their healing dolls after such powers. There was the demon, Varāki, with her distended belly and streaming hair, who made her victims' bodies swell; the demon Kutti Caittān (small Satan) holding his characteristic fork; a Christian demon, who, one healer claimed, killed "whomever the sorcerer ordered him to do," and the evil Kāṭṭēri, who was known to vent her frustrated maternal instincts by snatching unborn babies and infants, and was often depicted as holding the decapitated head of a baby in her hand.[32]

Indicating that the funeral worked to "remove" such malevolent powers, the iconography also fits in with general understandings of these demons. In Tamil cosmology demons are beings who have perished either before marriage or childbirth and hence have no direct descendants who can properly perform the funeral ceremonies that normally send off the dead to the hereafter.[33] Thus it would appear that Elmore was not mistaken when he understood back in 1913 that "the demon has been left buried," for such ritual action would constitute one sure way to banish these untimely dead from this world where they can trouble the living through recruitment by a sorcerer.[34]

That this "funeral" was really an exorcism of malevolent forces was clear to one woman who had undergone the *kaḻippu* ritual. But for her the injurer was not any demon but her "husband," whom she suspected of using sorcery against her. This was her reply when I asked about her participation in what paradoxically looked to me like a funeral that healed: "You ask why I did that death ceremony? I already told you, to break with my 'husband.' I want nothing more to do with him." She needed no decoding of symbols to tell her that this had been a funeral; she had no doubt that its purpose was the ritualized "death" of her living relationship with this "husband," who, I found out, had actually never married her and had returned to his legal wife right after this woman had given birth to their fourth child.

To eradicate these self-negations she had enacted the only ritual that could provide meaningful closure.[35] The "funeral" gave her permission to initiate retroactively an end to a relationship that her lover had already denied her. What was so interesting, however, was that to effect this separation she had actually participated in a rite that in social reality no Tamil woman in the South Arcot District would ever be allowed to perform or even witness. For at real funerals, under no circumstance can a woman ever break the "trickling pot" or watch a cremation.[36] Female mourners are even prohibited from entering the funeral grounds and must remain within the family threshold where, as we have seen, their collective mourning communicates acute feelings of sorrow over the death.[37] For her part, this woman had sat alone in the middle of a circle where, instead of wailing or evoking happier times, she had taken on the emotional and ritual posture of a male mourner. With no dramatic display of bereavement, she had coolly officiated over her "husband's" "removal" from her life.

Similar interpretations emerged from my conversation with another participant, the son of a village schoolteacher. Like the woman whom I have quoted, this young man did not consider himself victimized by any cosmological demon. In fact, he did not even believe he had been targeted by sorcery in the first place. This is what he told me the morning after his *kaḻippu*, the second he had undergone in the last five years: "I did the *kaḻippu* not because a sorcerer placed a spell on me. He did not. Not because there was a demon on me. There was none. I did the *kaḻippu* because I was getting crazy. I read too much, I think too much. I needed to forget, to let go *(pōnaviṭa)* of my thoughts. That's all."

From these accounts it would appear that this facsimile of a "funeral" functioned more as a kind of extractive surgery to "remove" the source of the affliction—be it a demon, a former lover, or a self-absorbing mind. However, it is interesting to note that this was not at all how the healer who performed the *kaḻippu* ritual on behalf of the woman whom I just quoted "read" its symbolism:

> That woman was seriously sick. She almost died. The *kaḻippu* was her last chance to come back to life. The goddess restored her life. . . . She is coming back to us. . . . She is like a new born. Because she died we had to perform her funeral and give the things required for a death ritual. . . . *The doll was a representation of the lady*. . . . This ritual was not dangerous for her. On the contrary, it brought her relief and a new life. . . The main message to the lady was "forget about your past! it is dead now, you are entering a new life where things will be better."

This specialist made it crystal clear that his ritual actions were not merely concerned with exorcising any demon, former lover, or other "commanding" force. Quite to the contrary, in his mind he had facilitated his patient's reincarnation, destroying her old life almost literally and "reconceiving" her into profoundly altered, and hopefully improved conditions of existence. Rather than strictly performing a healing rite, he had carried out what anthropologists call "a rite of passage," a "twice-born" experience that "moves" a person into a second life entirely dissimilar from the first.[38]

In this respect the healer's understanding was actually consistent with scholarly interpretations of the deeper, metaphysical basis of Brahmanic and Hindu death rites. The French Indologist, Charles Malamoud, for instance, argues that the old, Brahmanic funeral rite was "the *saṃskāra* par excellence"; this term, he explains, literally means perfecting *(perfectionnement)*, and designates rites of passage which, in the Brahmanical tradition, initiated individuals into new and better ontological states.[39] Other writers have confirmed that in modern ethnographic contexts, the "timely" death still constitutes the truest Hindu *saṃskāra*.[40] The healer's exegesis also confirmed Margaret Trawick's recent argument that four of the main Tamil healing systems are rooted in the "idea . . . that there cannot be birth without death."[41]

Yet when I replayed this man's tape-recorded response I realized its discrepancy with his actual procedures. True, he had accomplished three successive transformations: birth, death, and rebirth, but he had not exactly manipulated the symbolism of mortuary rites to predicate and effect the final transformation. First he had acted as creator by giving life to the effigy, which for him represented the victim because that was what it had stood for in the hands of the sorcerer. Then he had acted in the guise of a funeral specialist, officiating over the death of the afflicted self. And third, he had acted as midwife for his patient's rebirth.

But at this point the procedures that enacted this rebirth were no longer borrowed from mortuary rites. He gave patients the means (e.g. the nails) to commit an act of violence or personal revenge that would never figure at an ordinary funeral. Afterward, he invited them to inaugurate their recovery of personal freedom through a sequence of crushing, smashing, and slicing acts, which are constitutive of rites of consecration.

Now I understood that for all of his emphatic denials, this healer nonetheless had facilitated a kind of "removal." Not that he assisted in the elimination of enemies, but he had furthered a deathlike separation from the self. For the rebirth that he extended to his clients was premised on the repudiation of past experiences, on the irrevocable banishment of relationships that were constitutive of their former identities.[42]

Conclusion

Many scholars have noted how the Hindu funeral and its Brahmanic antecedents sought to obliterate not just the physical remains of the dead but their personal characteristics and biographies as well. Malamoud, for example, described the old Brahmanic crematory ritual as a "rite of suppression of the deceased's worldly person."[43] Jonathan P. Parry has documented how such representations still prevailed in contemporary Banares; as he writes, "No place is made in the mortuary rites for a celebration of [the dead's] individual achievements; no eulogies are delivered in praise of his particular virtues, and no recognition is given to the passing of a unique life."[44] The "usual" Tamil funeral also attempts to efface the individuality of the dead.[45] What is ceremonially lamented is an idealized and somewhat stereotypical relative, what is officially commemorated is a member of a kin group, and what is ritually preserved is an ancestor.

So when a facsimile of this funeral is performed without the context of kinship, it truly abolishes all that the person once was. For participants who feel victimized by sorcery, this replica of the imputed sorcery attack is thus the perfect means to erase injurers from social life and collective memory. Now they activate the funeral drum for people who in point of fact are not dead, expelling these enemies from their lives for good.

But this symbolic funeral may also attract those who are not victims of sorcery. In Hindu culture there are precedents for such transformative or "perfective" functions, as Valentine Daniel reports that prior to their yearly pilgrimage to Sabari Malai, male devotees of the God Ayyappan undergo "a miniature death ritual."[46] The prototypical Hindu renouncer *(saṃnyāsin)* is similarly said to perform his own funeral service at the time of his initiation.[47]

As far as I know, the countersorcery ritual did not secure temporary mergence with God or permanent deliverance *(mokṣa)* from the cycle of rebirths. On the contrary, for the healer I worked with it allowed participants to be reborn into the social world within their lifetime. But as in the case of the spiritual benefits obtained by pilgrims and renouncers, the pursuit of a revitalized existence was made possible by the obliteration of former identities and past actions. Much like the dead who undergo a real funeral, one did emerge "newly born" from the *kaḻippu* ritual, with no biography, no sense of continuity with the past, and no personal memories. The resumption of life that it facilitated was truly premised on "removal"—of both injurious others and the injured self.

Notes

1. Research for this chapter was conducted in Tamilnadu from August 1990 throughout October 1991. It was supported by a Junior fellowship from the American Institute of Indian Studies, in Chicago, to which I express my gratitude. It summarizes arguments presented in chapter 3 and 4 of my book (*Religion Against the Self: An Ethnography of Tamil Rituals*, Oxford University Press, 2000) and my article ("Deadly Power: A Funeral to Counter Sorcery in South India." *American Ethnologist* 27.1 (2000): 147–168). An earlier version of this chapter was presented at the 1994 annual meeting of the American Academy of Religion in Chicago.

2. There are two other Tamil glosses for sorcery. The first is *māntirīkam,* which the Reverend Carl Gustav Diehl translated as "that which has to do with Mantras." See Diehl, *Instrument and Purpose: Studies on Rites and Rituals in South India* (Lund: CWK Gleerup, 1956), p. 267. Mantras are syllables, words, formulas, names, curses, prayers, invocations, or songs that when properly uttered create power. See Andre Padoux, "Mantras—What Are They?" in *Mantra,* ed. Harvey P. Alper (Albany: State University of New York Press, 1989). That power can be used for beneficial or maleficent ends. On the one hand, mantras, for example, can help people secure a good marriage alliance, transfer to a better job, or retrieve stolen property. On the other hand, mantras can also destroy property, cripple an enemy, or separate lovers. Although mantras can be learned by anyone from widely available handbooks sold in train stations and bus stands, they are, as Diehl also observed, generally "in the hands of professional people." See Diehl, *Instrument and Purpose*; p. 268. The second Tamil gloss for sorcery is *pillicūṉiyam,* which Diehl (*Instrument and Purpose*, p. 267) translated as "black magic." The word is actually a compound derived from two foreign words. *Pilli* is the Malayalese term for sorcery and literally means "embryo child. " On this, see Nandadeva Wijesekera, *Deities and Demons. Magic and Masks*, part 2 (Colombo, Sri Lanka: M. D. Gunasena & Company, 1989), p. 181. This etymology suggests, as we will see, that the South Indian sorcerer's power derives not only from words or mantras but also from substances, such as the corpses of unborn babies or infants. As for the word *cūṉiyam,* it comes from the Sanskrit *śūnya* that means "destruction," confirming that the sorcerer's activities are indeed lethal.

3. Robert Hertz, *Death and the Right Hand,* trans. R. Needham and C. Needham: (London: Cohen and West, 1960); Richard Huntington and Peter Metcalf, *Celebrations of Death. The Anthropology of Mortuary Ritual* (Cambridge: Cambridge University Press, 1979); Maurice Bloch and Jonathan P. Parry, eds., "Introduction: Death and the Regeneration of Life," in *Death and the Regeneration of Life* (Cambridge: Cambridge University Press, 1982); Maurice Bloch, "Introduction: Death and the Concept of a Person," in *On the Meaning of Death. Essays on Mortuary Rituals and Eschatological Beliefs,* eds. S. Cederroth, C. Corlin, and J. Lindstrom (Uppsala, Sweden: Almqvist & Wiksell International, 1988); Parry, *Death in Banaras* (Cambridge: Cambridge University Press, 1994).

4. Bloch and Parry, eds., "Death and the Regeneration of Life," p. 4.

5. Aside from two dated studies [W. T. Elmore, *Dravidian Gods in Modern Hinduism.* New Delhi: Asian Educational Services, 1984 [1913]; and Diehl, *Instrument and Purpose*; there is not much literature devoted to the sorcery traditions in Tamilnadu. Sorcery, however, has been widely discussed in the ethnography of nearby Sri Lanka. But Tamil and Sinhalese sorcery traditions differ in several important respects. Whereas Gananath Obeyesekere and Bruce Kapferer present real evidence for the practice of sorcery in Sri Lanka, I was only able to record imputations of sorcery in Tamilnadu. I never encountered the songs known as *vas-kavi,* which Obeyesekere describes in "Sorcery, Premeditated Murder, and the Canalization of Aggression in Sri Lanka," *Ethnology* 14 (1975):1–23, 4, as "the most deadly form of sorcery practice in Sri Lanka." Nor did the key myths of Sinhalese sorcery seem to function as chartering narratives for Tamil sorcery (see Kapferer, *Legends of People, Myths of State. Violence, Intolerance and Political*

Culture in Sri Lanka and Australia. [Washington, D.C.: Smithsonian Institution Press, 1988]). Instead, one of my consultants associated the origin of Tamil sorcery with a version of a well-known Sanskrit story that relates how king Dakṣa (or Takkaṉ in Tamil) excludes the God Śiva from his sacrifice (see my book) *Religion Against The Self,* pp. 164–169, 449–57).

6. Diehl, *Instrument and Purpose;* p. 268.

7. John Beattie, "Sorcery in Bunyoro," in *Witchcraft and Sorcery in East Africa,* eds. John Middleton and E. H. Winter (London: Routledge & Kegan Paul, 1963), p. 28.

8. Stephen Inglis, "Possession and Pottery: Serving the Divine in a South Indian Community," in *Gods of Flesh. Gods of Stone. The Embodiement of Divinity in India,* eds. Joanne Punzo Waghorne and Norman Cutler (Chambersburg, PA: Anima Books, 1985).

9. For a detailed discussion of these specialists' initiatory visions and seances see my book, *Religion Against The Self,* 19–43, pp. 41–110.

10. This belief is so entrenched that in order to reduce the risk of such predation by sorcerers, the corpses of firstborn sons are not buried—as is the case with most Tamil Hindus—but are cremated instead. This practice crosses caste lines and may be quite old, as early in the century, Edgar Thurston, the superintendent of the ethnographic survey of the Madras Presidency, observed that "Among the Paraiyans (Untouchables), and some other castes, a first born child, if it is a male, is buried near or even within the house, so that its corpse may not be carried away by a witch or sorcerer, to be used in magic rites." See Thurston, *Ethnographic Notes in Southern India* (Madras: Superintendent, Government Press, 1906), p. 271.

11. For instance, I was told that the sorcerer utters his commands at night while standing naked in a water tank. Edgar Thurston reports a very similar practice among the Pulluvan caste of Malabar: Thurston, *Castes and Tribes of Southern India*, vols. 1–7 (New Delhi: Asian Educational Services, 1987 [1909]), p. 231. For another reference to sorcerers standing in water, see Diehl, *Instrument and Purpose,* p. 293).

12. For other spells, see Diehl, *Instrument and Purpose,* p. 269). For all of these spells the underlying principle was what Sir James Frazer termed *sympathetic magic,* the notion common to many ritual traditions that "like produces like," that whatever was said or done to the effigies affected their human targets. See Frazer, *Sympathetic Magic*, in *Reader in Comparative Religion: An Anthropological Approach,* eds. William A. Lessa and Evon Z.Vogt (New York: Harper, 1965 [1911–15], p. 301. There was another category of Tamil spells that corresponded to what Frazer called "contagious" magic, operating on the principle that affliction was transmitted via physical contact. Known in Tamil as *vaippu* (deposit), these spells involved infusing certain organic substances (egg, lime, and copper foil) with sickness or affliction and secretly placing them in the houses of victims or at a nearby crossroad. When human targets came into contact with these objects, the malevolent power began to work. The result was a slow but steady decrease of the victim's life-strength. Although this procedure was by far the best known to Tamil laypeople, it was *ēval* or the "control" acquired by the sorcerer over his victims' images that was the most common sorcery technique identified by the *cāmi*s I interviewed.

13. Marie-Louise Reiniche, "Les "démons" et leur culte dans la structure du panthéon d'un village du Tirunelveli," *Puruṣārtha* 2 (1975): 173–203, 182; Lionel Caplan, *Religion and Power: Essays on the Christian Community in Madras* (Madras: Christian Literature Society, 1989); Isabelle Nabokov, "Expel the Lover, Recover the Wife: Symbolic Analysis of a South Indian Exorcism." *Journal of the Royal Anthropological Institute* (n.s.) 3.1 (1997): 1–20.

14. Gananath Obeyesekere, *Medusa's Hair: An Essay on Personal Symbols and Religious Experience.* (Chicago: University of Chicago Press, 1981), p. 121.

15. David Scott, "The Cultural Poetics of Eyesight in Sri Lanka: Composure, Vulnerability, and the Sinhala Concept of Distiya," *Dialectical Anthropology* 16 (1991): 85–102, 96; Bruce Kapferer, *A Celebration of Demons: Exorcism and the Aesthetics of Healing in Sri* Lanka (Oxford-Washington, D.C.: Berg Publishers and Smithsonian Institution Press, 1991), p. 71; Kapferer, "Emotion and Feeling in Sinhalese Healing Rites." *Social Analysis* 1 (1979): 153–76, 156; Lionel Caplan, *Religion and Power: Essays on the Christian Community in Madras* (Madras: Christian Literature Society, 1989), p. 55; Margaret Trawick, "Untouchability and the Fear of Death in a Tamil Song," in *Language and the Politics of Emotion,* eds. Catherine A. Lutz and Lila Abu-Lughod (Cambridge: Cambridge University Press, 1990), p. 190.

16. This is also the case in Sri Lanka. See Obeysekere, "Sorcery, Premeditated Murder, and the Canalization of Aggression in Sri Lanka," *Ethnology* 14 (1975); 12–14; Kapferer, *Celebration of Demons,* p. 76, but see pp. 25–51.

17. Mary Douglas, ed., *Witchcraft Confessions and Accusations*, Association of Social Anthropologists Monograph 9 (London: Tavistock Publications, 1970); M. G. Marwick, "Witchcraft as a Social Strain-Gauge," in *Witchcraft and Sorcery: Selected Readings*, ed. Marwick (Harmondsworth: Penguin, 1964); John Beattie, "Sorcery in Bunyoro," in *Witchcraft and Sorcery in East Africa,* eds. John Middleton and E. H. Winter (London: Routledge & Kegan Paul, 1963). For a criticism of this functionalist argument, see Malcolm Crick, *Explorations in Language and Meaning: Towards a Semantic Anthropology* (London: Malaby Press, 1976), pp. 109–127. In a rare study of witchcraft beliefs in a South Indian village, Scarlett Epstein also observed that "not all tensions find expression in witchcraft accusation; only tensions which have no other outlet lead to such accusations. Wherever a judicial mechanism exists to settle quarrels between individuals or groups tensions in their social relations can be brought out into the open and therefore will not be channelled into witchcraft accusations." See Epstein, *A Sociological Analysis of Witch Beliefs in a Mysore Village,* in *Magic, Witchcraft, and Curing,* ed., John Middleton, American Museum Sourcebooks in Anthropology (Garden City, N.Y.: Natural History Press, 1967), p. 153.

18. In Tamilnadu there is nothing to be gained from making public allegations for, as Michael Lambek also discerns in Mayotte, it could "unleash forces whose consequences the accuser cannot predict." See Lambek, *Knowledge and Practice in Mayotte: Local Discourses of Islam, Sorcery, and Spirit Possession* (Toronto: University of Toronto Press, 1993), p. 263. Moreover, it is no possible to present tangible evidence of the spell and there is no legal procedure to punish the guilty party.

19. When I pointed out that they had actually not witnessed the evil sorcerer's ritual, the *cāmis* replied that they would be guided step-by-step by their tutelary goddesses— many of whom, like Kālī and Aṇkāḷaparamēcuvari, were known throughout Tamilnadu for heroic battles against demons. In this healing context, however, their supernatural assistants were not the goddesses who regularly spoke through them during their divining seances. One of them, for instance, interpreted "signs" with the help of Śakti twice a week, but it was the goddess Kālī who inspired his countersorcery rites. And when acting as an exorcist he did not attempt to identify with Kālī but retained his own consciousness and personality.

20. J. P. Fabricius, *Tamil and English Dictionary* (Tranquebar: Evangelical Lutheran Mission Publishing House, 1972 [1779]), p. 214).

21. Clarence Maloney, "Don't Say 'Pretty Baby' Lest You Zap It with Your Eye—The Evil Eye in South Asia," in *The Evil Eye,* ed. Maloney (New York: Columbia University Press, 1976); D. F. Pocock, *Mind, Body and Wealth. A Study of Belief and Practice in an Indian Village* (Oxford: Basil Blackwell, 1973).

22. Christopher J. Fuller, *The Camphor Flame: Popular Hinduism and Society in India* (Princeton, N.J.: Princeton University Press, 1992.

23. This is a grammatical phrase that literally means "making a verb active."

24. The exorcist might also trace Sanskrit and/or Tamil syllables *(uyirmey)* inside the enclosure. This was how one *cāmi* explained the significance of this writing:

> The combination of a vowel (*uyir* also the word for "life") and a consonant (*mey* also means "truth"), for example, h + a = ha, is the fusion of life and truth. Like the letters that the god Brahma, the creator, writes on people's foreheads at birth (*talaiviti*) they create order (*amaippu*: literally "structure") in the world. They are like a mother and protect us.

He seemed to be saying that the letters or mantras marking each ritual enclosure restored the personal fate that the creator had originally written for the victims, which had been disrupted by the spell. Along with these esoteric but positive symbols, some healers added others with different connotations. Inside each enclosure they placed small fruits from two shrubs. The first, *ūmattankāy* is known to have emetic and maddening properties (V. A. Vidya, personal communication). The second, *kumaṭikkāy,* is toxic when eaten raw (ibid). Usually both fruits were sliced in half and their insides then smeared with turmeric and vermilion powders. Since these two substances symbolize the manifestation of the goddess, their application onto the fruits' poisonous surfaces represented, in ways no words could achieve, her inevitable victory over noxious forces.

25. Anthony Good, *The Female Bridegroom: A Comparative Study of Life-Crisis Rituals in South India and Sri Lanka* (Oxford: Clarendon Press, 1991), p.135.

26. Gananath Obeyesekere, "The Impact of Ayurvedic Ideas on the Culture and the Individual in Sri Lanka," in *Asian Medical Systems: A Comparative Study,* ed. Charles Leslie (Berkeley: University of California Press, 1976), p. 205.

27. W. T. Elmore, *Dravidian Gods in Modern Hinduism* (New Delhi: Asian Educational Services, 1984 [1913]), p. 50.

28. Jonathan P. Parry, *Death in Banaras* (Cambridge: Cambridge University Press, 1994); David Knipe, "*Sapiṇḍikārana*: The Hindu Rite of Entry in Heaven," in *Religious Encounters with Death: Insights from the History and Anthropology of Religion,* eds. E. Reynolds and E. H. Waugh (University Park; Pennsylvania State University Press, 1977); Charles Malamoud, "Les morts sans visage: Remarques sur l'idéologie funéraire dans le brâhmanisme," in *La mort, les morts dans les sociétés anciennes,* eds., Gherardo Gnoli and Jean-Pierre Vernant (Cambridge-London: Cambridge University Press and Editions de la Maison des Sciences de l'Homme, 1982); Thomas J. Hopkins, "Hindu Views of Death and Afterlife," in *Death and Afterlife: Perspectives of World Religions,* ed. Hiroshi Obayashi (New York: Greenwood Press, 1992).

29. Knipe, "*Sapiṇḍikārana.*"

30. W. T. Elmore, *Dravidian Gods in Modern Hinduism* (New Delhi: Asian Educational Services, 1984 [1913]), p. 50.

31. For instance, see Eveline Meyer, *Aṅkāḷaparamēcuvari: A Goddess of Tamilnadu: Her Myths and Cult* (Weisbaden: Franz Steiner Verlag, 1986), p. 167; Alf Hiltebeitel, *The Cult of Drapaudī,* (Chicago: University of Chicago Press, 1991), 2(:)321–324; Isabelle Nabokov, "Who Are You?": Spirit Discourse in a Tamil World" (Ph.D diss., University of California, Berkeley, 1995), p. 425, n. 11.

32. According to Nur Yalman, the "painted clay images and figures" built by Sinhalese exorcists may also depict "particular demons." See Yalman, "The Structure of Sinhalese Healing Rituals," in *Religion in South Asia*. ed. Edward B. Harper (Seattle: University of Washington Press, 1964), p. 122. See also Obeyesekere, "Impact of Ayurvedic Ideas on the Culture and the Individual in Sri Lanka"; in Kapferer, *Legends of People, Myths of State. Violence, Intolerance and Political Culture in Sri Lanka and Australia* (Washington, D.C.: Smithsonian Institution Press, 1988). In Sri Lanka, however, the malevolence of sorcery effigies is extirpated not through funeral symbolism but through acts of violence and abandonment in the "jungle." See Nur Yalman, "The Structure of Sinhalese Healing Rituals," in *Religion in South Asia,* ed. Edward B. Harper (Seattle: University of Washington Press, 1964), p. 126; Kapferer, *Legends of People;* Kapferer, *Celebration of Demons.*

33. Knipe, "Night of the Growing Dead: A Cult of Virabhadra in Coastal Andhra," in *Criminal Gods and Demon Devotees: Essays on the Guardians of Popular Hinduism,* ed. Alf Hiltebeitel (Albany: State University of New York Press, 1989), p. 124).

33. Elmore, *Dravidian Gods in Modern Hinduism*, pp. 49–50.

35. The way she did this strikingly evoked the treatment accorded a missing person presumed to be dead in North India. According to Maurice Bloch and Parry, "(his) effigy . . . will be cremated, and his subsequent mortuary rituals performed. If he then reappears, he does so as an intrusive ghost who has no place in the world of the living. . . ." See Bloch and Parry, *Death and the Regeneration of Life*," p. 13.

36. However, according to Louis Dumont, among the *Piramalai Kaḷḷars* of Madurai it is a woman—either the widow or daughter of the deceased—who performs the "breaking of the trickling-pot" at the center of the village. The rite is repeated at the cemetery by the chief male mourner. See Anthony Good, *The Female Bridegroom: A Comparative Study of Life-Crisis Rituals in South India and Sri Lanka* (Oxford: Clarendon Press, 1991), p. 162; also see Manuel Moreno, "An Untouchable Funeral in a Village of South India," *Chicago Anthropology Exchange* 14: 1–2 (1981): 152–163, 158.

37. But I did observe that among low-castes close female relatives (especially daughters) were allowed to follow the funeral procession up to the village's boundary.

38. Arnold Van Gennep, *Les rites de passage* (Paris: Emile Nourry, 1909).

39. Malamoud, "Morts sans visage, p. 445.

40. Parry, *Death in Banaras;* Meena Kaushik, "The Symbolic Representation of Death," *Contributions to Indian Sociology* (n.s.): 10:2(1976): 265–92.

41. Margaret Trawick, "Death and Nurturance in Indian Systems of Healing," in *Paths to Asian Medical Knowledge,* eds. Charles Leslie and Allan Young (Berkeley: University of California Press, 1992), p. 132.

42. In this respect this healer perhaps had predicated his countersorcery rite upon his own initiation as a recruit of the goddess, for the rebirth of the self that he had also experienced within his lifetime had precipitated his separation from his wife and his withdrawal from village life.

43. Malamoud, "Morts sans visage," p. 443, translation mine.

44. Parry, *Death in Banaras,* p. 210.

45. I say "attempts" because the Tamil funeral does not always succeed in effacing the individuality of the dead who, through the medium of trance-possession, may assert their personality and emotions in many contexts. For many examples, see *Religion Against The Self.*

46. Valentine Daniel, *Fluid Signs. Being a Person in the Tamil Way* (Berkeley: University of California Press, 1984), p. 248.

47. Malamoud, "Morts sans visage, pp. 447–49; Thomas J. Hopkins, "Hindu Views of Death and Afterlife," in *Death and Afterlife. Perspectives of World Religions,* ed. Hiroshi Obayashi (New York: Greenwood Press, 1992), p. 151; Bloch and Parry, "Death and the Regeneration of Life," p. 13.

8

Dead Healers and Living Identities: Narratives of a Hindu Ghost and a Muslim *Sufi* in a Shared Village*

Peter Gottschalk

Why bump your head on the ground,
    why bathe your body in water?
You kill and call yourself 'humble'—
    but your vices you conceal.
What's the use of ablutions, litanies, purifications
    and prostrations in the mosque?
If you pray with a heart full of guile
    what's the use of *Haj* and *Kaaba?*
Twenty-four times the Brahman keeps the eleventh-day fast,
    while the Qāzī observes the Rāmzan:
Tell me, why does he set aside the eleven months
    to seek spiritual fruits in the twelfth?
Hari dwells in the East, they say,
    and Allāh resides in the West,
Search for Him in your heart, in the heart of your heart:
    there He dwells, *Rahīm–Rām!*
All men and women ever born
    are nothing but forms of yourself:
Kabīr is the child of *Allāh-Rām:*
    He is my Guru and my Pīr.[1]

* Portions of this chapter are reprinted from *Beyond Hindu and Muslim* by Peter Gottschalk, © 2000 by Peter Gottschalk. Used by permission of Oxford University Press, Inc. Each of the sites described as well as additional interviews with village residents can be seen on "A Virtual Village" (www.colleges.org/~village).

Typical of the iconoclastic songs of the Middle Period devotional poet Kabīr, these lines mock Hindu and Islamic traditions and those who follow them. Kabīr rhetorically questions Brahmans who keep their fasts and facetiously derides Muslims who practice *namāz,* the basic daily prayer, for only bumping their heads of the ground. He eschews mortal gurus and Sufi *pīr*-s (teachers) for the one, authentic spiritual guide. True faith, Kabīr argues, cannot be found in external places, practices, or teachers but only within the devout heart. Yet, Kabīr's portrayal of his belief in Allāh-Rām (and, obviously, that name itself) derives from, and is expressed in, language that comes from Hindu and Islamic traditions.

Although relatively few in contemporary North India consciously model their religious lives by Kabīr's caustic critique and unique synthesis of Hinduism and Islam, a great many exercise religious means quite apart from what many academic scholars portray. Just as Kabīr ignored orthodoxy and orthopraxy in his search for a mystical experience of the god he commonly called "Rām," many Hindus and Muslims throughout North India pursue their personal ends outside of the narrow religious categories that these scholars depict as "Hinduism" and "Islam." Too many scholars see Hindus and Muslims as inhabiting religious worlds of discrete practices and beliefs, and little overlap, without properly recognizing the intercommunal nature of so much of popular North Indian religiosity. As with our understanding of Kabīr whose unique religious vision cannot be entirely understood apart from its Hindu and Islamic context, we must recognize the traditional sources of current practices and beliefs *and* the manner in which many North Indians borrow freely from these sources without regard for their supposed religious identities as "Hindu" or "Muslim." This is particularly true in folk practices of visiting sites associated with the healing dead.

Previous scholarship has identified certain tombs and temples throughout South Asia that have become centers of spiritual healing through their association with the personality, space, and power of certain "dead" individuals. Devotees often learn of, and communicate these elements through, narratives describing events in the life, death, and afterlife of the healer. These narratives demonstrate that many dead healers belong neither to just one tradition nor to no tradition at all. In order to explore the tradition-specific and intercommunal aspects of religious healing in India, this chapter examines the folklore surrounding the temple of a *brahm* and the tomb of Sufi in one Bihar village and analyzes the uses of narrative by local residents to describe both the authority and the efficacy of the powers that they seek to access. Whereas the parts of narratives that demonstrate *authority* often ascribe a particular religious identity to the "Sufi" or *brahm,* the narrative elements that depict the *efficacy* of these men commonly reflect the intercommunal nature of their various sites of healing.[2] In other words, local narratives demonstrate both the authority and abilities of these dead healers and, in so doing, express the multiple identities of local residents and devotees. It is a crucial element of the social dimension of death in this area that beliefs, practices, and narratives regarding the dead who heal work to affirm both inclusive and exclusive religious identities as well as intercommunal local identities.

Ignoring the busy traffic of the bazaar, Sūrya Tiwārī sits on the porch of his family home and describes for me the local centers of spiritual healing among the many temples and tombs in his village of Arampur. Above, on the wall behind him, a painted advertisement encourages pilgrims to enlist the services of his brother who serves as a priest in the nearby temple of Śāstrī Brahm, as his father and grandfather had before him. Sūrya narrates the origins and development of this temple that attracts devotees from far beyond the borders of his native Bihar. Yet, despite its considerable powers, he explains, this *brahm,* or vengeful Brahman ghost, had limitations.

> Any Muslim who is not buried after death can seize a Hindu (for example, someone going to the toilet). They can cause the person to go nude, be crazy, or act like a Muslim by doing *namāz* or *wuẓū.*[3] These people can come to Śāstrī Brahm's temple and be judged [diagnosed], but they are then sent to the places said to control *jinn* because there is no system to control *jinn* in this temple. So they are sent to a Muslim saint's tomb where there is *jinn* control, or the Muslim ghost is asked what it wants since it's possible that the *jinn* will take that and abandon the person.

I leave the conversation wondering whether spiritual healing practices had long been divided along such communal lines or whether the recent national tensions exacerbated by Hindu and Muslim chauvinists had even penetrated the realm of the dead, such as *bhūt-pret*[4] and *jinn.*[5] Only later do I realize that my question was shortsighted. It relied too much on the descriptions of Sūrya Tiwārī and on those others who declare the religiously exclusive character of religious healing sites. I had failed to appreciate the narratives of yet other devotees that imply the intercommunal nature of these sites. More precisely put, while describing the authority of a Sufi or *brahm* to heal, Hindus, Muslims, and Christians who frequent these sites usually refer to an exclusive religious identity for each of these dead healers, yet when describing his ability to heal (all the dead healers in this area are male) they portray the multiple identities associated with the dead healer as well as with those of the devotees themselves. Commonly, area residents make these claims to authority and efficacy through narrative and, in so doing, create an intercommunal public sphere.

An important, shared factor among the healing *brahm* and Sufis of Arampur is that they are dead. Stuart Blackburn has observed that "As a source of Indian religious thought, death is probably unsurpassed."[6] Of course, death becomes primarily important insofar as it affects the living and one way in which the dead do so—for many Hindus and Muslims—is through healing. Many believe that these dead individuals act as animated agents who can affect, for good and ill, the health of the living. If, as Blackburn argues, death plays such a central role in much of Indian religious thought and behavior, it is partly because it denotes neither the end of life nor its opposite but, rather, marks a milestone in an individual's life. This milestone marks the appropriation, for some, of remarkable powers that can influence the lives of others in the community in which they formerly resided. A wide variety of the dead actively inhabit the Arampur area. We might roughly divide these between those socially incorporated and those that are not. Among the latter that residents identify are the *bhūt, brahm, pret, Paṭhān, śayid, jhureyal, pahalvān,* and *jinn* that roam the area or inhabit solitary places like trees or graveyards. Anyone who bothers them —intentionally or not—may become possessed or otherwise troubled. The socially incorporated dead include the various *ḍīh bābā*-s that protect the entrances to villages, Śāstrī Brahm, Sufis, and *shahīd* (Islamic martyrs).[7] A key difference between the two groups is that, whereas the former are seldom associated individually with any particular place, the latter have shrines *(sthān),* temples *(mandir),* courts *(dargāh),* or tombs *(mazār)* dedicated to them where devotees can propitiate them.[8]

Because these sites are often established by local devotees at places associated with the life or death of the active dead, they act not only as locales for devotion but also as spatial and temporal markers for the current community. Such sites serve as spatial intersections between the life of an individual healer and a local community. Meanwhile, annual festivals at these sites, often commemorating the death and expanded empowerment of the healer, create a temporal intersection. With its time fixed on a community's annual calendar, these festivals relate the mortal life of the healer to his continuing presence in the community. A date, perhaps associated with a singular event in the mortal life of the healer (e.g., his death) becomes an annually repetitive holiday observed by, and demonstrative of, the continuous community. These temporal and spatial elements as manifested at the places associated with dead healers establish them as a permanent part of the social order that they had been on the verge of departing. As such, they reflect the nature of that order.

Before a community establishes such intersections between itself and a healer however, it first recognizes the healer's authority and efficacy to heal. We shall explore the ways in which residents do this through narratives for two local healers in order to demonstrate how reverence for dead healers helps mold both communal and intercommunal social contexts for the living. First, an examination of the authority invested in local healers reflects how they can represent traditions uniquely Hindu or Muslim. Later, an analysis of the efficacy that devotees ascribe to these healers will reflect the intercommunal dimensions of both devotional/healing practices *and* the village environment. We will detail how the authority to heal (which creates a socially sanctioned potential for power following certain conditions of the person's life, death, and afterlife) differs from the ability to heal (which demonstrates, through anecdotes, the publicly recognized actualization of this authorized power). Both dynamics result in the construction and affirmation of an intercommunal public sphere.

*The Limits of "*Jinn *Control" and Other Aspects of the Authority to Heal*

If we can briefly define authority as "the social sanction to exercise power," then the event of death becomes, when socially recognized in particular ways, an important step in gaining the authority to heal. Both Hindus and Muslims believe that death can initially or further empower a person as a healer. Of course, death alone does not sanction a healer because, otherwise, all the dead would be considered capable of healing the living and this is not the case. Among the additional criteria by which devotees judge a healer's credentials we discover the differences in authority ascribed to Hindu and Muslim healers. A more detailed examination of two examples of these healers, Śāstrī Brahm and Asta Auliyā, will illustrate this point.

For most residents of Arampur, no one among the empowered dead commands more respect than Śāstrī Brahm. For at least a century, pilgrims from across North India have traveled to Arampur village for the sake of worshiping and petitioning him. Situated on the southern edge of the Gangetic Plain in western Bihar, Arampur stands about sixty miles east of Banaras. Large numbers of pilgrims, if they do not come from the city itself, make use of Banaras as a transportation hub to reach the cobblestoned main street of Arampur. A walk of twenty minutes brings them through the busy central bazaar of the village, where residents of the surrounding area come to buy merchandise, sell grain, drink tea, eat snacks, and trade gossip. If they do not stop first to obtain the help of professional Brahmans such as Sūrya Tiwārī's brother, they soon reach the end of the street that is overshadowed by a mammoth, open gateway at the edge of a large, eroded mound of earth. Inaccessible from one side due to a barrier of low, whitewashed shops, this mound is all that remains of the once proud fort of the local ruler Rājā Vicitra who local residents attribute to have built, hundreds of years ago, practically every large structure and reservoir currently left in the area, including the gate.

A path leads the pilgrims through this heavy sandstone portal, past merchandise-ornamented shops, to the mound's rounded top over which the tall white steeple of Śāstrī Brahm's temple towers. After ringing the bells hanging above the temple entrance, the pilgrims join others either in the large courtyard dominated by an expansive shade tree or within the much smaller inner temple where Brahmans direct the proper offering of prayers and gifts to the small stone which is Śāstrī Brahm's *mūrti* (embodiment). The courtyard seldom empties entirely of people. Devotees, most of them women, beseech this ghost of a Brahman for various favors, among them the healing of mental instability, spirit possession, and various physical illnesses. Many of the devotees suffering possession rely on the powers of exorcism practiced by professional Brahman men who work at the temple although some arrive with their own *ojhā* (exorcist) who may be neither Brahman nor male. In either case, the exorcist positions the client, surrounded by the family members and friends who brought him or her, in the courtyard facing Śāstrī Brahm's *mūrti.* This proximity with the *mūrti* may cause the possessing spirit to induce its host to tremble, shake, gyrate, weep, sing, and/or shout. The exorcist attempts to speak with the spirit, often physically provoking its attention by prodding the host with a short stick. *"Bhūt bole!"* (Speak ghost!), the exorcist commands, "Who are you? What do you want?" He warns the ghost that it is in the *darbār* (royal court) of Śāstrī Brahm. When the exorcist thinks that she or he understands the nature of the possessing spirit and what needs to be done to extricate it from the client, she or he will command it to say and accept that Śāstrī Brahm is *mālik* ("lord"). When the spirit finally affirms this (it may take awhile if it resists), the Brahman leads the victim to the *mūrti* and to the sacrificial fire pit so that the proper offerings can be made.[9] Small, engraved marble tiles comprise much of the temple's floor, each attesting to the devotion and thanksgiving of one of Śāstrī Brahm's supplicants. Outside, the whitewashed walls of the temple, short, semispherical *piṇḍ*-s (lumps of baked mud, concrete, or other materials established at a site for worship) make a similar witness.

The narratives of authority and efficacy by which devotees explain the importance of the temple of Śāstrī Brahm portray this temple as a locus of personality, space, power, and the past. The variations among these narratives demonstrate the variety of perspectives among the devotees who tell them while the endurance of the core elements of the basic story suggests the narrative's local importance. Although stories about how Śāstrī Brahm came to be a powerful healer told by contemporary residents of the Arampur area differ in various details (including or excluding a range of characters and events), they all share elements that remain completely consistent with a version told to Alexander Cunningham more than a century earlier.

As we sit with another member of his household in the shade of a thatch canopy overlooking the family fields, 'Uṣmān Ḵẖān explains his story of Śāstrī Brahm in his native Urdu:

> He lived in the time of Rājā Vicitra. Arampur is a very historical place. Śāstrī Brahm was Rājā Vicitra's guru. Rājā Vicitra was a Rājpūt[10] and Śāstrī Brahm was a resident of [another village]. His house was tall and a light shone from it. One day the rani saw this and asked people whose

> light it was, then ordered the house to be destroyed. And so it was. Śāstrī Brahm was troubled and began to fast. Rājā Vicitra explained to Śāstrī Brahm that he would make an even better house for him and that he did not know what the rani was doing. But Śāstrī Brahm did not believe him and died by his own hand.

Like most other Muslims of the area, 'Uṣmān K̲h̲ān concludes his narrative of Śāstrī Brahm's life with his death. However, most Hindu residents extend this narrative with a final story which gives testimony to the *brahm*'s powers. For them, the narrative does not conclude until Śāstrī Brahm, as a ghost, goes to Delhi and leads the sultan's army back to Arampur in order to precipitate the raja's ultimate demise. At first glance it would seem as though the omission of these postmortem activities reflects 'Uṣmān K̲h̲ān's doubts or disbelief concerning the powers ascribed to the dead Brahman, both at the time of the raja's defeat and currently. But note must be taken that, throughout his narrative, he referred to Śāstrī Brahm in the polite, plural third person of Urdu in contrast to the informal, singular third person with which he referred to the raja. Although Muslims with a strictly orthodox theology may be unable or unwilling to acknowledge any authority by which a dead Hindu—or any dead person—can hurt or heal,[11] many accord some of the dead with the possibility of power and, so, talk about them with cautious deference. Less doctrinally constrained Muslims and most area Hindus accept the power of Śāstrī Brahm based on their respect, if not for his authority, then for his efficacy—a point that we will develop later.

Within the realm of authority we observe a definite distinction among Muslims and Hindus based on their religious traditions. Stuart Blackburn notes that the power of the deified dead in folk Hinduism derives from the nature of their death. They must have died a premature, unjust (preferably) violent death.[12] Blackburn emphasizes that the deification of the Hindu dead in no way depends upon the moral stature of the deceased. Indeed, we find that devotees to Śāstrī Brahm emphasize not his life, but his suicide that he felt compelled to perform due to the unjustified crime of jealousy committed against him by the rani and/or raja. The authority imparted by this type of death is demonstrated in the variety of modern and ancient Sanskrit texts that many Hindu devotees refer to as evidence of the *brahm*'s authority. These include *purāṇā*-s and books seldom, if ever, seen and said to be in the care of special Brahmans in places away from Arampur.[13]

Arampur is also home to healers less famous than Śāstrī Brahm. Residents associate the local tombs of *shahīd*-s and Sufis with the healing powers that these men are said to have exercised in their lives. Many of the Hindus, Muslims, and Christians who frequent these sites describe through narratives the powers of the healer to whom they entrust their well-being. Whether these supplicants believe that the Sufi performs the healing himself or acts as an intermediary for Allāh varies according to the individual. Whichever the case might be, the concern for, and evaluation of, authority and efficacy remains equally important. In the increasingly polarized climate of Indian religious politics, one might expect that such narratives would reflect an exclusive religious identity of the site, its healing practitioners, and its devotees. This is, indeed, the case for many of the narratives which depict the authority by which the dead can heal. The narratives of Śāstrī Brahm rely on a common trope in Hindu folklore of the Brahman who dies an unjust death and returns as a powerful spirit. Similarly, the narratives of the Sufi Asta Auliyā often rely on the Islamic folklore trope of the Sufi who clears the jungle and civilizes its residents, which we will explore in greater detail later.

Among the dozens of tombs of Sufis and *shahīd*-s local to the area, the *dargāh* (or shrine) of Asta Auliyā stands among the most important. Situated on the edge of Arampur on a well-developed path leading from the nearby bazaar, this Sufi's whitewashed tomb rests atop a raised concrete platform surrounded by a low wall that is itself set within an enclosed garden of untended plants and trees. Faded banners, waiting for the next *'urs*[14] celebration to be changed, hang from the large tree that shades the tomb. To the left of the eastern gate into the garden is a small, open mosque. Because the *miḥrāb*[15] of the mosque looks immediately over the Sufi's tomb, those praying inside face not only distant Mecca but also the tomb outside. Above the garden gate entrance an inscription provides Asta Auliyā's full name and the spiritually significant number "786."[16] A house farther east from this compound houses the current *faqīr* who, as a blood descendent of Asta Auliyā, is said to continue his powers.

Asta Auliyā draws devotees daily. Men and women can be found anytime between morning and night bowing or kneeling before the tomb, hands pressed or spread wide with palms up in the fashion of a Muslim prayer form, *du'ā*. Occasionally a family will arrive with a disturbed member whom they hope and pray can be relieved of her or his confounding *bhūt*-s, *pret*-s, or other malicious, marauding entities. As at Śāstrī Brahm's temple, some of these distressed people arrive in ropes or even chains, bound by their family to prevent them from harming themselves or others. Unlike the temple, no professional intermediaries work at this or at any of the area *dargāh*-s. Supplicants make their requests directly to the dead healer. Very often, a devotee comes to make a prayer in front of the tomb and, then, places a bottle of water or oil on the tomb's raised floor or tall walls. She expects the Sufi's power to energize the liquid so that it can be used as a remedy for some family member's physical ailment, whether it be sickness or infertility.

When asked about Asta Auliyā, many local residents describe his sanctity according to established patterns of Islamic religious authority. They may claim that he belongs to either a familial or educational Sufi lineage. That is, they may describe his connection to a Sufi *silsila* or "chain" of teachers either by claiming that his father and/or other ancestors were important Sufis or by describing him as the student of a famous Sufi teacher like the nationally renowned Mu'īnuddīn Chishtī of Ajmer. They may also relate his travels to, and studies in, Arabia, particularly Mecca. His authority may further be demonstrated through the common South Asian Islamic trope that describes the spiritually powerful and religiously devout Sufi who clears the jungle for civilization and converts nonbelievers to Islam.[17] Like the colored bottles of water carefully perched along the sides of Sufi tombs, the Sufis themselves absorb power through their association with important places (e.g., Mecca) and/or the *silsila* of family or teachers who are markedly Muslim. In the minds of their clients, this power authorizes them to heal according to some understanding of Islamic traditions.[18]

Salmān A'lam alludes to some of these claims to authority when, during the carnival atmosphere of the *'urs* or death celebration of Asta Auliyā, he answers my question as to where the Sufi had come from. "Either from Ajmer or Pakistan," he replies. When I ask where in Pakistan, he continues,

> Near Lahore. Others came with him. The ruler of Arampur was Rājā Vicitra. Islam was not common then. Rājā Vicitra did not think that Asta Auliyā was powerful so he decided to test him. A living woman was sent to Asta Auliyā who was told that she was a dead Muslim servant and that *jināẓī kī namāz* ("funeral prayers") should be said for her. Asta Auliyā said "no" but he was pressured to agree. He told Rājā Vicitra that the woman would die as a result of the prayers. The raja told him to go ahead. . . . The woman, who was alive, had been sent a *kafan* ("burial shroud") by the raja. Asta Auliyā told people to line up for the prayer and did the *namāz*. The woman died. Asta Auliyā was a powerful man. The body of the woman was put in a grave that is there today. The woman was a *ṭ̤awā'if* ('dancer' or 'prostitute'). Her tomb is right in front of where Asta Auliyā's is and was oriented north-south. But when he died, it changed direction by itself.

Indeed, today the tomb attributed to the *ṭ̤awā'if* stands unusually skewed southeast-northwest in contrast to the surrounding Muslim tombs that are all oriented north-south.

Salmān's narrative accomplishes a number of general descriptive tasks. It associates Asta Auliyā with Rājā Vicitra as an important local entity, prompting a proud association with one of Arampur's most famous figures. Despite the renowned injustice of the raja against Śāstrī Paṇḍey, residents speak of him with a pride that reflects their lofty regard for their village and for its legendary past grandeur. The narrative implies the importance of both Asta Auliyā's devotees (because of their faith in a Sufi spiritually powerful enough to foil the politically dominant Rājā Vicitra) and Arampur's residents (because their village includes a powerful Sufi within its boundaries). It is worth noting that Salmān's story does all of this without explicit communal exclusivity. None of the many devotees, either Hindu or Muslim, who provided me with some version of this narrative made any mention of the raja or the woman as being Hindu. The narrators' intentions seemed more focused by the trope of the humble spiritual leader overpowering the proud political leader, a theme common to Sufi narratives throughout the world.[19]

More specifically for our concerns, Salmān A'lam's narrative establishes the Sufi's authority. First, it associates him with Ajmer and Lahore, both homes of important South Asian Sufis such as Mu'īnuddīn Chishtī and 'Alī ibn 'Uṣ̤mān al-Hujwīrī. Second, the narrative strengthens this authority with an allusion to the Sufi's Islamic character, suggesting that he arrived in the Arampur area because "Islam was not common then." Third, it furthers this notion as it demonstrates the spiritual and compassionate powers of Asta Auliyā who attempted to avoid the lethal result of the raja's deviousness but who exercised his powers when left without an option. Throughout the world, Muslims celebrate Sufis who live lives of compassion, but do not expect them to be passive. When facing an injustice against other Muslims or Islam, Sufis are expected to act decisively, as Asta Auliyā did.[20]

Narratives such as those of 'Uṣ̤mān Ḵẖān and Salmān A'lam depict a disjunction at several points between the authority to heal of Śāstrī Brahm and local Sufis. While the devotees of Sufis in Arampur emphasize the nature of the Sufi's life that is usually described as devoted to religious learning and compassionate acts of healing and/or teaching, devotees ascribe power to the *brahm* according to the manner of the *brahm*'s death. Furthermore, devotees commonly refer to the Sufi's knowledge and veneration of the Quran and other religious books in Arabic while the quality of Śāstrī Brahm's scholastic or devotional life seldom, if ever, arises.

Consistent with broader Hindu cultural expectations, only three elements of Śāstrī's life determine his authority to heal: he was (1) a male (2) Brahman who (3) died an unjust death. The implied basis of a *brahm*'s authority to heal, therefore, does not derive from the manner of his life, as with Sufis, but rather from the nature of his death. Many Hindu traditions pay great attention to the successful migration of the dead away from the society of the living into *pitṛ lokā* ("realm of the ancestors") until reincarnation returns them to the realm of the living. Sanskrit texts such as the *Garuḍa Purāṇa* detail the nature of this passage. In separate works, David Knipe has explored contemporary rituals performed in order to both facilitate this passage[21] and to cope with the dangerous consequences of untimely death.[22] Although the *manner* of a *brahm*'s life might not matter, his social status (as a male Brahman) most certainly does. Inversely, devotees prove the Sufi's authority to heal with reference only to the manner of his life, not to his inherited social position. Consistent with general Islamic ideals, a person obtains religious stature through the equal opportunity that Allāh grants all believers to truly submit—to be true Muslims—regardless of class, age, or gender.[23] Classical Islamic thought pays little concern to "bad deaths" like Śāstrī Brahm's. The *shahīd,* who certainly suffers an untimely death, proceed immediately to the paradisaical Garden, and so do not threaten the living in any way. Despite some discrepancies between the Quran and Ḥadīth, the general understanding is that the dead remain in or near their graves awaiting the Day of Judgment, their contact with the living limited to the medium of dreams.[24] But these understandings changed over time and some Muslims came to accept the ability of dead saints to intercede on behalf of the living.[25]

All of these differences, therefore, clearly demonstrate that the *brahm* and Sufi do, indeed, appear to be religiously defined and communally distinct on the basis of authority. Ultimately, we see that a religious community recognizes religious power within and according to the parameters that its tradition allows. One way in which Hindus and Muslims portray a dead healer's authority in regard to these parameters is through narratives that use tropes specific to their respective traditions. As they tell or accept such stories while among others from their religious community—whether it be in the home, place of worship, or tea stall—they affirm their membership in that community.

Intercommunal Elements in Narratives of the Healer's Efficacy

Yet, to halt our analysis here would be to ignore a social dimension of Indian religious life in which the common worship of the dead unites the living beyond the confines of communal boundaries through intercommunal activities, perspectives, and identities. Almost to the same degree that devotees recognize and refer to specifically Hindu and Muslim traditions while describing the authority of dead healers, they ignore communal differences while portraying the effectiveness of these men.

If we return to Salmān A'lam's narrative, we notice that the elements that demonstrate the Sufi's efficacy, in juxtaposition with those proving his authority, do not rely on any specifically Islamic character. We have already noted that Asta Auliyā showed his compassion, when he attempted to avoid harming the woman, and his stridency, when he exercised his powers when left without an option—powers effective enough to kill her. Significantly, Salmān's story avoids explicit communal exclusivity. None of the many devotees I interviewed, either Hindu or Muslim, who provided some version of this narrative made any mention of the raja or the woman as being Hindu or Muslim. Presumably, one might argue, the fact that the raja sent her corpse for burial instead of cremation implies that she was Muslim. Even if this is the understanding of Arampur residents, they made no indications in their narratives to me that the point is important. No one hinted at any injustice served upon the woman by the Hindu raja because she was Muslim. And although residents widely recognize the raja as having been Hindu, no narratives suggested that the outcome would have been any different had he been Muslim. This feature becomes all the more significant when considering that local Muslims could have celebrated Asta Auliyā's success against the Hindu raja and identity as a warrior Sufi by depicting him as a *shahīd* (Islamic martyr) or *gāẕī* (victor against non-Muslims) popular in hagiographic folklore and literature.[26] Yet, no one suggests such an identity.

A similar intercommunal dynamic operates in narratives regarding Śāstrī Brahm. The lengthy and detailed version that Sūrya Tiwārī shared before making his above comments about the limits of Śāstrī Brahm's powers serves well to illustrate this dynamic. While providing a protracted history of Arampur stretching from Gupta rule to the local victory of a king around 1180, Sūrya explains in a fluid mix of Hindi and English:

> So [that king] picked Arampur fort as his new capital and built a seven-story tall fort. He buried his [wealth] there. Three or four generations later Rājā Vicitra. . . . ruled. Śāstrī Pāṇḍey was his priest and chief minister. After 22 to 25 years without issue from his first wife, he consults Śāstrī Pāṇḍey concerning the future pure Hindu son. . . . Śāstrī Pāṇḍey suggests a second wife and this angers the first who then tries to create friction between the king and priest. She convinces the king to be against the priest. As a result, Śāstrī Pāṇḍey's house was damaged. . . . The king also took back the villages given by the king's ancestor to the priest's family. Śāstrī Pāṇḍey became angry and said that he would have no peace until he defeated the king. So he sent his family away . . . Śāstrī Pāṇḍey went to see the king but was refused. So Śāstrī Pāṇḍey entered the fort through the moat canal and commenced to do a *dharnā* ("fast"). He said he would do an . . . indefinite . . . hunger strike while awaiting the king's return of his property. Otherwise he would destroy the raja, the fort, and [the raja's] family. On the twenty-second day Śāstrī Pāṇḍey died and became a *brahm* or Brahman ghost. Accidental deaths lead to *brahm* or *brahmaṇapret* ("spirits of Brahmans").

Sūrya Tiwārī continues,

> The raja began to get more problems. He sought relief through *tāntrik*-s ("practitioners of tantra") but with no success. Before a visit by Śāstrī Pāṇḍey's grandson, Sudarśan, a mysterious incident happened. There was an attempt to bury Śāstrī Pāṇḍey's body but local tradition holds that it turned to stone. Many priests were asked to come from Banaras and asked how to do *śrāddh* (the Hindu ceremony for the recently deceased). Some suggest doing a *samskār* (a Hindu rite of passage)

with a priest using a *putlā* ("human image") made out of grass. Śāstrī Pāṇḍey's grandson and his family priest go to Maṇikarṇikā Ghāṭ [in Banaras]. All see Śāstrī Pāṇḍey there in human form. . . . while others prepare the funeral pyre. They were scared. Śāstrī Pāṇḍey said that he would not be happy until the raja was dead or had quit the fort. The raja didn't believe the story. People saw Śāstrī Brahm from Banaras to Arampur.

> In Delhi at this time was the Muslim dynasty of Mubārak Shāh. The raja paid the Sultan of Jaunpur protection money. Meanwhile the Delhi Sultan was thinking of taking Jaunpur in July or August 1427 or 1428. During the planning a simple Brahman, who was Śāstrī Brahm, said that the rule of Jaunpur would fall if the Arampur raja was defeated. No one in Delhi knew who the simple Brahman was. He came in a dream to the Sultan to assure him . . . On October 1427, after five days [of fighting], the [Jaunpur] ruler's forces ran away. All the Hindu rulers were defeated along the way. . . . the Delhi Sultan remembers Śāstrī Brahm and constantly thinks of him. As he does so invisible powers increase through non-human inspiration. A three-day battle occurred and the Arampur raja was destroyed. Mubārak Shāh looted the fort. He made someone who was . . . not a pure Rājpūt into a small king or *jāgīrdar* of Arampur after giving Mubārak Shāh a lot of the loot.

> Yet the *jāgīrdar* began to feel a shadow in the fort and suffered from Śāstrī Brahm's curse for one week or a month. An astrologer or demonologist explained that the soul of Śāstrī Brahm is present. It is necessary to make complete satisfaction of Śāstrī Brahm's revenge. Adhināth and other Brahmans from Banaras came to question Śāstrī Pāṇḍey's soul. They promise to establish him as a *brahm* and the residents and king will establish a home for him and worship him as a god in exchange for the destruction of the curse. Śāstrī Pāṇḍey's soul was ready so Śāstrī Brahm was established in a room in the fort. A *yajña* ("sacrifice") was done in the fort and this was the first day of the worship of Śāstrī Brahm in the form of Lord Śiva.

At first glance the story seems anything but noncommunal. Sūrya made great effort to explicitly identify certain figures as either Hindu (Śāstrī Pāṇḍey, Rājā Vicitra, the *jāgīrdar,* and other Hindu rajas) or Muslim (Mubārak Shāh and the Jaunpur "Sultan"). He describes the lineage to which Mubārak Shāh belonged as a "Muslim dynasty" and the rulers whom Mubārak Shāh defeated on his drive toward Arampur as "Hindu kings." As one of the most formally educated individuals to come from Arampur, Sūrya has read many Indian textbooks and Western histories that depict South Asia's political history as a competition among various Hindu and Muslim factions. His narrative reflects the overall picture that these texts often paint of the slow yet inevitable conquest of "Hindu kingdoms" by "Muslim invaders." Yet, despite this obvious attention to religious identity, he portrays Śāstrī Brahm's powers as indiscriminately applied. Note that Śāstrī Pāṇḍey, transformed by death into Śāstrī Brahm, revenged himself not only against Rājā Vicitra (who craved a "pure Hindu son") but also against the *jāgīrdar* who is "not pure Rājpūt" because of their respective infractions committed by damaging his house and looting the fort. Meanwhile he aided without prejudice the Muslim Sultan of Delhi against the Muslim "Sultan" of Jaunpur, the Hindu Raja of Arampur, and the Hindu kings unfortunate enough to stand in between these two. In summary, Sūrya Tiwārī (and most other Arampur residents) narrates a story about how Śāstrī Pāṇḍey came to be a *brahm* that demonstrates the efficacy of his powers for or against individuals without regard for their religious identity, *despite the obvious concern on the part of the narrator to identify them in this way.* Not only does Sūrya Tiwārī's awareness of religious difference not necessitate communalist antagonism, but it reflects the social reality that Śāstrī Brahm aids those who respect him no matter what their religious identity. This allows for an intercommunal identity among his devotees.

Significantly, the power of seemingly disempowered spiritual figures to successfully wrestle with political and social figures finds a parallel in both religious traditions. In the realm of efficacy, we notice interesting parallels between the narratives concerning Śāstrī Brahm and Asta Auliyā. Although the authority for his powers derives from specifically Hindu traditions, Śāstrī Brahm's abilities are demonstrated in a narrative in which he destroys a Hindu raja through an alliance with a Muslim sultan. This notion of the humble spiritual person overpowering the proud political leader is a theme common not only to Sufi narratives throughout the world but also to many oral and written narratives in North India that depict animosity between Brahmans and Ṭhākurs (lords of the land).[27] Brahmans often overcome the Ṭhākurs' economic and political power through the exercise of their spirituality in ways similar to Sufi victories over abusive rulers.[28] Therefore, the efficacy of both the *brahm* and the Sufi is demonstrated through their confrontation with the local political leader whose religious identity plays no part in the outcome.

It is consequential that both narratives depict their protagonists as proving their efficacy through conflict with Rājā Vicitra. Each vies proudly for a place in popular memory through an association with the raja, perhaps the most well-remembered figure in the area. In turn, each narrative implies the importance of the devotees of both Asta Auliyā or Śāstrī Brahm because of their faith in a man spiritually powerful enough to foil the politically dominant Rājā Vicitra.

But doesn't Sūrya Tiwārī's initial comment about Śāstrī Brahm's inability at *"jinn* control" seem to suggest that efficacy *is* tradition specific? When he acknowledged that professional Brahmans at Śāstrī Brahm's temple could diagnose a person's possession as caused by a Muslim ghost or *jinn* but that the *brahm*'s powers could not exorcise it while a Muslim saint could, was he not admitting that the religious association of a ghost disables Śāstrī Brahm's efficacy? Simply put, the Hindu *brahm* seems to exercise no authority over a Muslim ghost.[29] What would seem to reflect the tradition-specific nature of efficacy, however, actually demonstrates the intercommunal nature of efficacy within the limits of tradition-based claims to authority. But how?

Although Śāstrī Brahm may not be considered effective against Muslim ghosts, we must consider first that devotees of area Sufis never suggested that a dead Muslim healer could not be effective against a Hindu ghost. This one-sided limitation reflects the lopsided activity of local Hindus and Muslims at the *brahm*'s temple and Sufi shrines. Whereas most Hindus show little hesitation to seek healing or exorcism at a site associated with a Muslim healer, many Muslims consider it inappropriate to request help at a Hindu temple. As many Indian Muslims hew a course of greater conservative orthopraxy in response to national communalist politics and international revivalist movements, they refuse (increasingly, I suspect) to accept (or, at least, admit) the authority of Hindu spirits.[30] Just as Hindu residents of Arampur will as likely accept the authority of a dead Sufi as that of a *brahm* because doctrine constrains them less, so too the Hindu ghosts who afflict them. But Muslim ghosts, like their pre-mortem co-religionists, are more likely not to accept the authority of Hindu healers. In this way then, traditional notions of authority do limit the realm of an individual healer's efficacy according to the religious identity of the healer and the afflicting ghost.

This demonstrates that the issue of authority exists within a large context, one that determines the relative characteristics of the various members in the community of the dead. The question of a Hindu ghost's efficacy over Muslim ghosts derives from a vast domain in which different powers, both malevolent and benevolent, are ascribed to spirits of deceased humans depending upon their place in life and manner of death. No one suggests that rancorous spirits have any religious preference regarding whom they possessed or otherwise afflicted. Although some ghosts do prefer certain victims (e.g., *cuṛail,* ghosts of barren women, who out of envy attack pregnant women), most spirits of the dead—whether Hindu or Muslim—seemingly pounce on the living without regard for their religious tradition. Although Muslim ghosts may not accept Śāstrī Brahm's authority, the fact remains that Hindu ghosts inflict Muslims as well as Hindus and that members of both communities, despite the resistance of more orthodox Muslims, can be found at Śāstrī Brahm's temple seeking respite.

Finally, it is significant that, although neither Śāstrī Brahm nor Asta Auliyā nor most of the several other dead Sufi healers local to the area originated from the area, their presence acts as a significant source of local pride for Arampur residents. Almost all Hindus and Muslims of this large village and the many surrounding villages know their stories and respect their powers, even if they do not personally rely on them for healing. Local residents interweave the narratives of these important healers into the narrative of the area itself. Beyond their demonstration of the healers' authority and efficacy, narrators at times promote their pride of belonging to a village with such important and effective powers. In this manner, these Hindus and Muslims often use these narratives to forefront their shared village identity while de-emphasizing their religious, caste, and class identities.

Constructing and Affirming an Intercommunal Public Sphere

Although Arampur's neighbors are acutely aware of one another's communal differences, they share a common public sphere in their village. The narratives regarding local healers, the daily rituals that attempt to access their healing powers, and the ceremonies that ritually commemorate them at Śāstrī Brahm's temple and at Asta Auliyā's *dargāh* (court) play a role in the integration of villagers into a common identity as residents of Arampur and devotees of one or both of these healers.

Scholars have rightly made much of the interreligious communion that Sufis—both living and dead—have generated across South Asia since the first large-scale arrival of Muslims at the turn of the first millennium. From the role of Sufis in creating an Indo-Islamic culture in thirteenth-century Bengal as described by Richard Eaton[31] to the intercommunal healing services provided by the female *pīr* (teacher) Amma in modern Hyderabad analyzed by Joyce Burkhalter-Flueckiger,[32] Sufis have played a prominent part in forging a foundation of common memory, ritual, and identity among Hindus and Muslims.

One occasion demonstrated the shared devotional space that Asta Auliyā's *dargāh* affords. While sitting with Druma Yādav, Rātī K̲h̲ān, and other members of the K̲h̲ān family—all residents of Naugrah, a village neighboring Arampur—I ask about a recently discovered temple near Śāstrī Brahm's temple that some Arampur residents are excavating from beneath a building atop the mound of Rājā Vicitra's fort. One member of Rātī K̲h̲ān's family answered, "The temple surrounded by the pipal tree is a Śiv temple."

> A second K̲h̲ān family member added, "That is nothing to us. We must keep our hearts clean."
>
> Druma Yādav, in Hindi: "A pandit lived there, and a raja too. Then it was destroyed. Before, there was an *akhāṛā* ('wrestling ground') there. When they were removing soil there, they found the Śiv *mūrti* ('image')."
>
> Me: "Is that true?"

Druma: "Yes. To the east of Arampur is a village where my *birādarī log* ('caste folk') have a neighborhood. Asta Auliyā is a great *buzurg* ('venerable person'). He is above everyone. No temple or mosque is greater than him."

Me: "Who was he?"

Druma: "A *faqīr* ('Muslim ascetic')."

Me: "Why was he famous?"

Druma: "There are so many temples and mosques but none are as great as he is. There is Bhagwān and Śaṅkar and there is Allāh, and *nabī rasul*[33] (Muhammad). *Cāroṅ mālik* ('All four are lords')."

Second Ḵẖān: "Allāh is Lord of all."

Once again, a local resident responds to a question regarding an Arampur site with a narrative (i.e., the pandit and raja) and, in so doing, successfully negotiates a common ground between his Hindu beliefs and the Islamic ideas of his Ḵẖān neighbors. He accomplishes this in three ways.

First, despite the conflicting beliefs of some of his Muslim landowning neighbors (or, perhaps, because of them), Druma, a Hindu field-worker, successfully shifts the conversation away from the potentially troublesome topic of the new temple to Śāstrī Brahm's temple to the *dargāh* of Asta Auliyā before suggesting common cause with these neighbors through a statement of theological fraternity. What might seem to be a haphazard connection between the temples and the *dargāh* is quite intelligible to residents in the area fluent in the narratives which connect the derelict fort, Śāstrī Brahm, and Asta Auliyā to Rājā Vicitra. Despite the class and religious differences between them, Druma and the Ḵẖāns can share a local identity through their mutual group memory of the area's most renowned figures. This strategy of narrative association lends some of the local significance of the raja-*brahm*-sultan story to less well-known group memories and identities such as those surrounding Asta Auliyā. Devotees of Asta Auliyā, by narrating stories that depict his involvement with the raja, graft their identity as the Sufi's devotees onto that of being Arampur residents to the exclusion of communal, caste, and class identities.

Second, Druma creates a common ground with the Ḵẖāns when he alludes to the current power of the Sufi. Although the second Ḵẖān family member, not brooking the idea that Allāh has any peers, rebutted Druma's claim that Bhagwān, Śaṅkar, Allāh, and Muḥammad were all lords, he did not contradict Druma's lengthier comment regarding the efficacy of Asta Auliyā. Druma praised the Sufi's grandeur in the present tense, clearly claiming that his power survived his death and resides still in his *dargāh*.

Finally, we take note how Druma, a resident of an adjoining village, made a personal connection both to the Sufi and to the Arampur area. Although he could have simply started talking about Asta Auliyā, Druma initiated his conversation first with reference to his fellow caste members and then to their neighborhood in a village just opposite from the *dargāh* in Arampur. In so doing he revealed the interrelatedness of his caste, area, and devotional identities. The manner in which Druma effortlessly transposed the *dargāh* as a metonym for the Sufi demonstrates that Druma's regard for the Sufi is inexorably tied with a specific local place. For Druma the *dargāh* is the locus of the Sufi's powers in life and afterlife, while for others it is the Arampur area itself wherein these powers are associated. Salmān A'lam's earlier narrative demonstrated how the Sufi comes to be related with the place of Arampur through his triumph over Rājā Vicitra to whom is often attributed the creation of a monumental and successful Arampur. Yet other residents connect him with Arampur by depicting him as the founder of the village. They narrate how the Sufi cleared the jungle, established Arampur, civilized its *janglī* inhabitants, and brought Islam to many of them.

These dual efforts of devotees in the Arampur area to associate the person, power, place, and the past of Asta Auliyā with the Arampur area may conflict. A discussion between the current *faqīr* (Muslim ascetic) and three other Arampur residents leads to an impasse after a check of a marble engraving affirmed for them that Asta Auliyā had died ca. 1384 C.C.E.[34] One person claims that Arampur did not exist when Asta Auliyā first arrived in the area, that he had civilized the *janglī log*[35] (uncivilized people), and that Rājā Vicitra had lived before his arrival. Another person argues that it was impossible for Rājā Vicitra to have lived before Asta Auliyā because Bakhtiyār Khiljī had arrived at the time of the raja, and the Sufi—not the Delhi Sultan—was the first Muslim in the area. Eaton's work on thirteenth-century Muslim expansion into Bengal has recognized the prevalence of this trope of Sufi as jungle-clearer and civilizer:

> In popular memory, some [Muslim holy men] swelled into vivid mythico-historical figures, saints whose lives served as metaphors for the expansion of both religion and agriculture. They have endured precisely because, in the collective folk memory, their careers captured and telescoped a complex historical socioreligious process whereby a land originally forested and non-Muslim became arable and predominantly Muslim.[36]

In the case of the conversation in front of the current *faqīr,* debate ensued when the story depicting Asta Auliyā in the familiar role of jungle-clearer and civilizer could not be accommodated within the narrative associating the Sufi with Arampur's most famous son. These men wrangled with their narratives in order to produce a uniform group memory to suit their identities both as devotees of

Asta Auliyā and as residents of the Arampur area while also insinuating how the manner of the Sufi's life led to his authority to heal.

These narratives about Asta Auliyā establish not only the well-known story of his life but also his postmortem effectiveness as a healer. The annual *'urs* (death day celebration) pays homage to both and shows that an intercommunal devotional identity and public sphere forms not only through discourse but also through ritual. Like these stories, this ritual couples the dead healer with place and power. Because tradition regards the death of a Sufi as the rending of the final veil separating him or her from God, residents of the Arampur area and devotees from outside the state celebrate the day, venerating Asta Auliyā's past life and present efficacy. Pushcart merchants position their vehicles laden with fruits and sweets along footpaths near the *dargāh* while itinerant merchants display their wares on spreads of cloth. Children shoot balloons with a small air rifle. In two huge cauldrons, cooks prepare the free community meal for all who wish to partake.

After sundown, a small group of men perform the evening *namāz* (Muslim prayer perrformed five times a day) in the mosque. Then a group of devotees, evenly divided between women and men, gather on the eastern side of the tomb and begin the hours-long process of respectfully offering coins, incense sticks, and platters of food. Individuals and groups of devotees offer *cādar*-s (a tomb-covering sheet) which young men attending to the tomb spread carefully along the length of the barrow. Often these are given in fulfillment of a vow. Long chains of fresh flowers commonly accompany these *cādar*-s that can be devoted by individuals, families, or whole *muhalla*-s (neighborhoods). Most *muhalla*-s in Arampur are populated by one or a few specific castes and, therefore, are religiously distinct. Yet, *muhalla*-s of both Hindu and Muslim castes send their men with one or more *cādar*-s as physical evidence of their respect for the Sufi and their unity as a *muhalla*. When the offerings have been completed, a group of about fifty men cover their heads with whatever they have available and gather on the tomb's eastern side to offer *du'ā* (informal prayer) under the leadership of the contemporary *faqīr*. Finally, the offerings presented to the tomb earlier are returned to their owners who identify the changed and charged substances as both *prasād* and *baraka*—terms derived from Sanskrit and Arabic, respectively.[37] Throughout the *'urs* Hindus and Muslims of all castes and classes intermix, converse, and pray together. This and other religious celebrations provide the rare moments when village men and women freely mingle in public. Many are drawn by the *melā* (festival) atmosphere of eating, shopping, music, and socializing. Others combine these activities with their devotional practices. Whatever the case, the *'urs* of Asta Auliyā, and some of the other major Sufis in the area, provides an opportunity for area residents, regardless of identity, to celebrate this personage collectively. They express their pride in both him and in their home territory in a space that is defined by narratives as significant, shared physically in ritual once a year, and, through the gift of *muhalla cādar*-s, connected with the rest of Arampur.

Arampur area residents take a similar pride in their spatial association with Śāstrī Brahm. Any resident can point out the local places associated with the raja-*brahm*-sultan story, including Rājā Vicitra's defunct fort, Śāstrī Brahm's active temple, and Ba<u>kh</u>tiyār <u>Kh</u>iljī's mammoth mausoleum. But most will clearly consider Śāstrī Brahm as the most important feature of both the narrative and the area. The raja may be considered the architect of many of the oldest and most notable features in the local region and the sophistication of the sultan's mausoleum has attracted the attention of national and international scholars since the days of British rule. However, the primary site associated with the raja—his fort—serves now only as the setting for the *brahm*'s temple while the Suri-era tomb has no greater significance for residents than as a picnic place. Clearly, these centuries-old sites have remained associated with the raja and sultan only through their connection with the contemporary, though dead, healer—Śāstrī Brahm. These associations continue through both oral histories told in family homes and tea stalls and *Brahm Prakāś,* a short pamphlet detailing a local Brahman's version of the story which sells in Arampur's main bazaar.[38] As with Asta Auliyā's *dargāh,* the temple often acts as a metonym for the *brahm* in people's conversations.

Like Asta Auliyā, Śāstrī Brahm's fame as an important character of the past and an effective healer of the present empowers any place associated with his person and power. His temple, situated atop the barren mound where the raja's palace had once stood would be the most obvious locus. But another place benefits from Śāstrī Brahm's reputation. A few times, a resident of the Muslim *muhalla* of Loharani in Arampur village stopped me, pointed to an overgrown pile of unremarkable rubble in a nearby field, and asked if I knew what it was. "It is the cremation site of Śāstrī Brahm," the self-appointed informant would say, showing his pride that it was in "our Loharani." Although the cremation site plays a very small role, if any, in most narrations by Arampur's inhabitants regarding the raja, *brahm,* and sultan (and contradicts stories of his cremation in Banaras and his body's transformation into stone), many residents of this one Muslim neighborhood seize the opportunity to associate themselves with a character who helps define Arampur as a significant place past and present. In so doing, they forefront their identification with their neighborhood (i.e., we-of-Loharani) through a narrative that simultaneously associates them with their village (i.e., we-of-Arampur), demonstrating how the residents of this neighborhood share an identity that overlaps with those of local Hindus even if they do not share in the belief that the *brahm* has spiritual powers. In many such cases, even if a recitation of the story cannot be considered a confession of faith in the powers of the *brahm,* it is an affirmation of local territorial identity. Yet again, the veneration of an active member of the dead helps affirm an identity among the living that goes beyond—though without denying—the identities of *Hindu* and *Muslim.*

Ultimately, which-identity-local-residents-express-when depends on how they want to assert themselves in a particular social context. Some may derisively narrate these stories in order to mock them and demonstrate their religious chauvinism. However, those who respect the powers of these healers cannot help but express their own multiple identities in their narratives of authority and efficacy. Contemporary Arampur residents explain that Śāstrī Brahm helped kill a Hindu raja and supported a Muslim sultan despite his personal religious identity. Many of those same residents patronize Śāstrī Brahm and Asta Auliyā without conflict with their own religious identities. These religious identities, themselves, come into question as many self-proclaimed "Hindus" and "Muslims" follow practices and beliefs that borrow from one another's "traditions" as strictly defined by many orthodox/orthoprax coreligionists and secular scholars.

Once again, we are reminded of Kabīr's religious vision that could transcend these religious categories only through the use of language and practices learned through them. Daniel Gold writes that the followers of Kabīr and other Sants devoted themselves to their gurus whose "sanctified personality . . . could then serve for some as an object of devotion both readily believable and close at hand."[39] Most residents of Arampur do not have the lofty ideals of Kabīr but, like his followers, seek a more tangible center for their devotional lives. When searching for relief from illness, they may frequent the worship places of one or more dead healers. Although some will refer to a healer's tradition-specific authority to justify their faith in his power, others will rely on the stories that demonstrate his efficacy and reflect the intercommunal life of the temple, *dargāh,* and village. Generally, then, Arampur residents live interrelated lives with their neighbors—alive and dead—aware of religious differences only within a much larger context of multiple identities, some shared and some not.

Notes

1. Charlotte Vaudeville, *A Weaver Called Kabir: Selected Verses with a Detailed Biographical and Historical Introduction.* (Delhi: Oxford University Press, 1997 [1993]), pp. 217–18.

2. All of the dead healers in and around Arampur were men. However, examples of dead female healers exist in other regions. For example, see Paul Courtright, "The Iconographies of Sati," in *Sati, the Blessing and the Curse: The Burning of Wives in India*, ed. John Stratton Hawley. (New York: Oxford University Press, 1994), pp. 27–48. Although numerous, large monuments to women who committed *satī* stand at one end

of Arampur, I neither saw nor heard of anyone worshiping there as Courtright describes in regard to Rajasthan. Also see Diane Coccari, "The Bir Babas of Banaras: An Analysis of a Folk Deity in North Indian Hinduism." (Ph.D. diss., University of Wisconsin–Madison, 1986), pp. 117–26.

3. Muslim daily prayers and ritual ablutions, respectively.

4. A general term for ghosts and spirits that are often malevolent. Both terms derive from Sanskrit roots: *bhū* (becoming) and *pre* (to come forth).

5. Entities mentioned in the Quran as created from fire that become, in South Asia, synonymous at times with ghosts of the dead.

6. Stuart Blackburn, "Death and Deification: Folk Cults in Hinduism," *History of Religions* 24:3 (February 1985): 255.

7. Residents often conflate Sufis with *shahīd.*

8. Maurice Bloch and Jonathan Parry, Introduction to *Death and the Regeneration of Life* (New York: Cambridge University Press, 1982), pp. 32–38. It is useful to observe that the socially unincorporated dead become dangerous as they assert themselves in the lives of the community by causing illness or possession. Living members of the community may opt to create a shrine for them and propitiate them should they become too unmanagable, thus settling them back as a recognized part of society, as we shall see Śāstrī Brahm accomplish successfully.

9. A compelling examination of similar spiritual interogations among Indian charismatic Catholics can be found in Matthew N. Schmalz, "Sins and Somatologies: Sexual Transgression and the Body in Indian Charismatic Healing" (Paper presented at the annual American Academy of Religion conference, San Francisco, November 1997).

10. A Hindu high caste associated with the *kṣatrya* or warrior/king class of society.

11. For example, a Pakistani Shī'ī pamphlet instructing Muslims on the facts of death and funerals cites several Quranic passages regarding the condition of the dead between the time they die and are resurrected. It adamently concludes, "The above mentioned verses are sufficient to refute the claims of the so-called spiritualists and occultists to *[sic]* who pretend to talk with the dead." *Death and Death Ceremonies* (Karachi, Pakistan: Peermahomed Ebrahim Trust, 1972), p. 47.

12. Blackburn, "Death and Deification," 260.

13. Narayana Rao points out that such vague references to supposed books represent a common strategy in India and demonstrate the authority that many contemporary Hindus give to the written word over the oral. Personal conversation, September 27, 1996.

14. The annual celebration of a particular Sufi's death day.

15. The niche in a mosque's front wall that indicates the direction of Mecca and, thus, prayer.

16. The number inscripted on the Sufi tomb, ٧٨٦ ('786'), probably derives from *abjad,* a numerological science that attributes a number to each letter of the Arabic alphabet. The number 786 is the *abjad* equivalent of the *bismillāh* (the prayer, "In the name of Allāh"). However, most Muslim residents whom I asked about this did not recognize it as such and usually guessed that it represents the Sufi's death date.

17. Richard Eaton, *The Rise of Islam and the Bengal Frontier, 1204–1760* (Delhi: Oxford University Press, 1994), pp. 207–19.

18. The development and role of authority within institutional Sufism has recently been examined by Arthur Buehler in his *Sufi Heirs of the Prophet: The Indian Naqshbandiyya and the Rise of the Mediating Sufi Shaykh*. Columbia: University of South Carolina Press, 1998. Buehler, too, notes the importance of genealogy.

19. Many scholars have explored the role of devotional narratives that juxtapose Sufis and political leaders. These include Michael Gilsenan's treatment of Lebanese *shaykh*-s in his *Recognizing Islam (*New York: Pantheon Books, 1982); and Clifford Geertz's depiction of Sīdī Laḥsen Lyusi in *Islam Observed: Religious Development in Morocco and Indonesia (*Chicago: University of Chicago Press, 1968).

20. The manner of life of local Sufis often also includes their retreat into the forest and the appropriation of spiritual powers as a result. Although no one made such a claim for Asta Auliyā (other than his arrival in the jungle as a proselytizing civilizer), such elements comprise parts of the narratives of two other dead Sufi healers—one in Arampur and another three miles nearby.

21. David Knipe, *"Sapindikarana:* The Hindu Rite of Entry into Heaven," in *Religious Encounters with Death: Insights from the History and Anthropology of Religion,* eds. E. Reynolds and E. Waugh (University Park: Pennsylvania University Press, 1977), pp. 111–24.

22. Knipe, "Night of the Growing Dead: A Cult of Vīrabhadra in Coastal Andra," in *Criminal Gods and Demon Devotees: Essays on the Guardians of Popular Hinduism,* ed. Alf Hiltebeitel (Albany: State University of New York Press, 1989), pp. 123–56.

23. "The Believers, men and women, are protectors, one of another: they enjoin what is just, and forbid what is evil: they observe regular prayers, practice regular charity, and obey God and His Apostle. On them will God pour His mercy" (Quran 40.71). Although ideally true and the famed examples of such female figures as Rābi'ah of Basra notwithstanding, the comparative lack of female Sufis, living or dead, in India demonstrates the actual limits of this notion.

24. Jane Idleman Smith and Yvonne Yazbeck Haddad, *The Islamic Understanding of Death and Resurrection* (Albany: State University of New York Press, 1981), pp. 47–61.

25. Ibid., pp. 183–90.

26. Richard Eaton, *Sufis of Bijapur, 1300–1700: Social Roles of Sufis in Medieval India* (Princeton: Princeton University Press, 1978), pp. 19–37.

27. Perhaps the fact that the generic terms *darbār* and *dargāh* used for the *brahm's* temple and the Sufi's shrine, respectively, can also mean "royal court" also reflects this power struggle.

28. Coccari, "The Bir Babas and the Deified Dead," in *Criminal Gods and Demon Devotees: Essays on the Guardians of Popular Hinduism, ed.* Alf Hiltebeitel (Albany: State University of New York Press, 1989), p. 254.

29. This dynamic is reported in other areas as well. Jonathan P. Parry refers to the issue of authority when he writes in regard to Banaras: "[Hindu guardian spirits] do not, however, have jurisdiction over Muslim spirits; and here the exorcist (whatever his religion) will enlist the help of a Muslim *Sayyad,* or one of the *Panchon pir* ('the five Islamic saints')." Parry, *Death in Banaras* (Cambridge: Cambridge University Press, 1994), p. 231.

30. This increasing concern for orthopraxy among many Muslims does not limit itself to criticism of "Hindu" practices alone but also the practices of other Muslims that seem unacceptable. A large number of local Muslims, with the complaint that it was "un-Islamic," refused to participate in the annual Muḥarram commemoration although many admitted that in previous years they had. The rise of Hindu revivalist groups such as the Rāṣṭrīya Swayaṁsevak Saṅgh and Vishwa Hindū Pariṣad may be creating a similar dynamic among increasing numbers of Hindus.

31. Eaton, *Rise of Islam and the Bengal Frontier.*

32. Joyce Burkhalter-Flueckiger, "Religious Identity at the Crossroads of a Muslim Female Healer's Practice" (Paper presented at the annual South Asian Studies Conference, Madison, October 1996).

33. A messenger from Allāh who brings a divine book.

34. As concluded from their reading of the "786" engraved in Arabic numerals mentioned earlier.

35. Literally: "jungle people."

36. Eaton, *Rise of Islam and the Bengal Frontier,* pp. 207–8.

37. Both terms, the first from Sanskrit and the other from Persian and Arabic, denote "blessing."

38. Lalji Tripathi, *Brahm Prakāś* (Bhabua: Ruchika Printers, 1993).

39. Daniel Gold, "Clan and Lineage among the Sants: Seed, Substance, Service," in *The Sants: Studies in a Devotional Tradition in India,* eds. Karine Schomer and W. H. McLeod (Delhi: Motilal Banarsidass, 1987), p. 305.

Contributors

Peter Gottschalk is Assistant Professor of Religion at Southwestern University in Georgetown, Texas. For the 2002–3 year, he is also Visiting Assistant Professor of Religion at Wesleyan University. Gottschalk is author of *Beyond Hindu and Muslim: Multiple Identity in Narratives from Village India* (Oxford Universitty Press, 2000). A recent project is codesigning a website entitled, "A Virtual Village" (www.colleges.org/~village) which allows computer users to virtually investigate a North Indian village.

David M. Knipe is a historian of religions with specialization in South Asia. His field research since 1980 has focused on the religious life of the Godavari Delta in coastal Andhra Pradesh, including the living traditions of Vedic Brahmans (a thirty-two-hundred-year-old textual and ritual legacy) and the interplay of contemporary Hindu rituals and symbols with folklore, traditional medicine, and astrology. He is Professor Emeritus at the University of Wisconsin, Madison where he served as Chair of the Department of South Asian Studies, Director of the South Asian Area Center, and Director of the Program in Religious Studies.

Isabelle Nabokov is Associate Professor of Anthropology at Princeton University. She is the author of *Religion against the Self* (Oxford University Press, 2000). She is currently writing an ethnography of Tamil funeral songs.

Gregory Schopen has taught at Indiana University, University of Texas-Austin, and Stanford University and is currently Professor of East Asian Languages and Cultures, UCLA. He is the author of *Bones, Stones, and Buddhist Monks: Collected Papers on the Archaeology, Epigraphy, and Texts of Monastic Buddhism in India* (Honolulu: University of Hawai`i Press, 1997), and coeditor of *From Benares to Beijing: Essays on Buddhism and Chinese Religion* (Mosaic Press, 1991).

Jonathan S. Walters is Associate Professor of Religion and Asian Studies, and Paul Garrett Fellow at Whitman College in Walla Walla, Washington. He is the author of *The History of Kelaniya* (Social Scientists' Association, 1996), *Finding Buddhists in Global History* (American Historical Association, 1998), *Buried Treasure in Sri Lankan History,* and coauthor of *Querying the Medieval* (Oxford University Press, 2000), in addition to numerous articles and reviews. He is currently completing a book on the legend and cult of Arahant Mahinda, "apostle of Buddhism" to Sri Lanka, and continuing his work on rural healing and sorcery traditions in Sri Lanka.

David Gordon White is Professor in the Department of Religious Studies at the University of California, Santa Barbara. He is the author of *The Alchemical Body: Siddha Traditions in Medieval India* (University of Chicago Press, 1996), editor of *Tantra in Practice* (Princeton University Press, 2000), and author of *Kiss of the Yogini: "Tantric Sex" in Its South Asian Contexts* (University of Chicago Press, 2002).

Liz Wilson is Professor in the Department of Comparative Religion and Affiliate in Womens Studies at Miami University in Oxford, Ohio. She is the author of *Charming Cadavers: Horrific Figurations of the Feminine in Indian Buddhist Hagiographic Literature* (University of Chicago Press, 1996) and is currently working on a book on attitudes toward sexuality and family life among contemporary Western Buddhists.

Richard K. Wolf has conducted ethnomusicological research in India and Pakistan since 1982. He is Assistant Professor of Music in the Music Department at Harvard University.

Index